Living by the Word of God

Davis Byrd

Larry,

This might well have
never come to be without
your help. Thanks for all
you've done and for
your friendship.

Davis

Living by the Word of God

Davis Byrd

Parson's Porch
Books
Cleveland, TN

Parson's Porch Books

121 Holly Trail, NW
Cleveland, TN 37311

Copyright (C) 2010 by Davis Byrd

ISBN: Softcover   978-0982-6337-1-7

This book was printed in the United States of America.

Unless otherwise noted, biblical quotations are taken from *The New English Bible*, copyright 1970 by The Delegates of the Oxford University Press and The Syndics of the Cambridge University Press.

Other biblical quotations are taken as noted from the following:

New Revised Standard Version Bible, copyright 1989 by the Division of Christian Education of the National Council of Churches of Christ in the United states of America.

The Message, Eugene Peterson, copyright 1993, 1994, 1995, 1996, 2000, 2001, 2002. Used by permission of NavPress Publishing Group.

The New Testament in Modern English, trans. by J. B. Philips, copyright 1962 by The Macmillan Company, New York.

To order additional copies of this book, contact:
Parson's Porch Books
1-423-584-9261
www.parsonsporch.com

To
Kay,
the love of my life.

TABLE OF CONTENTS

ACKNOWLEDGMENTS

Over the years of my life that lie behind this book, I have accumulated a wide variety of clues to understanding the meaning of my wanderings and wonderings. These clues have come both through personal experiences and through the lives and influences of others with whom I have traveled portions of the path or whose path mine has crossed. I have come upon many of these other paths in the process of reading what others have written. Some of these paths I have sought out intentionally (knowing something about the authors) and some I have stumbled across by accident or through the providence of God. From these sources I have borrowed readily and extensively. In so doing, I do not intend to claim I am being true to their intent in writing. Rather I am only being true to what their writings have said to me. Often they said what I wish I could have said, but the reality is that they said it better than I. So rather than try to say the same thing poorly, I am happy to give full acknowledgment of these sources and quote them frequently.

I confess my creativity lies less in my ability to create *ex nihilo* than in my ability to weave together the threads I have pulled from many different people and places into new combinations that express a new idea, or a new nuance, or at least something that comes fresh from my heart. In this process I have long since lost track of all of the influences on my thinking. In addition to being influenced by the writings of those whom I acknowledge, I am quite certain I have borrowed from many others who have faded in my memory and whose contributions have melded into what I now think are my own thoughts and words. I apologize in advance to anyone whose contribution to my thinking thus goes unacknowledged. I will appreciate any corrections in quotation or attribution that readers may wish to call to my attention, and I will make appropriate corrections in any future printings or editions of this book.

Many people have contributed personally to my faith development, often without my awareness at the time and without my ability at this time to name them to give appropriate credit. However, there are a few whose role was sufficiently clear in its impact that I not only can name them, I would be remiss not to do so. My parents and wife were foundational in my faith emergence and maturation. I have acknowledged them and expressed my gratitude in my "Author's Note." People of First Baptist Church, Florence, South Carolina, were influential in their tolerance of me as the son of their pastor for 27 years. Many went beyond tolerance and gave me encouragement. Quite a few of them participated in Bible surveys that I taught in Sunday school in the 1970s. My study and preparation for teaching those classes were key to deepening my understanding and love of the Bible. The eagerness of their responses to my teaching encouraged me more than they knew. Among those people, Dorothy Murphree played a pivotal role by asking a question that changed the direction of my life: "Have you thought about going to seminary?" At the time she asked the question, I had never thought about it, but once the question was asked, it wouldn't go away. Within a few months, I closed my architectural practice and moved my family to Louisville, Kentucky to enter seminary. At seminary, many professors helped me grow, none more so than Glen Stassen and Ken Chafin.

There is a special group of friends from a Sunday school class at First Baptist Church, Nashville, Tennessee who kept my soul alive and nurtured during a time when that was greatly needed. I will always be grateful to them. (You know who you are.) Two of them I must single out by name. At the time of my retirement, Fred Heifner said, "Don't spend your time playing golf. You need to write." So, Fred, here it is. Thank you, I think. Wayne Ozment gave generously of his time and editing talents to help me improve the early drafts of the manuscript. Thank you. Of course, the remaining errors are mine.

Finally, I want to express special thanks to David Tullock at Parson's Porch Books, without whom this book might never have made it into print.

"One does not live by bread alone,
but by every word that comes from the mouth of God."
Matthew 4:4

AUTHOR'S NOTE

In order to appropriate one's beliefs fully one must articulate them.
David J. Lose [1]

In a very real sense, the writer writes in order to teach himself, to understand himself, to satisfy himself.
Alfred Kazin [2]

It cannot be too strongly emphasized that all witness necessarily involves the use of the first person singular.... It is never somebody in general who bears witness; it is always an individual with an individual consciousness.... The method of evangelism is inevitably the method of testimony. Each man has only one story that is worth telling.
Elton Trueblood [3]

For several years I have thought about writing this book, but the task has been sufficiently daunting that I have successfully avoided it until now. The sheer magnitude of the work involved in writing a book has always been overwhelming, almost paralyzing. But even more intimidating than the work involved is the presumptuousness of writing a book in the first place. I like books. No, the truth is I love books. I love reading books. I love holding a book. I love being in a room that

---

[1] Lose, *Confessing Jesus Christ*, p. vii.
[2] Kazin, *Think*, quoted by Ralph Keyes, *The Writer's Book of Hope*, p. 188.
[3] Trueblood, *The Company of the Committed*, pp. 49, 55.

11

contains lots of books. Books are restorative for my soul. But, until now, books have always been something for me to read, never something for me to write. I have been a happy reader from early childhood on, but rarely have I been a writer and never a writer of a book. Nonetheless, despite my misgivings, I have now set forth on this journey of writing.

Any writing necessarily reflects the author's subjectivity. This is especially true in this case, because this book is confessional. For a while I felt a little defensive about not being scholarly in my writing and only being confessional. However, a statement by Robert McAfee Brown has helped me be more comfortable with the confessional nature of my writing. In his book *The Pseudonyms of God* Brown suggests "Christian theology will be a *confessional theology*. The one who speaks is himself grateful [for God's love and grace]."[4] Now I certainly lay no claim to being a theologian, but if a theologian can be confessional, surely being confessional is okay for the rest of us who struggle to understand God and are grateful for God's love and grace. This means, therefore, that my writing is quite subjective. This is my testimony to my faith and my reflections on the implications of my faith for understanding God's Word and for living life in light of that Word.

While I have been informed and influenced by the work of many scholars, I have been very eclectic in my selections of scholars and my selections from their writings. Even more, my use of others' writings may well stray from the authors' original meanings. So by citing them, I do not intend to imply they meant what I now mean when I reference their thoughts. Nor would I contend I am presenting a comprehensive treatment of any of the subjects I address. At best I am sharing what I know of the truth as I know it. In this regard I can identify with the account of a Native American who was giving testimony in court and was asked through a translator if he promised to tell the court "the truth, the whole truth, and nothing but the truth." After struggling for a while, the translator gave the man's reply: "I don't know what the whole truth is… I only know what I know."[5] That's all I can claim for my writing: I don't know the whole truth; I only know what I know.

This book is an outgrowth of my lifelong journey with the Bible. Its roots can be traced to some time around 1970, when it was only a train

---

[4] Brown, *The Pseudonyms of God*, p. 16, emphasis in the original.
[5] Related by John Buchanan, "Truth Claims," *Christian Century*, January 29, 2008, p. 1.

of thought and a brief outline resulting from an extended time of concentrated Bible study. The more I read and studied the Bible, the more I came to appreciate the Bible as Word of God, while at the same time growing to understand that the Bible *as a book* has no exclusive claim to being *the* Word of God. I came to realize God's Word has been and is still being uttered in many ways and forms. Many of these utterances, it is true, are accessible to us only through the Bible, and *one* of them indeed *is* the Bible. But the Word of God is more than the Bible.

From the mid-1970s through the early 1980s, my train of thought was side-tracked; and the outline was set aside while I pursued seminary degrees, where my study agenda was set by seminary curricula rather than my own independent interests and pursuits. Those years made lasting and invaluable contributions to my understanding of the Bible and of God's Word. Graduate studies in theologies of liberation and hope and in the field of peacemaking particularly influenced and enriched the development of my belief structure and have contributed to this endeavor in writing; but my outline of earlier thoughts remained largely untouched during seminary years due to lack of time. In the years since seminary I have only sporadically updated and expanded it, never taking it beyond outline form until now. Nonetheless, it has evolved along with my spiritual pilgrimage of faith over the past forty years of adult life.

As I reflect on these past years I realize that "pilgrimage" may not be the right word to describe my life. Pilgrimage implies a known destination toward which one is always moving. A more apt term for my life might be spiritual wandering rather than pilgrimage. I have wandered along a way that can only be described in hindsight as a path. I have moved under a sense of God's will in the moment more than as a grand scheme. One of the joys of such a life is being surprised as to where it leads. Most of these surprises have led to times of wonder at the emergence of meaning and blessing along the way.

This book is an expression of my personal understanding of God's Word and of my faith that is built on that Word. At least part of the motivation for writing comes as an effort to give voice to my faith so I may more fully understand it myself. I expect the process of writing will necessitate that I give clearer voice to what has up until now happily existed in my mind and in various jottings as "random thoughts" from a life of wondrous wandering in somewhat spontaneous outbursts of thought and self expression. In his book, *A Room Called Remember*,

Frederick Buechner suggests the notion of life as

> a kind of traveling, of seeing the sights. And the more sights
> you see, the more feelings those sights call up in you, the more
> alive you become to what is going on in the world both
> around you and inside you, then the more profoundly you
> need to put a word to it. [In] some important sense the thing
> you are seeing or feeling doesn't even fully exist for you until
> you have given a word to it.[6]

And as Wilfred Cantwell Smith has suggested, "Faith is not one element in the total pattern of that person's life; rather, it *is* the pattern that the other elements form. To understand a man's faith is to ascertain how he sees the world (and feels it)—all of the world."[7] So my journey into writing is partially to give "a word" to my faith and partially to reveal the pattern of my life.

Native American Pulitzer Prize winning author and poet N. Scott Momaday has been widely quoted as saying,

> an Indian is an idea which a given man has of himself. And it
> is a moral idea, for it accounts for the way in which he reacts
> to other men and the world in general. And that idea, in order
> to be realized completely, has to be expressed [in language].[8]

When I first read these words, they struck me as being true about anyone's self identity. I would paraphrase and adopt Momaday's concept and say, "Being a follower of Christ is an idea I have of myself. And it is a moral idea, for it accounts for the way in which I react to others and to the world in general. And that idea, in order to be realized completely, has to be expressed in language." Whatever else this venture into book writing may be, it is my attempt to give expression to my idea of myself and how I relate to others and to the world. Simple honesty requires that I acknowledge I do not always follow faithfully or act and react consistently with my self-idea, but it is that idea that lets me know when I have failed.

---

[6] Buechner, *A Room Called Remember*, p. 166.
[7] Smith, *Religious Diversity*, p. 72, emphasis in the original.
[8] I saw this in 2008 on a poster in the Funk Heritage Center at Reinhardt College in Waleska, GA.

I also believe the incentive for writing comes partially from the growing awareness that I am aging and that I will not always be around to share my thoughts with whoever might be interested in them. In 2002 the reality of my inevitable death was presented to me in a new and rather attention-getting way. In his book, *Soul Salsa*, Leonard Sweet calls attention to a web site, www.deathclock.com. When you go to that website, you can enter your birth date, gender, and general outlook toward life (pessimistic, normal, or optimistic). Then the website gives you your "death date." It is a little unnerving to see a date identified as the date you are going to die. To make it even more unnerving, there is a countdown clock, showing your future life span in seconds; and as you sit and watch, the seconds tick away. When I first visited the site, I selected "normal" as my outlook; but when I saw the outcome, I quickly decided I would be "optimistic," which extended my life span significantly. The web site has been further refined since that first visit and now it takes into account your BMI (body mass index) and whether or not you smoke. (It has also added "sadistic" as another option regarding attitude toward life. I didn't even dare to check that out.) Based on my visit to the site as I was writing these words, my death date is January 13, 2038, with 926,578,817 seconds left (and counting down) as I exited the site. I know this is only a variation of the old actuarial table concept, but it does tend to drive home the reality of a finite span of life ahead of me. I can certainly identify with the feeling expressed by Sam Keen:

> The clock is ticking the minutes away. My minutes. Each tick synchronizes with a heartbeat. Now inside and out the measured movement of time carries me forward toward, toward, toward, toward (my mind stutters to avoid the end of the sentence, to avoid the end, to avoid the sentence). [9]

Try it yourself: www.deathclock.com. You have nothing to lose but a few seconds of life.

With my time ticking away, I feel a growing sense of urgency to make the remaining time count for something that will outlast me. In 2004, in one of my momentary successes at journaling (which, for me means that I actually wrote something down), I jotted down some thoughts and feelings about a dream of the previous night in which I

---

[9] Keen, *To a Dancing God*, p. 6.

had committed some minor infraction of a "rule" or "law"—something inconsequential like not paying a bill on time. The "authorities" (whoever they were) decided to make an example of me, and I was sentenced to 30 years in prison. I was devastated, because I knew that this would surely be the rest of my life, and all I had hoped to do in the rest of my life would now be impossible to accomplish. These are my reflections which I wrote down the next morning: "That was a dream. It was only a dream. I have the rest of my life, however long it may be, still ahead of me." And then came the question: "What will I now do to make use of it?" As I was growing up, my father would frequently urge me: "Give a good account of yourself, Son." Ever since that dream, I have felt a growing need to give an account of myself while I still can. So this book gives my account of my self, while I still have time to give it.

> I am not asking you tonight Lord, for time to do this and then that,
>
> But your grace to do conscientiously, in the time that you give me, what you want me to do. [10]

Not only is my future "ticking away," but I realize further that I do not remember the events of my life as securely as I did in earlier years. This may mean that I, myself, may turn out to be my primary audience—later reading (between now and January 13, 2038) some of the thoughts that I set down on these pages and reading them as if I had not first written them myself. This may result not just from fading memory, but also from the fact that whenever we revisit our own past, we do so as different persons, changed by the experiences and circumstances of intervening years. As the poet Hugh Prather has observed, "What I just was doesn't quite apply. What I just intended is in the past. This is not a lack of resolve, it is the way life flows… [I am] always a new me."[11] I am still a work in progress. My journey with the Word continues, which changes me as I move forward. When at some future date I look back on this account of my self, I will be a new me. (Sidebar: As I was writing this, my mind took off on a flight of fancy. The apostle Paul wrote: "My knowledge now is partial; then it will be whole, like God's knowledge of me" (1 Cor. 13:12b). I would paraphrase

---

[10] Michael Quoist, "Lord, I Have Time," *Prayers*, p. 96.
[11] Prather, *I Touch the Earth, the Earth Touches Me*, n. p.

Paul to say, "*I am now partial; then I will be whole, like God's knowledge of me.*")

Yet there is still another reason for writing this book. It is more than just a private project of self-understanding and expression; it is also an effort to give voice to my beliefs as a personal testimony to be shared with others. In this regard, a comment by Peter Gomes from his book of sermons, subtitled *Biblical Wisdom for Daily Living*, has both challenged and encouraged me: "If God is to be known, that knowledge will be in the lives of ordinary people who are redeemed by his extraordinary message of love."[12] God knows I am certainly one of the ordinary people, and I know I have been redeemed by God's extraordinary love. With the assurance of this love I have strived to work out my own salvation in fear and trembling (Phil. 2:12-13); but, with Paul, I have also found that it is God who is at work in me. Through the years and along the way I have managed to find a faith that falls far short of certitude, which means it is still faith, but which nonetheless gives me peace. That my faith seems to hold me rather than I hold it gives me a sense of humility and keeps me from trying to impose my beliefs on others. I can testify to my faith. I can even share it with conviction and heartfelt passion, but I more often end up in tears at the wonder of it all than in a missionary zeal to convey it to, much less impose it on, others. By sharing my testimony—my story—I simply hope that others will be helped to articulate their own stories and that their stories too will be stories of knowing God's love. In the words of Robert McAfee Brown, "As we see how others read the Bible, we may get a new understanding of what the biblical message says to us."[13]

So I continue down a path that I have wandered along for a lifetime. I hope anyone who may follow my steps down this path will find yourself, as well as me, along the way in my wanderings (and wonderings). Shakespeare has been quoted as writing, "Not everyone who wanders is lost." I would add, "Not everyone who wonders is lost." I like the way David James Duncan writes of wonder:

> Wonder is my second favorite condition to be in, after love—and I sometimes wonder whether there's even a difference: maybe love is just wonder aimed at the beloved.

---

[12] Gomes, *Sermons: Biblical Wisdom for Daily Living*, p. 119.
[13] Brown, *Unexpected News*, p.14.

Wonder is like grace, in that it's not a condition we grasp:
wonder grasps us. [14]

I have been grasped by love, and I am amazed at the wonder of it as I continue to wander.

Words from three hymns have special meaning for me and express my heart in better words than mine. The first words come from a Christmas carol by John Jacob Niles:

> I wonder as I wander, out under the sky,
> How Jesus the savior did come for to die
> For poor ornery people like you and like I;
> I wonder as I wander out under the sky. [15]

And words from the pen of Elizabeth C. Clephane:

> Two wonders I confess—
> The wonders of redeeming love
> And my unworthiness. [16]

The other words come from a hymn by Fred Pratt Green:

> For the wonders that surround us,
> For the truths that still confound us,
> Most of all, that love has found us,
> Thanks be to God. [17]

Thanks be to God, indeed!

*****

[14] Duncan, *God Laughs and Plays*, p. 8.
[15] Niles, "I Wonder as I Wander," *The Hymnal for Worship and Celebration*, ed. Tom Fettke.
[16] Clephane, "Beneath the Cross of Jesus," *The Hymnal for Worship and Celebration*, ed. Tom Fettke.
[17] Green, "For the Fruit of All Creation," *The Hymnal for Worship and Celebration*, ed. Tom Fettke.

PROLOGUE

For some people, it might be hard to identify the beginning of their spiritual pilgrimage. For others, it might easily be identified with a sudden life-changing encounter with God. For me, it began with my birth. I was born into a pastor's home, and I grew up as a pastor's son, a PK (preacher's kid). This means Christianity, church, and all of the related trappings have been the context of my life and faith development from the beginning. I have never known life without Jesus Christ, church, and the Bible at its center. As a child, what we were going to do as a family on Sunday morning, Sunday night, and Wednesday night was never a matter of question. It was a given: we would go to church. Every day ended with a time of family Bible reading and prayer just before going to bed. Every meal was preceded with a blessing. Every issue in life was assessed in spiritual and ethical terms drawn from the Bible and the life of Jesus. These were all fixed points along my spiritual path from the cradle on through childhood and adolescence.

Unlike some PKs, I never wandered very far from this path. This is not to say that I always behaved in ways that I would have wanted my parents to know, but there was never a rebellion of spirit against what I was taught and what I saw lived in my home and what I heard from my father's pulpit. My father loved God, God's Word, and God's people; and he loved his family. There was a wholeness and consistency to his life that shaped me in ways that I am still coming to realize. Through him, I came to know of a God of love—and of God as deserving our love. Through Dad, I also came to know that God's love is for everyone, not because of our merit, but because of God's nature. This was no cheap love I learned from him, however. This was a saving love, but it was also a costly love. From Dad I learned that there is always a corrective element in God's love that carries with it requirements of repentance, commitment, and faithfulness.

From the beginning of my life I also knew my mother's love; and through her love, I knew of the tenderness of God's love. A verse in 1 Samuel contains a phrase that I have come to see as an image of how God loves us. It is part of Abigail's blessing for David, in which she prays that if anyone should seek to take David's life, "the Lord your God will wrap your life up and put it with his own treasure" (1 Sam. 25:29). This is the love I knew from my mother: I was wrapped up in her love as a special treasure. Another passage further communicates this understanding, this time from a psalm attributed to David:

> Bless the Lord, my soul;
> my innermost heart, bless his holy name.
> Bless the Lord, my soul,
> and forget none of his benefits.
> He pardons all my guilt
> and heals all my suffering.
> He rescues me from the pit of death
> and *surrounds me with constant love,*
> *with tender affection.* [1]

Mother always surrounded me with constant love and tender affection. She modeled for me the tender love of God.

It is fair to say that my life's path was a spiritual journey long before I ever realized it. In a very real sense, God's Spirit was "born within me" when I was born. Knowing the saving love of God in Christ was never far from me. As a fish swims in water without "knowing" anything about water, I swam in God's love long before I "knew" anything about God. So when I reached what my father always referred to as "the age of accountability," the natural next step along my spiritual path was to testify formally to my knowledge of and acceptance of God's saving love. At the age of eight I made my "public profession of faith," but that occasion was not a significant marker for me alongside my spiritual path. In truth, I have no real memory of the experience. I guess it was such a natural event in my life that my memory of it has faded into the general haze of the distant past. My profession of faith as an eight-year-old does

---

[1] Psalm 103:1-4, emphasis added.

20

not matter in my testimony nearly so much as the years of life I have spent experiencing time and again the infilling of God's Spirit.

Probably 30-35 years ago I jotted down some thoughts about the nature of the spiritual life. A new-born baby is filled with the "breath" of life when it is slapped on the bottom (or, at least, that's how it was done when I was born) and draws its first breath. But, in order to sustain life and to grow, that baby must *continue* to have new infillings of life's breath. That first breath is just the first of countless breaths of life-giving air. It marks the beginning of life, but it is not sufficient for sustaining life. In much the same way, the experience of salvation, which is a spiritual "new birth," begins with an infilling of the soul with the breath/Spirit of God. But this "new creature" must *continue* to experience new infillings of the Divine Breath if it is to live and grow. We stay spiritually alive only because God keeps breathing into us.

The flip side of the spiritual life is what *we* do to keep it alive. For me, in this regard, the spiritual life can be likened to married life. A marriage begins with a wedding, but it only begins there. A true marriage results from a lifetime of getting up every day and living the vows of the wedding all over again. Similarly, a Christian life may "begin" with a commitment made after the age of accountability, but it must be lived by getting up every day and committing to that life all over again. St. Augustine has been quoted as saying something to the effect that you have to start your relationship with God all over from the beginning, every day. In 2007, *Image* journal asked writers, artist and musicians why they believe in God. One response I particularly liked: "I keep deciding to believe in God, even on bad days. In this, my seventh decade, faith seems to me not certainty but commitment, a renewable vow."[2] I, also in my seventh decade, would say the same thing.

Since I just used the metaphor of marriage, I want to acknowledge the influence of my own marriage on my spiritual journey. For the past 43 years I have walked the path in the company of the dearest person in my life, my wife Kay, whose love for me has modeled God's love most intimately. Her tenderness and faithfulness have nurtured me on the journey. She has allowed my journey in large measure to set the parameters for her own journey. She has supported me even when she had doubts. She has trusted my sense of God's call even when she could not hear it herself. She has forgiven me when I have failed her. She has

---

[2] Cited in "Imaging God," *Christian Century*, November 13, 2007, p. 6.

gotten up each day and loved me all over again, even when that was not easy to do. I am grateful for and humbled by her unconditional love. She has caused me to be a better person than I would ever have been without her. "I will arise and call her blessed and sing her praises."[3]

During my college years at Rice University my childhood faith, largely inherited without question from my parents, began to become *my* faith. This transition in faith was part of the overall process of leaving home and creating my self as an independent identity. At Rice I was no longer the son of the pastor of the First Baptist Church of a small Southern county seat town, a role which had included both spotlight and privileges. At Rice I could be whoever I wanted to be. This was both an exciting and intimidating opportunity, one that I had not anticipated before arriving there. In fact, the very process of arriving there first made it clear that I was on my own, a long way from home. After a twenty hour train ride of over 1000 miles and a taxi ride from the train station in Houston to the Rice campus, as I stood by my suitcase surrounded by strangers, I knew in the depth of my being that I had started a new chapter in life.

In looking back on my college years, I confess I did not always behave in ways consistent with my upbringing; but even in those years of exploring independence, I never wandered away from my faith. Rather, it was through those experiences (and maybe despite a few of them) that my faith began to mature. One important influence in my process of becoming more conscious and intentional about my beliefs was a class in cultural anthropology. In that class I became increasingly impressed with the universality of religion in the primitive cultures we studied. I came to see religion as a basic human experience that transcends time and space, and I came to believe human beings cannot live without transcendent meaning in their lives. The universality of the religious impulse was reassuring to me of the validity of religion in my own life. In ways I cannot explain even now, the awareness of the very universality of human religious searching deepened my faith in the particularity of my own religion.

A second insight that came during that class, which was not related to the course material at all, was my sudden awareness that the people of the Bible were just ordinary people, very much like the ancient and primitive people I was studying, not some unusual species of spiritual humanoids with unique and unrepeatable ways of experiencing God. I

---

[3] My rephrasing of Proverbs 31:28.

came to realize in a new and profound way that if *they* could experience God in *their* lives, then *I* could experience God in *my* life. The people in the Bible didn't know they were living the Bible. They were just living in relationship with God. Even the writers of what we now have as the Bible didn't know they were writing Holy Scripture. They were simply writing about their lives and encounters with the Holy One of Israel. They were just ordinary people with, perhaps, an extraordinary openness to God; but the flash of insight for me was the awareness that they put their "spiritual pants" on one leg at a time just like I do. That was quite an epiphany for me! I know. It seems pretty obvious. But when I realized that the people in those Sunday school pictures from my childhood were just ordinary people—like all of the other people I was learning about in anthropology and art and architecture history classes and also like me—I was encouraged. I, too, could know God on my own, not just through the faith of my parents, and not just through the biblical record of others' experiences with God, but through my own experiences with God.

That's where my adult faith adventure began, but it hasn't ended yet. This book is an attempt to give a progress report of where I have gotten in the nearly half a century since I got out of the taxi at Rice.

*****

23

INTRODUCTION

My faith is inseparable from my understanding of the Bible. Through the years, story has become my primary category for understanding the Bible, and I have tried to place my own story in the biblical story. Only recently I came across a book by John I. Durham on the biblical art of Rembrandt. In that book Durham gives a fascinating and compelling account of Rembrandt's frequent practice of painting his own portrait as one of the characters in his portrayal of a biblical scene. According to Durham, Rembrandt saw himself in the biblical stories:

> [He] saw those stories as real, the narrative accounts of real persons whose experiences were not that different from his own, and whose difficulties and mistakes and triumphs and celebrations had value for his own life.... The Bible became so real to Rembrandt that he found himself knowing that he might have lived its drama, might have been one of its people. And that knowing joined to his humanity, reached out toward and into meaning. [1]

A key to appreciating Rembrandt's participation in the biblical story is recognizing that he did not paint *others* into the story; he painted *himself*. Therefore, when we view his masterworks of confessional art, we see Rembrandt; but if we let his art speak to us, we, too, can enter the scene with him. Like Rembrandt, I need to place myself in the biblical story; but without his artistic talent, I can only place myself in the story in my

---

[1] Durham, *The Biblical Rembrandt*, pp. 64-65, 106.

imaginings and express the results in words.

Before I get to the main story, in the spirit of full disclosure, I want to identify briefly some of the key components of my approach to understanding the Bible. I can't trace the origin and development of these components; I simply know they affect my way of seeing life and experiencing God. The first of these components is the role of perspective in our seeing. When dealing with a visual art, such as Rembrandt's paintings, we are fully aware of the concept of perspective. But perspective is not restricted to visual art. Perspective is an integral part of all of our "seeing," both literally and figuratively. One's perspective always influences how anyone "sees" and understands anything, including how we understand the Bible. Even more significant, I am persuaded that perspective was involved in how the people *in* the Bible saw things as well. Therefore, when I read the Bible, I am seeing from my perspective what the biblical writers saw from their perspectives.

Secondly, I believe that reading the Bible as story provides the most constructive context for understanding the Bible, because it both contains stories and *is* story. Further, I see the biblical story as *the* grand story not only for my life individually but also for human life in general. Biblical scholar Walter Brueggemann has cautioned, "Trouble surfaces in the community of faith whenever we move from the idiom of story."[2] Therefore, reflecting on the role that story plays in all of our lives is important. And, finally, I want briefly to explore the role played by myth and metaphor in our efforts to express the meaning of the inexpressible.

As I seek to understand the Bible as Word of God, I trust that I do not do violence to the Bible in the process, although I will be amazed if some do not think that I have done so.

****

The Role of Perspective

The truth is there are multiple ways of seeing the world.
Perception is everything.
Leonard Sweet [3]

---

[2] Brueggemann, *The Creative Word*, p. 22.
[3] Sweet, *Postmodern Pilgrims*, p. 144.

[Events] themselves are in their turn conditioned by the
human experience of them.... [History is] in its very essence a
process of action and reaction between external circumstance
and human response.
John Baillie [4]

[Only] when an occurrence is supplemented by an
interpretation does a happening become an event.
Howard Clark Kee and Franklin W. Young [5]

We do not see things as they are, but as we are.
Jewish Proverb

No matter how much anybody sees, nobody sees it all.
Robert McAfee Brown [6]

We tend to think we know what we see and that what we "see" is
the real thing. But this is simply not the case. First, there is an event in
all of its neutral reality and, second, there is our perception of it. Yet
even this is not quite true. In the course of our days, innumerable events
escape our notice entirely. The truth is, unless an event is sufficiently
compelling that we are forced into awareness of it, we tend to notice
only those events and things that fit naturally into our already
constructed ways of seeing. This came home to me years ago in one of
those rare moments of startling insight that come when you least expect
it. In the late 1960s I attended the annual meeting in Washington D. C.
of the World Future Society. One of the speakers told a story of a group
of marine biologists who dragged a seine made of six-inch mesh through
all of the world's oceans. After examining their catch, the scientists'
report of their findings included the conclusion that there was nothing
living in the ocean smaller than six inches in size. Of course, what they
"saw" was based on their method of perceiving reality; and they were
totally oblivious to the things their method failed to see. This insight
into the connection between method and perception became one of the

[4] Baillie, *The Idea of Revelation in Recent Thought*, p.
66.
[5] Kee and Young, *Understanding the New Testament*, p.
63.
[6] Brown, *Theology in a New Key*, p. 85, emphasis in the
original.

"stack poles" around which I process life.

In short, what we "see" depends on our past, our context, our frame of reference, and our methodology. Every experience is inseparable from our interpretation of it. We can see only what our pre-existing experiences and perceptual models enable us to see. For example, our eyes send signals of patterns of light and dark and color to the brain; but our mind "sees" these patterns and colors as a dog or a cat only because the patterns and colors fit our preexisting perceptual models of a dog or a cat. Over time and mostly subconsciously, but rarely without self interest, we build a whole portfolio of images and sort them into categories for ready reference based on the cumulative impact of our experiences. Eventually, we come to rely without much conscious thought on our portfolio, "seeing" only what we expect to see based on the categories established by our prior experiences. In other words, we don't believe what we see as much as we see what we believe; and then we support our beliefs with what we see. To put it in words adapted from the humorist poet Ogden Nash, I believe we believe what we believe we believe.

Our expectations shape our perceptions, which then lead to our behavior. Repeated behavior reinforces our expectations, establishes our "reality," and becomes our destiny. Once in a while we will have a category-defying experience that challenges our habitual schemes and requires expanding and reorganizing our "reality" portfolio to make room for a new schema. As we now begin to see with "new eyes," our life is changed, until the new portfolio is challenged later by yet another category-defying experience. In the words of the Jewish proverb quoted above, we see things not as *they* are, but as *we* are. Ninian Smart identifies what I am calling our "reality portfolio" as a "worldview": "Whether we have spelled it to ourselves or not, each of us has a worldview, which forms a background to the lives we lead."[7] And as significant events impact us, such as the death of a loved one, the birth of a baby, a diagnosis of cancer, a betrayal of trust by a friend, or the events of September 11, 2001, we are changed. From that time forward, "reality" for us has also changed.

We see differently, feel differently, and respond differently. We have a new perspective, a new worldview. But, even then, as Robert McAfee Brown reminds us in the quote cited above, no one sees it all. We each can "see" only from where we stand, which is only one point of view;

---

[7] Ninian Smart, *Worldviews*, p. 34.

and from our point of view we are always standing in the center of the world looking out. But we are also at the same time standing in some other part of the world when our position is seen from someone else's point of view.

We get in trouble when we think we are the center of things and that the center of *our* world is the center of *the* world. It takes a truly selfish arrogance never to accept the limitations of one's own point of view. Novelist Ray Bradbury, in the new introduction written for the 1976 edition of his book *Dandelion Wine*, provided a wonderfully picturesque way of seeing from someone else's point of view:

> The people there were gods and midgets and knew themselves mortal and so the midgets walked tall so as not to embarrass the gods and the gods crouched so as to make the small ones feel at home. And, after all, isn't that what life is all about, the ability to go around back and come up inside other people's heads to look out...and say: oh, so that's how you see it!? Well, now, I must remember that. [8]

Bradbury's right. We must always remember how others see things, particularly when it comes to religious beliefs, faith, and biblical understanding.[9]

A second component of perspective results from the fact that we do not live our lives only as individuals but also, consciously and unconsciously, as part of the context of our time, race, gender, nationality, and economic status. As anthropologists are aware, a culture doesn't perceive itself as being a culture; it is simply understood as just being the way the world is. Similarly, individuals within the culture see the world in light of their culture's definitions of reality, as just being how life is. In the words of Robert McAfee Brown, "*How* one makes up

---

[8] Bradbury, *Dandelion Wine*, p. xii.
[9] I would name just three of many books that have helped me read and understand the Bible through others' eyes: *Unexpected News: Reading the Bible with Third World Eyes* by Robert McAfee Brown; *The Rich, The Poor— and the Bible* by Conrad Boerma; *Good News Is Bad News Is Good News* by William K. McElvaney. Also, see the books listed in the Bibliography and anything by John Howard Yoder.

his mind is partly conditioned by *where* he makes it up."[10] So we not only see things as *we* are but also as our community of significant others are. We simultaneously see our lives both as individuals and as persons in time, place, and community. Walter Brueggemann is well aware of the role community plays in our individual identity:

> Our identity is secured in the places of cost and joy in which we have been involved.... And when we ask who we are, we answer in terms of those events which have happened in our common past and which continue to happen in our common life.[11]

This component of community is especially important when seeking to understand the perspectives of those individuals whose writings make up the Bible. What we have in the Bible are the writings of peoples' experiences of God and with God which were shaped by their community context and which, in turn, shaped that community context.

A third component of perspective, often related integrally to the circumstances of our lives in community, is our translation of experience into language. Walker Percy asserts that "language is the very mirror by which we see and know the world."[12] Amos Wilder goes even further in stating the importance of language in shaping our world: "There is no 'world' for us until we have named and languaged and storied whatever is."[13] We live, therefore, in a story-world, a language-world that is the only world we know. David James Duncan has given a concise example of the relationship between the world and our story-world:

> There is an old, broken ponderosa pine tree, backlit by evening sunlight, outside the window.... This tree is real. It is 'nonfiction.' But the words 'pine tree, backlit by evening sunlight' are neither the tree nor the light: they are signals telling the imagination to create an imaginary tree and light.[14]

---

[10] Brown, *The Pseudonyms of God*, p. 24, emphasis in the original.
[11] Brueggemann, *The Bible Makes Sense*, p. 20.
[12] Percy, *The Message in the Bottle*, p. 12.
[13] Quoted by Brueggemann, *An Introduction to the Old Testament*, p. xiii.
[14] Duncan, *God Laughs and Plays*, p. 189.

The influence of language on our understanding of the world is both powerful and inevitable. Language is the expression of the soul of a community, and "reality" comes to us in the terms of our cultural language. Whenever we give expression to our experience, we generally use the words and syntax of a language we have inherited and learned from our family and community. As we grow, our perspectives on life are inevitably shaped by the language of our childhood, and this shaping happens so subtly that we are not even aware of how the language we use has shaped the way we have perceived the event that we are now describing. As Rubem Alves has noted, things come to us already clothed in language, which influences how we experience the world, and "because of their power to define our world, they ultimately condition what we do."[15] Further, although language shapes our world, we must always remember that language cannot substitute for the world. No matter how eloquently we express ourselves, our words are never the same as the reality we are seeking to understand and express. Once again, this must be kept in mind as we read the Bible. Even the "red letter" words of Jesus are not the same as the reality they express.

As Diana Eck has pointed out, our language is only *our* language. She goes on to make clear the limitation and cultural context of human speech: "Human speech is limited. It may be profound, rich, and imaginative, but finally it is limited." And this limitation is nowhere truer than when we speak of God: "[In] imagining and speaking of God, we human beings choose the idea of God that will ground our being. [And our] particular language for God…is shaped by our particular cultures and particular times." And Eck then cautions that we must take care not to mistake our word images of God as God, setting up a language idol of God in the process: "[Many] of us who are Christians and Jews have preferred to think that those who address God through material images are idolaters, while those whose images are shaped by words are not."[16] Duncan sums this point up quite nicely:

> God is Unlimited. Thought and language are limited….The instant we define this fathomless Mystery [who is God] it is no longer fathomless. To define is to limit. The greater a person's confidence in their definition of God, the more sure I feel that their worship of 'Him' has become the worship of their own

[15] Alves, *Tomorrow's Child*, p. 38.
[16] Eck, *Encountering God*, pp. 61, 74, 78.

definition.[17]

A final component of perspective is memory. As we become further removed from an event with the passage of time, our experience of the event is further modified by our memory; and our memory has been influenced by our experiences subsequent to the prior event. We should keep in mind that the act of remembering is exactly that: "re-membering," putting the pieces together again; and we almost always get it wrong. Memories come with the label, "some assembly required," and unfortunately, there are no assembly instructions to help us. In the absence of instructions, we tend to default to re-membering in ways that help preserve the status quo of our self and our worldview; and we are usually oblivious to the strangeness of the contraptions we come up with. I know that my memory is full of Rube Goldberg-like contraptions that bear little resemblance to the original event.

We erroneously tend to think of memory as a kind of camera that records everything it observes with the objectivity of a lens and preserves it accurately on film for later reviewing. But this is a flawed analogy that ignores the fact that our "memory lens" fails first of all to record everything we experience and then it adjusts what it does record to fit our "memory story." Our memory is less a photographer than an artist, giving us an expression of an ever-changing web of relationships and associations. Or it is like a movie always being filmed, edited and censored by an anonymous creative director running around in our heads. I was particularly impacted by an illuminating description of the way memory works that one of the characters gave in a novel by John Darnton:

> We think of memories as replicas of events that happened to us. Almost as if we made little films of our daily lives and stored those films away in our brain cells somewhere, canisters that can be opened at will. But now we know that it doesn't work like that. *Memories are not recaptured—they are made new each time.* Our brain tries to construct them out of the fundamental elements that were there because they touch us on some deep emotional level. And each time we construct it, the memory is different in some way or other, but we are unaware of the difference. So, strictly speaking, the memory is not of some past event, something over and done with that we are

---

[17] Duncan, *God Laughs and Plays, p. 19.*

recollecting afterward. It's a current event, a new experience happening in real time. The part of you that creates the illusion that you are recreating it—the projectionist for the film that isn't there—is your consciousness. [18]

Our memories are illusory at best and sheer illusions at worst.

Dominic Crossan makes this same point in his autobiographical book, *A Long Way from Tipperary*: "Between story and history lurks memory. It speaks like story, but claims like history." He goes on to give a fascinating account of the results of a psychological experiment at Emory University in which a group of freshmen were asked the day after the Challenger explosion to record details of how they had learned about the explosion. Then the same students were asked the same questions four years later, and the two sets of accounts were compared. The findings were quite surprising and disturbing. Many of the students never remembered making the earlier record and for the ones who did, their second record was either somewhat different or utterly different from their first. Even more alarming, many students asserted that their second record was correct, while the first record was dismissed as mistaken. In other words, the later memory completely replaced the earlier one. The most disconcerting finding of all was not only the frequent lack of any positive correlation, but often a negative correlation, between their certainty and their accuracy. For instance, a student who scored zero for accuracy by getting all the details of her first record wrong in her second record had scored her own certainty about her accuracy as 5 out of a possible 5.[19]

We not only have flawed memories of events, we can, in fact, even have "memories" of events we never actually experienced. The work of psychologist Elizabeth Loftus has demonstrated that memories can easily be planted in a person's mind— sometimes just by asking if they remember having experienced an event that never even happened. Subjects in her study would initially deny having had the experience, but about a third of them would later remember the experience as certainly as if it had taken place. In short, "to remember anything whatsoever…is

---

[18] John Darnton, *Mind Catcher*, pp. 135-136, emphasis added.
[19] John Dominic Crossan, *A Long Way from Tipperary*, p. 155.

to create not a work 'of reality' but of the human imagination."[20] My wife accuses me of this with some regularity.

We should note that all of the above aspects of perspective are present even when we are trying to be objective and fair. When bias, self-interest, self-deception, and deliberate distortion are factored into the process, our perceptions may often have very little indeed to do with "reality," especially if we are dealing with something ultimately beyond our knowing, such as God. I know that my own memories, my constructs of "reality," my personal worldview, and my writing are not exceptions to these aspects of perspective. I hope what follows is clear and understandable, and even persuasive; but I freely acknowledge that it is my testimony to my faith alone, from my perspective.

*****

The Importance of Story

> We all live by powerful, resounding stories, stories so true that they reveal to us God's purpose for the whole creation and the whole human family.
> Diana Eck [21]

> Story-telling matters enormously because it is story...which stands at the heart of our faith and which more perhaps than any other form of discourse speaks to our hearts and illumines our own stories.
> Frederick Buechner [22]

> Each of us acts today and hopes for tomorrow in the light of past experiences that have been woven into a life-story.... To be a self is to have a personal history.
> Bernhard W. Anderson [23]

> To be ourselves we must *have* ourselves—possess, if need be re-possess, our life stories. We must 'recollect' ourselves, recollect the inner drama, the narrative, of ourselves.
> Oliver Sachs[24]

---

[20] Cited by David James Duncan, *God Laughs and Plays*, p. 191.
[21] Eck, *Encountering God*, p. 90.
[22] Buechner, *A Room Called Remember*, p. 47.
[23] Anderson, *Understanding the Old Testament*, p. 1.
[24] Sachs, *The Man Who Mistook His Wife for a Hat*, p. 111, emphasis in the original.

God made man because he loves stories.
Elie Wiesel [25]

No matter what we talk about, we are talking about ourselves.
Hugh Prather [26]

Human beings are storytellers. Stories are one of the earliest ways we begin to construct our understanding of life: "Mommy, tell me a story." My childhood was certainly filled with stories that my mother told me, as well as the endless stream of Bible stories I heard at church, which were always illustrated with the most wonderful artwork. In my daughter's home, part of the bedtime ritual required by her first child when he was a two-year-old was his nightly request to "talk today," which meant that she was to tell the story of the day's significant events, discoveries, and moments in the life of the child and the family. For all of us, whether we consciously "talk today" to ourselves or not, narrative becomes the typical means of ordering our lives. We each build our life story as we move along through life, being shaped by our experiences and then shaping other experiences accordingly, telling and re-telling our story. The individual and community stories that we create then, in turn, re-create both our selves and our culture anew.

According to Elie Wiesel (who was perhaps quoting 18th century Rabbi Nachman of Bratzlev), God made us to be storytellers; it's our God-given nature. Theologian Harvey Cox goes so far as to assert that *"without our stories we would not be human.* Through our stories we assemble our pasts, place ourselves in a present and cast a hope for the future. Without our stories we would be bereft of memory or anticipation."[27] This has been true from long ago as primitive peoples developed the ceremonies and myths that formed them into communities. Through most of human existence, the foundation of personal identity was participation in the shared stories, legends, and myths of a tribe, nation, cult, or religious group. The shared memories and hopes of a person's group bound together the past, present, and future of the individual in community. In their collective stories, people developed their sense of shared existence—how they came to be, why they came to be who they were, and what this meant for how they would live their lives together. Those who told the stories may possibly have been aware of their communal importance from the first telling. More likely, they started off

---

[25] Wiesel, *The Gates of the Forest*, frontispiece.
[26] Prather, *I Touch the Earth, the Earth Touches Me*, n. p.
[27] Cox, *The Seduction of the Spirit*, p. 12, emphasis added.

just recalling and telling about interesting and significant events with little awareness of how the stories would linger and grow in importance.

In a 1979 NBC program called *Centennial*, the narrator spoke of a woman's letters from years earlier which were now to be published. As I recall, the narrator commented to this effect: "She'd laugh if she knew she was writing American history all that time. But that's what history is: women writing letters, men telling tales, people dying." That's certainly how primitive "history" came to be. For thousands of years, such stories were told and retold in tents and in temples and became the basis for civilization and for individual and communal self-identity. According to Ninian Smart, human beings "have the impulse to find out who they are by telling a story about how they came to be. Myth thus is the food which feeds our sense of identity."[28]

In his book *To a Dancing God*, Sam Keen links the death-of-God theology of the mid-1900s to a loss of confidence in all transcendent reference points:

> Modern man has lost his way in the forest, he cannot light the fire or say the prayer, and he is dangerously close to losing his ability to see his life as part of any story.... [Telling] stories is functionally equivalent to belief in God, and therefore, 'the death of God' is best understood as modern man's inability to believe that human life is ultimately meaningful by being incorporated into a story. [29]

In other words, the so-called death of God was in reality the death of our understanding of our relationship with God. To use Karl Barth's words, "humanity appears strangely lost in its history."[30] These words remind me of the widely quoted folk wisdom expressed by a Siberian Elder: "If you don't know the trees you may be lost in the forest, but if you don't know the stories you may be lost in life." Without a memory of a shared past and the hope of a shared future, it is difficult to place the current moment in a temporal context, unless we can tell a story.

As "modernism" itself seems to be dying, many postmodernists still seem to reject the notion of the grand story— the metanarrative— that gives context and meaning to life. This may be due, in part, to a commendable modesty that rejects the notion of any one story that is grand enough and big enough to provide a place for everyone. However this may be, there is ample evidence of the continued lack of the grand

---

[28] Smart, *Worldviews*, p. 95.
[29] Sam Keen, *To a Dancing God*, pp. 85-86.
[30] Barth, *Church Dogmatics IV.3.2*, p. 694.

story today, because many people do indeed seem to have lost their sense of identity and are "bereft of memory or anticipation." As theologian Jurgen Moltmann has noted, "We live more fragmentarily and experimentally than our fathers and mothers did....Our life story is no longer a long novel but rather a short story."[31] For some, I might add, life stories have been reduced to bumper stickers or the streaming minutiae of Facebook entries, YouTube tales, and "Tweets."

After several centuries of dominance by rationalism and science in western society, however, some observers suggest story may be experiencing a new chapter in postmodern life. In his book *A Whole New Mind*, Dan Pink argues that recent decades have belonged to the kind of person with a certain kind of mind found in computer programmers, lawyers, and MBAs. But, Pink believes, the future belongs to "a very different kind of person with a very different kind of mind—creators and empathizers, pattern recognizers and meaning makers...artists...storytellers...big picture thinkers."[32]

I think, perhaps, that a storyteller has said it best:

> It's no coincidence that just at this point in our insight into our mysteriousness as human beings struggling toward compassion, we are also moving into an awakened interest in the language of myth and fairy tale. The language of logical arguments, of proofs, is the language of the limited self we know and can manipulate. But the language of parable and poetry, of storytelling, moves from the imprisoned language of the provable into the freed language of what I must, for lack of another word, continue to call faith. [33]

*****

Myth, Metaphor and Meaning

> The word 'myth' has [a] connotation in common language [as] something that is not really true, or that it is only figuratively true. That connotation is...an expression of modern sophistication. The idea that one can stand outside oneself, as it were, and examine the fundamental beliefs by which one lives one's life (i.e., one's myth) was unknown in earlier times.

---

[31] Moltmann, *The Passion for Life*, p. 40.
[32] Quoted by Tom Peters, www.tompeters.com, posted 10/15/04.
[33] Madelaine L'Engle, http://www.storyteller.net/articles/160, accessed 6/20/08.

Primitive people…had no such critical distance from their myth. In fact, they did not even know they had a myth. Their society itself *was* the myth, fully articulated to form and guide all of human life.
John Biersdorf [34]

Typically a religion has a story or stories to tell. But they are not just any old stories—they are ones which quiver with special or sacred meaning. In the field of religion such stories are called myths.
Ninian Smart [35]

Man's ultimate concern must be expressed symbolically, because symbolic language alone is able to express the ultimate…. Myths are always present in every act of faith, because the language of faith is the symbol…. [There] is no substitute for the use of symbols and myths: they are the language of faith…. Christianity speaks the mythological language like every other religion.
Paul Tillich [36]

Throughout most of church history, biblical stories have been taken as both myth and history. Only with the rise of modern intellectualism and rationalism did we begin to make a distinction between the two terms and to think of history as dealing with truth and myth as dealing with fiction. For most people today, "myth" simply means an untrue story, the subject matter of television shows like "MythBusters" and web sites like snopes.com. In common usage today, a myth is only an urban legend or some other false account that has no basis in fact. In everyday language, saying "It's a myth" is just another way of saying "It's not true." But in theology and the comparative study of religions, "myth" is not a term that relates to the truthfulness or falsity of a story. The term "myth" simply refers to any story of divine or sacred significance, with no indication as to whether it is true or false. As Ninian Smart has said, it "is artificial to separate supposed false myths about the divine from 'true' stories as found in the Bible or elsewhere."[37] Wilfred Cantwell Smith, sounding a lot like Harvey Cox in the earlier quote, has argued the mythical is not in contrast to the historical. Rather, it is the mythical

---

[34] Biersdorf, *Hunger for Experience*, p. 14, emphasis added.
[35] Smart, *Worldviews*, p. 7.
[36] Tillich, *Dynamics of Faith*, pp. 41, 51, 54.
[37] Smart, *Worldviews*, p. 80.

that has made "human history human."[38]

In its origin, the word "myth" simply means "story." However, whereas a story can relate only to an individual, myth has a communal meaning: "A myth is not just about me: it is about us."[39] A myth is a shared story that makes sense of ourselves and our participation in community. "One absorbs the myth by learning to live and function in the community."[40] Our myths give meaning to our lives, our actions and our relationships with one another.

For me, it is only a short journey from myth to metaphor, because metaphor also involves us in a web of meanings, in much the same way as does myth. Metaphor means to "see as," to see one thing in terms of another thing. We can hardly speak of the experiences of life without resorting to metaphors: "mortgage meltdown," "housing bubble," "ten-foot pole," "road map to peace," "search engine," "sunset years"—I could go on like this until "the Lord returns," but you get the point. Metaphors abound in everyday conversation and are the playground of headline writers: "Fear slices into sales," "Demise of honeybees may sting sales," "Baker set to expand footprint," just to cite a few from a recent newspaper. Leonard Sweet describes metaphors as "the software of thought" and "the stuff of which our mind is made"—using two pretty good metaphors to make his point.[41]

Metaphors are by no means limited to casual communication. At their best and truest, our songs and stories, our myths and metaphors are all attempts to plumb the depths of human experience and to give some expression to what we find at the core of our being. But when we start considering the use of metaphors in religion, we are treading on sacred but shaky ground, because as Eugene Peterson points out, a "metaphor is literally a lie. It is simply not true."[42] How can we use a "lie" to tell a truth? In fact, we do it all the time. Metaphors (lies?) are the stuff of our hymns (A Mighty Fortress Is Our God), our prayers (Father, we lift up our hearts to you this morning.), our scripture (Jesus said, "I am the real vine, and my Father is the gardener." John 15:1), and our professions of faith (I have been born again.). Metaphor scandalizes because it seems to be wrong, and as Walter Percy has observed, "it is wrongest when it is most beautiful."[43] It seems that the most beautiful

---

[38] Smith, *Religious Diversity*, p. 54.

[39] Smart, *ibid*, p. 94.

[40] John Biersdorf, *Hunger for Experience*, p. 14.

[41] Sweet, *Soul Tsunami*, p. 201, using another good metaphor as the title of his book.

[42] Peterson, *The Jesus Way*, p. 215.

[43] Percy, *The Message in the Bottle*, p. 66.

truth can best be told with words that are "wrong," that are, factually, "lies."

All language that we apply to God is actually metaphorical language. In fact, the word *God* is itself a metaphor, because the word points beyond itself to infinite, divine Being and Mystery. Truth, especially religious truth, is inexpressible without symbol and metaphor, because of the inadequacy of language. Although she was speaking of song writing, Roseanne Cash could have been referring to metaphor when she spoke of the limitations of language:

> We are so deeply limited by language.... Songs are the attempt to convey what is under and behind language, and so it is counter-productive, if not counter-intuitive, to clutch at the exactitudes of circumstances that retreat further in meaning the more desperate we become to quantify them. [44]

I need at this point to be clear about my understanding of the difference between "true" and "truth." On the one hand, metaphors can be profoundly true whether or not they are literally or factually true. On the other hand, many things in life are literally or factually true but have minimal or no truth value for life. This is particularly applicable for stories, which makes them "dangerous stuff," as Dominic Crossan has pointed out. He says that some stories are literally true, but "literal stories fill our newspapers each morning and our garbage cans each evening." Others, he goes on to say, "are only metaphorically true.... It is by them we live and we die. They are *only* metaphor as around us is *only* air—try living without it."[45] To believe that a metaphor *is* true is not so important as being able to *see* truth in the light of the metaphor. It is for this reason that Jesus spent so much time telling stories as a means of conveying truth. "Jesus taught in parables, analogies, figures of speech, and startling metaphors to stir the sediment of people's hearts and open their eyes to the deeper meanings of life."[46]

Roseanne Cash has given as good an account of the profound difference between "facts" and "truth" as one could want:

> An amalgamation of facts strung together, even as a poetic narrative, is not necessarily the same thing as truth.... The

---

[44] Cash, "The Ear of the Beholder," http://measureformeasure.blogs.nytimes.com/2008/05/22 the-ear-of-the-beholder/, accessed June 27, 2008.

[45] Crossan, *A Long Way from Tipperary*, p. 142, emphasis in the original.

[46] Leonard Sweet, *Soul Tsunami*, p. 203.

'truth' (or 'honesty') and the 'facts' are not necessarily the same, they are not necessarily equal and one often requires the suspension of the other.... [It] is an immutable 'truth' in art and music that facts are not necessarily the best indicators of the deepest human experience. [47]

Similarly, the meaning of our deepest human experiences of religion and spirituality rarely comes to us as simple, straightforward "facts of life." Meaning is always a byproduct of living and searching, of finding and being found by truth.

---

[47] Cash, "The Ear of the Beholder," ibid.

PART ONE: THE BIBLE AS STORY

The Bible is the memory book for Jews and Christians.
Walter Brueggemann [1]

The Bible is not the story of ideas about God, but the story of the
people of God.
Leslie Newbigin [2]

The world that we now read of in our Bibles was an essentially oral
world.... Language in itself, in its origins and in most of its practice,
is oral. We *speak* words long before we write and read them.... In
our Holy Scriptures story is the primary verbal means for bringing
God's word to us. For this we can be grateful, for story is our most
accessible form of speech.
Eugene Peterson [3]

Readers of the English Bible continue to have a difficult time
with the notion that they are reading a book not written by or
for them nor in their own language, and so, conveniently, they
forget that inconvenient fact.
Peter Gomes [4]

---

[1] Brueggemann, *The Bible Makes Sense*, p.79.
[2] Newbigin, Quoted by Robert McAfee Brown, *The
Significance of the Church*, p. 33.
[3] Peterson, *The Jesus Way*, pp. 62, 71, emphasis in the
original.
[4] Gomes, *The Good Book*, p. 73.

The Bible as Story

The Bible is full of stories, containing relatively little expository prose. By some assessments, narrative story is the most common single type of writing in the Bible, accounting for 40 percent of the biblical material.[5] Even more important, the Bible itself *is* story, "the unfolding narrative of God at work in a violent, sinful world, calling people…into a new way of life."[6]

We tend to approach the Bible as the written text of a book. In fact, the very word "Bible" means "book," which presents us with a fundamental problem. (No pun intended.) If we are going to approach the Bible on its terms rather than ours, however, we must understand most of the words that we are now reading were spoken and heard long before they were ever written and read. The stories of the Bible were spoken and then re-spoken countless times as part of a long tradition of oral transmission. This is particularly so of the narratives of the Old Testament, where generations of orally transmitted traditions were finally written down long after the stories were first told. One of the few things I remember from my seminary class on biblical Hebrew is that Hebrew was first and foremost an oral language, lacking even the linguistic elements required for it to be written. In ancient Israel, an event, either private or corporate, was first experienced, and then remembered, told, re-told, adapted, collected, and only much later written down, copied and, finally, read. Every phase of the transmission, including the final writing, added new layers of interpretation and understanding—all of this reflecting that these were "truth" stories, rather than stories that were merely "true." In the Old Testament literature, we have what Walter Brueggemann has described as a "traditioning process" of "interpretive history" that is "confessional and not reportorial in character."[7]

Historians have come to recognize that *all* history is interpreted history—perceived, formed, and told in light of an overarching understanding of life. As Old Testament scholar Bernhard Anderson stresses,

> History is not a series of naked facts arranged in chronological order like beads on a string. It is absurd to suppose that an event is a kind of 'thing in itself' which can be recovered after

---

[5] I don't remember where I picked this up, but I believe it is probably a fair assessment.

[6] Brian McLaren, *A Generous Orthodoxy*, pp. 167, 171.

[7] Brueggemann, *An Introduction to the Old Testament*, p. 8; *The Bible Makes Sense*, p. 50.

all interpretation is stripped away. An event is a meaningful
happening in the life of a people. And history is the narration
of those experienced events—events so memorable that they
are preserved in the oral memory and eventually written down
in records. [8]

"History" is itself something of an ambiguous term. We commonly use
it to refer to the process of events or to the story of that process, and
sometimes to both. We often forget, however, that history is never free
from interpretation. History never gives us the bare bones reporting of
the "actuality" of an event as it "took place." "Facticity" is always
secondary to meaning. There is always an element of interpretation even
on the part of the first observer or eyewitness.

As I have already asserted, the process of human consciousness
cannot isolate observation from interpretation, so even the "eyewitness
report" of an honest and consciously unbiased observer presents an
edited (and, often, an editorialized) version of the "actuality." What we
call the events of history are always seen through the interpretive
judgment of the eyewitnesses and, more often, through subsequent
layers of interpretations of later generations. The original observer's
interpretation itself becomes a new "fact" of history. These interpreted
"facts," in turn, subsequently impact later historical happenings as a
result of their shaping influences on the lives and minds of succeeding
generations.

History is always made up of event *plus* meaning, and the meaning is
subject to change with the passage of time and change of circumstances.
Later interpreters of history make their selections from the "received
history," and then make new judgments and interpretations according to
some current principle or faith that is their guide. The best we can do in
trying to uncover the actual original event is to try to "read backwards"
through the series of interpretations, hoping eventually to arrive at a
likely understanding of the human reactions to the original event and the
reasons for the various subsequent interpretations. This process can
certainly be informed by the work in related fields such as archeology,
but a true understanding also requires the capacity to enter
sympathetically into the minds of those who have left the records of
their experiences and reactions and understandings.

To read beyond the words to the meaning of the words and then to
go beyond the reported events to the divine truth revealed through the
events takes spiritual imagination. One of my favorite examples of
interpreted event is recorded in the 12th chapter of John's Gospel,

---

[8] Anderson, *Understanding the Old Testament*, p. 22.

where Jesus was wrestling in turmoil of soul with the approaching hour of his death. In John's telling of the story (John 12: 27-29), Jesus accepted what lay ahead as the fulfillment of his purpose and prayed, "Father, glorify thy name." And then, John wrote, "A voice sounded from heaven: 'I have glorified it, and I will glorify it again.' The crowd standing by said it was thunder, while others said, 'An angel has spoken to him.'" My guess is that the ears of the bystanders heard thunder. The hearts of some of the bystanders heard the voice of God's angel. Vibrations of their eardrums registered thunder. Vibrations of their heartstrings resounded with the voice of God. Jesus heard the words of God, and his heartstrings vibrated with the Word.

*****

The Bible as Story: Narrative Theology

In looking at the Bible as story I stumbled unknowingly into the field of "narrative theology." At the time I first came up with the notion of seeing the Bible as story (in the 1960s), I was totally unaware of both the term "narrative theology" and its emphasis on understanding the Bible as story. In recent brief readings in the field, I have found myself in agreement with much that I have read. In fact, in recent years, I have even unknowingly read from some of the authors who are associated with the field, which probably means that I have absorbed some of the content of narrative theology without knowing it. However, I make no claim that I am being consistent with the premises and positions of narrative theology. Here, as elsewhere throughout this book, I am seeking only to be consistent to my own confessional beliefs. And, since narrative theology in any formal sense had little, in any, influence on me, I will leave more extensive treatment of the subject to others.

46

Understanding the Biblical Story

To read is to interpret.
Peter Gomes [9]

[There] are no innocent interpretations and no innocent interpreters.
Walter Brueggemann [10]

The language of the Bible is a language to be read and reread,
to be pondered and scrutinized. To the eyes and heart of faith,
after all, it is a love letter, one long love letter.
Jaroslav Pelikan [11]

If we study the whole Bible, its central concerns come through
clearly enough. We learn that we are all sinners, that God
loves us anyway, and that knowing our salvation rests on grace
frees us to live in service of God and neighbor without
worrying about how we will be rewarded.
William C. Placher [12]

The Bible is a constant best seller. Yet, the book that practically everybody owns is a book that relatively few read. It may well be true that never has there been a book so widely owned and so rarely read. The book that everybody knows about is also one that relatively few know much about. Speaking about the New Testament (although their words could apply to the entire Bible), Howard Clark Kee and Franklin W. Young have said, "There is no book in the English language that we quote oftener and understand less than we do the New Testament."[13] A major reason for this lack of reading and understanding the Bible is that it is not an easy book to read or to understand. It is an anthology of diverse ancient writings in languages other than English, spanning nearly two millennia and separated from us by another two millennia, serving a variety of sometimes obscure purposes, and originating in a part of the world about which we generally have little understanding and frequently have little interest (except for how it affects our oil supply and national security). Further, the collection was assembled by unknown editors in

---

[9] Gomes, *The Good Book*, p. 25.
[10] Brueggemann, *An Introduction to the Old Testament*, p. 400.
[11] Pelikan, *Whose Bible Is It?*, p. 231.
[12] Placher, "Struggling with Scripture," *Struggling with Scripture*, p. 37.
[13] Kee and Young, *Understanding the New Testament*, p.1.

an unfamiliar literary format lacking any obvious plot.

Unlike most books, the Bible is not best read by starting at page one and reading through to the end. Few have the endurance to complete this process, and even those who do will not necessarily achieve much understanding. Nor is it properly read by what New Testament scholar A. M. Hunter has called the "lucky dip" method, where a text is selected at random with the expectation that somehow God will guide your finger to just the passage you need for the moment. This method may have been helpful in some instances, but it is does not lead to a proper understanding of the Bible. Neither is the Bible to be broken into selected isolated verses and passages which are then treated like fortune cookies to break open and read for moral and spiritual guidance, although the devotional value of such reading may be worthwhile. More dangerous still is to read isolated verses and passages and use them as bullets in a spiritual ammunition belt to win arguments and defeat opposing points of view. In the words of William Sloane Coffin, "Too many Christians use the Bible as a drunk does a lamppost—for support rather than for illumination."[14]

A proper understanding of the Bible requires that it be viewed in its entirety. This means we must uncover the basic story line, the "plot," if we are to link the diversity of material into a cohesive unit. It is at this point that we need to recall the influence of perspective on how and what we see. Earlier I cited a Jewish proverb that reads: "We do not see things as they are, but as we are." This is not only true in general, it is also true of how we read and understand the Bible. There is a big word for this: "hermeneutics." Hermeneutics is the term used for the formal process of establishing principles of interpretation and explanation of meaning. When used in the fields of theology and biblical studies, it applies to the general principles used to determine the meaning of the Scriptures. Informally, it applies to the less structured, but no less real, method we all use in approaching the Bible.

Peter Gomes, minister of The Memorial Church at Harvard, has this to say about our hermeneutical method:

> Everyone who reads the Bible, whether they acknowledge it or
> not, does so within a hermeneutical theory, for interpretation
> is what we do when we read.... [We] apply either explicitly or
> implicitly a theory of interpretation to which we submit the

---

[14] Coffin, *A Passion for the Possible*, p. 63. Coffin was probably paraphrasing humorist Robert Orben's comment about how people use statistics.

We each bring to our reading of the Bible an assortment of presuppositions, information, biases, prejudices, emotions, memories, and experiences that inevitably influence our reading. Old Testament scholar Walter Brueggemann says quite frankly, "There is no interpretation of Scripture…that is unaffected by the passions, convictions, and perceptions of the interpreter."[16] Even more bluntly, Eugene Peterson says, "These words given to us in our Scriptures are constantly getting overlaid with personal preferences, cultural assumptions, sin distortions, and ignorant guesses that pollute the text."[17] And as with other aspects of our lives, our model for reading the Bible is influenced by our life experiences and relationships with others: "[How] we read the Bible, each of us, is partly a plot of family, neighbors, and friends…and partly the God-given accident of long-term development in faith."[18]

Finally, reading and understanding the Bible is always a work in progress. We never have the final reading or understanding. As Brueggemann says, it "is inescapably provisional reading. It is rightly done with modesty that belongs to those who are yet to be surprised always again by what is 'strange and new.'"[19] I can testify to this in my own experiences of reading the Bible, where a text that I know I have read many times suddenly speaks a new Word to me.

All of this also applies not just to reading the Bible, but also to knowing God. In his book *He Who Lets Us Be*, Geddes MacGregor frankly acknowledges that our "concept of God…reflects the model we are using."[20] As with the hermeneutical method of our Bible-reading, our "God-knowing" is always influenced by our passions, convictions, and perceptions; it is also part of a "family plot;" and it is always provisional, never final.

So, how do I read the Bible and how do I understand God at this point in life? The foundational hermeneutic with which I read the Bible and base everything I know about God is summed in three words: **GOD IS LOVE** (1 John 4:8, 16); and 1 John 4:16 continues, "he who dwells in love is dwelling in God, and God in him." This affirmation of love as

---

[15] Gomes, *The Good Book*, p. 357.

[16] Brueggemann, "Biblical Authority," *Struggling with Scripture*, p. 20.

[17] Peterson, *Eat This Book*, p. 53.

[18] Brueggemann, *ibid*, p. 10.

[19] Brueggemann, *ibid*, p.13.

[20] MacGregor, *He Who Lets Us Be*, pp. 96-97.

the nature of God and the nature of life lived in God is my starting point and the filter through which I pass every reading of Scripture, every assessment of meaning in life, and every statement about God. While the storyline of the Bible has multiple threads, I believe the working of the God's love in creation and history is the underlying plot of the biblical story, and all other threads of the story are subplots that must be understood in light of this main plot. To borrow a phrase I recently came across from Leonard Sweet, the Bible is "the 'I Love You' Story."[21] As Paul Tillich has put it:

> God and love are not two realities; they are one. God's Being is the being of love and God's infinite power of Being is the infinite power of love.... The criterion, the ultimate criterion, is love. [22]

I know that God is love not because Paul Tillich tells me so. I know it not even because the Bible tells me so. In fact, in the Old Testament (and to be honest, in places in the New Testament) a first time reading (or even repeated readings) will not necessarily lead one to define God as love. Many readers of the Bible, and even many Christian believers, come away with a God more of judgment and wrath than of reconciliation and love.

I know that God is love because of the Bible's witness to the life of Jesus. And I know it because I have found it to be true in my own life. Undoubtedly, my affirmation of God's nature came partially through years of reading and trusting the Bible. But my belief now is not propositional; it is confessional. I now believe that "God is love" not because of the authority of Scripture; rather, I now believe the authority of Scripture because I find there the story of God's love that I have come to know in ever richer and deeper ways in my own life. I can affirm in my own experience these words from William Sloane Coffin:

> Socrates had it wrong; it is not the unexamined but finally the uncommitted life that is not worth living. Descartes too was mistaken; 'Cogito ergo sum'-- 'I think therefore I am'? Nonsense. 'Amo ergo sum'—'I love therefore I am.' Or, as with unconscious eloquence St. Paul wrote, 'Now abide faith, hope, love, these three; and the greatest of these is love.' I believe that. I believe that it is better not to live than not to

---

[21] Sweet uses this as the title of Part 2 of his book, *The Three Hardest Words*.

[22] Tillich, *The New Being*, p. 26.

love."[23]

I believe that also.

*****

The Void in God's Heart

We find [God] as runaway children, weary of their escapade,
find their father. *They consent to be found by him.*
Harry Emerson Fosdick [24]

The deepest truth is that there is nothing we can do to make
God love us more than God already loves us and nothing we
can do to make God stop loving us. The One who is behind
all things is nothing but love, always has been and always will
be.
John Claypool[25]

While my wife, Kay, and I were in Greece in the fall of 2003, we
visited the royal tombs near Verria (the biblical town of Berea) and saw
the tomb of Phillip II of Macedon, father of Alexander the Great. The
museum at the tomb displayed many of the objects (gold, weapons,
jewelry, etc.) that had been placed in the tomb to ease Phillip's existence
in the afterlife. I was reminded of the consistency with which human
beings throughout the millennia, around the world, and from virtually all
religions (and from virtually no religion) have sought assurance of
meaningful existence after death and some measure of promise
regarding that existence. Looking at all of the objects from the tomb, I
was struck in a new way by the futility of our search for these
assurances.

Then, with clarity like never before, came the assurance! We don't
have to search! We simply have to be found, by the "hound of heaven,"
to use Francis Thompson's term for the Holy Spirit. This has become a
key component of my biblical hermeneutic. In the words of Robert
McAfee Brown,

It wouldn't be enough to say that the Bible is the record of
man's search for God.... It is much closer to the truth to say that

---

[23] Coffin, *Credo*, p. 5.
[24] Fosdick, *The Meaning of Being a Christian*, p. 259,
emphasis added.
[25] Claypool, *God the Ingenious Alchemist*, p. 18.

the Bible is the record of God's search for man. Throughout the Bible people seem bent on trying to escape from God. And in spite of this, God continues to seek after those same people, refusing to give up, continuing the pursuit in spite of countless rebuffs and evasions. [26]

In the words of the Psalmist, "Goodness and love unfailing, these will follow me all the days of my life" (Ps. 23:6a). In commenting on this psalm, Walter Brueggemann wrote of God's pursuing love this way:

> We are being chased by God's powerful love. We run from it. We try to escape. We fear the goodness, because then we are no longer in control.... [But it is time to quit running], to let ourselves be caught and embraced in love.... 'I will dwell in the house of the Lord forever,' that is, 'my whole life long.'... The last line of the psalm asserts that *the true joy and purpose of life are to love God and be loved by God....* [27]

This is so amazing that it risks being incredible—not only unbelievable, but also untrue.

Along with this reassurance of God's searching and pursuing love came a new understanding. Pascal has been quoted as having said something along the lines of, "There is a God-shaped void inside each of us, and our hearts are restless until it is filled." The new understanding was this: there is a "Davis-shaped void" inside the heart of God, and God's love for me makes God's heart restless until the void is filled. And this is true not just for me, but for each person who is created in God's image—in other words, for each of us, for all of us. Our God-created nature comes with a void for God only because God's nature comes with a void for each of us. Love always has a void until it is met with a response of love from the beloved.

Before I met and fell in love with Kay, I had no "Kay-shaped void" in my heart; but now I do, and only she can fill it. No one else can love me enough to fill the void that has her shape. Before I had children and grandchildren, I had no voids in my heart with their shapes; but now I do, and only each one of them can fill his or her individual void in my heart. If that is true for me, whose love is as flawed as it is, it must be infinitely true for God, who *is* love.

Not everyone is comfortable with this concept of God, because it

---

[26] Brown, *The Bible Speaks to You*, p.15, emphasis in the original.
[27] Brueggemann, *The Threat of Life*, p. 95, emphasis added.

suggests that God is incomplete without us. They say things like "God has no needs." "God needs no friends." "God doesn't need us." As great a theologian as Thomas Aquinas argued that God has no needs, including no need of us.[28] Maybe God doesn't need us, but God apparently loves us. And the very nature of love is that it is costly for the lover. It seems odd to declare that God is love, and then maintain that God's love is not a love that is affected by the response of the one who is loved, even when the response is rejection that would bring about suffering in the heart of any lesser lover. I like what Jurgen Moltmann has to say about God at this point:

> The God about whom the people spoke from experience in the Old and New testaments...is no cold, silent, heavenly power that sits self-sufficiently upon his throne and scatters gracious alms among his subjects. He displays a great passion for creations, for human beings, and for the future.... He is not immutable in the sense of being incapable of being hurt by human refusal of his love. Neither is he perfect in the sense of being perfectly content whether or not his searching love actually finds those whom he seeks and loves. [29]

This means that God's heart longs for each of us, individually, personally—not in theory, not in general, not as humankind, but as specific individuals who each has a place in God's heart, shaped around each person's own shape (soul). This is the Good News, that God longs for *EACH* of us so much that God gave God's heart (in Christ) for each of us! This, I suggest, is the nature of what the New Testament calls *agape*. As Paul Tillich has expressed it, "*Agape* seeks that which is concrete, individual, unique, here and now. *Agape* seeks the person, the other one who cannot be exchanged for anything or anyone else."[30]

This foundational understanding of God as love runs head on into the notion of God as unlimited power. Once we start with the affirmation that "God is love," everything we go on to say about God's power must be subordinate to this primary affirmation. In his book *He Who Lets Us Be*, Geddes MacGregor has some helpful insights into the

---

[28] From what I understand, Aquinas said that God creates out of love, not out of need, which may not be that different from what I am saying. However, I am not qualified to parse, much less correct, the theology of Aquinas; I must leave that to others.

[29] Moltmann, *The Passion for Life* pp. 22, 92.

[30] Tillich, *Biblical Religion and the Search for Ultimate Reality*, p.50.

relationship of love and power:

> Only love can let another being be.... God must not only
> occasionally restrain himself in the exercise of his power; he
> must never exercise it at all except in support of love, and love
> without freedom is impossible. Love *is* the abdication of
> power.... To say that God is omnipotent can only mean that
> nothing diminishes his love.... Since the root metaphor is
> love, the other dependent metaphors cannot be used apart
> from it. The only kind of wisdom God can exhibit must be
> whatever kind is compatible with love. The only kind of
> knowledge he can be said to have is the kind that springs from
> love. [31]

I would add that whatever kind of holiness that God has must also
be the kind that is compatible with love. Some people have a
hermeneutic for understanding God based on God's holiness, and they
say that God's holiness means that God can have nothing to do with sin
and with sinners. They may say it more eloquently and in complex
theological language, but the essence of their message is that before God
can allow me to be close, I must be "cleaned up"—and, according to
this view this is what God does for me in Christ on the cross. This
sounds good, but it still distances me from God. And I believe that it is
not consistent with God's incarnation in Jesus, which is the result of
God's love for us while we were still sinners (John 3:17). The
incarnation is God setting aside the divine holiness that would maintain
distance and coming among us and getting down and dirty with us out
of love. As one of my ethics professors in seminary has expressed it,
"God's *holiness* is revealed not in distance from all sinners but in being
with us to redeem us... [Holiness] is seen in redemptive compassion
rather than in being separate from whatever is unclean."[32]

Back in the 1960s Ivan Tors was an animal trainer and producer of
the television series "Gentle Ben" and "Daktari," along with numerous
other animal films and programs. The method commonly used in
training animals in that day and time could be summed up as "whip-and-
fear." In contrast, Tors used a technique that he called "affection
training," which began in the nursery where attendants spent the day

---

[31] MacGregor, *He Who Lets Us Be*, pp. 57, 120, 128,
emphasis in the original. This book is well worth reading
for a full treatment of this relationship between God's
love and God's power.
[32] Glen Stassen, *Living the Sermon on the Mount*, pp. 26,
105, emphasis in the original.

fondling young animals in keeping with Tors' concept that "you cannot love without touching." That phrase has lingered in my mind over the years: "You cannot love without touching." I suspect that those words express an eternal truth about the nature of all love, including the divine love. I believe that God loves us while we are still sinners; and this means that God takes me—dirty hands, dirty feet, dirty heart and all—into God's very heart. Because even God cannot love in the abstract and from a distance, separated and isolated.

There is no precondition on God's love except the willingness on my part to come to God: "Whosoever will may come." God loves me *first* and cleans me up *later*. God's own holy self was sacrificed in the incarnation in Jesus' life as well as in his death. "God was in Christ reconciling the world to himself," and he *touched* people and allowed *them* to touch him.[33] He loved people up close and down and dirty. Someone has described the life of Jesus beautifully as "a sacrament of intimacy." In the life of Jesus as well as on the cross of Jesus, God's own purity and holiness got dirty with *our* dirt—because God knows that you cannot love without touching.

To sum it up, for me the basic plot of the Bible—of God's story, of the story of Israel's and the Church's experiences of God, and the story of my experiences of God—is *a love story*, the story of God's love for humankind, for each of us and all of us, for me, for you. In the words of Leonard Sweet: "The grand narrative…is the story of 'I love you' like no other love story."[34] God's love for us is what Robert McAfee Brown refers to as the "fundamental miracle": "the fact—the miraculous, inexplicable, fact—that God loves stumbling, sinful people like us."[35] This is for me both the fundamental and foundational miracle of my life and faith. In identifying myself as one who lives *by* the love of God and one who is called to *live* the love of God, I find the basic unity in my life that links past, present and future. In my understanding of love as relational and communal I find not only unity in my life; I find my life in comm*unity*. It is in love and in community that I have my story.

History provides the setting for the biblical story and for the working out of God's love despite all of our individual and collective efforts to resist and oppose it. In Sam Keen's words, "The whole of history is a story for which God has provided the script."[36] With this basic clue to understanding, we may now be able to establish an

---

[33] See, for example, Mark 1:31, 1:41, 3:10, 5:27-31, 5:41, 6:56, 7:33, 8:22-23, 9:27.
[34] Sweet, *The Three Hardest Words*, p. 24.
[35] Brown, *The Bible Speaks to You*, p. 86.
[36] Keen, *To a Dancing God*, pp. 90-91.

overarching view of the biblical revelation that will provide a workable framework within which we can gain understanding of both the biblical story and its major subplots. It is in this story that I find *my* story. And, in the process of exploring the biblical story, we may even find *our* story.

*****

The Biblical Back-Story

In a very real sense, the first eleven chapters of Genesis provide the "back-story," or prologue, of the main story of the Bible. These chapters contain the opening scenes of history and of the whole biblical drama. If we are to understand the biblical story, we have to back up to the beginning. Interestingly, there are two beginnings to the story, both of which are poetic accounts of occurrences for which there can be no literal account. The first creation account (Gen. 1:1-2:4a) declares and celebrates the power of God in creation. The second account (Gen. 2:4b-25) declares and celebrates fellowship as the purpose of God in creation.

In the first account, which is a poem of powerful majesty, we are given an account of God's creative acts that call the entire universe into being. The story begins with the storyteller: "In the beginning, God." And without delay the story gets underway in the powerful, creative acts of God. God created. For six days God created, and in those six days God created the cosmos out of chaos. This was not creation out of nothing (although there are many more qualified than I who believe that it is creation *ex nihilo*, "out of nothing"), but creation that gave order to the undifferentiated mass and mess of pre-creation chaos. For six days God created, and every day God declared that the result of the day's work was "good." On the sixth day, humankind, the crowning achievement of the creative process, was created in the image of God. And on the sixth day, after all was said and done, God looked upon "all that he had made, and it was very good" (Gen. 1:30).

The stage is set, the cast is on stage, and the drama begins to unfold. But, before we rush into the story, we need to consider briefly a basic question about the nature of the lead characters the author of the story has created. What is meant by the declaration that we human beings are created in the image of God? At the very least, I think it suggests that human beings more closely resemble God than do any of the other creatures. Out of all of the creatures, only human beings have the potential for hearing, communing, and relating to God. In his book *The Message in the Bottle*, Walter Percy explores the question "Why is it that

56

men speak and animals don't?"[37] While reading that book I was struck with the notion that our being created in the image of God has to do with our capability for language. God (who may be known as Word) speaks creation and us into being; we, in turn, speak in ways that no other of God's creatures can even come close to doing. We human beings are the speaking creatures of the creative God who speaks.

Further, we share a trace of God's creativity and are given responsibility for a derivative sovereignty to have dominion over the earth in a continuation of God's creative work, "participating in God's creation under God's direction."[38] This derivative sovereignty is not permission for exploitation, which treats God's creation as belonging to us (which is an attitude that has brought us to the brink of ecological crisis), but it is an assignment of stewardship to care for God's good creation which still belongs to God. We are to be mediators of God's presence in the world, acting toward creation on God's behalf as God would act. We have been entrusted with the care of both the stage and the plot of the story. In a sense, the drama that is about to take place is a sort of improvisation, where the actors and the author interact in the development of the storyline. The nature of the story as a love story has been determined by the nature of the author, but, like most love stories, the plot of this story will take many a twist and turn. In fact, it is not long before the actors try to recast the story and rewrite the script. But, I'm jumping ahead.

There are really two "Scene Ones" in the back-story. While the first creation account is, perhaps, better known, and is certainly essential to understanding the nature of all that exists in the universe of the story, it is the second creation account that best sets the stage for reading the Bible as a love story. Walter Brueggemann points that "We are prone to think of creation as an act that simply lets people be. But creation is a call to be in relationship with the caller."[39] It is nothing less than a call to participate in the creative passion of God. This second account is a wonderfully and simply told tale of the intimacy of God's involvement in the creation of human selfhood. In this account there is no powerful voice declaring the universe into existence with sovereign pronouncements of "let there be." In this story, God is more of a sculptor who literally breathes God's own breath into the nostrils of a clay figure, so that "man became a living creature" (Gen. 2:7). Eugene Peterson notes, in an image that I find both wondrous and humbling, we

---

[37] Percy, *The Message in the Bottle*, p. 8.
[38] Eugene Peterson, *Christ Plays in Ten Thousand Places,* p. 77.
[39] Brueggemann, *The Bible Makes Sense*, p. 22.

"breath [sic] the same air that God breathed over the deep" in the beginning of creation.[40] In this intimate moment of in-breathing the divine breath, human life begins:

> From the damp soil, Yahweh scoops up earth and molds the figure of the first man. He breathes breath into this inert form and it becomes a living self, a 'soul.' Selfhood in the Bible is the result of a union of body (flesh) and divine breath. The man does not *have* a soul; he *is* a soul, a self, when and only when the union of body and spirit has taken place. [41]

Scott Cairns has given a wonderful version of this creation account in his poem "YHWH's Image," capturing the intimacy of the Creator with human creation, which is in the Creator's own image:

> And YHWH [42] sat in the dust, bone weary after days of strenuous making, during which He, now and again, would pause to consider the way things were shaping up....

> But when YHWH Himself finally sat on a dewy lawn—the first stage of his work all but finished—He took in a great breath laced with all lush odors of creation. It made him almost giddy.

> As He exhaled, a sigh and sweet mist spread out from him, settling over the earth.... Then YHWH lay back, running His hands over the damp grasses, and in deep contemplation reached into the soil, lifting great handsful [sic] of trembling clay to His lips, which parted to avail another breath.

> With this clay He began to coat His shins, cover His thighs, His chest. He continued this layering, and, when He had been wholly interred, He parted the clay at His side, and retreated from it, leaving the image of Himself to wander in what remained of that early morning mist. [43]

I like that. But my all-time favorite retelling of this creation event is the

---

[40] Peterson, *Christ Plays in Ten Thousand Places*, p. 69.

[41] Walter Harrelson, *Interpreting the Old Testament*, p. 46, emphasis in the original.

[42] Note: "YHWH" is the representation of the name "Yahweh," which is the Hebrew name for God in this passage from Genesis and in many other passages in the first five books of the Bible.

[43] Scott Cairns, *Recovered Body*, p. 39.

one expressed by James Weldon Johnson in the inimitable style of the African American preacher in a sermon poem entitled "The Creation:"

> And God stepped out on space,
> And he looked around and said:
> I'm lonely—
> I'll make me a world....
>
> [And after creating everything but humanity,]
> God looked around
> On all he had made...
> And God said: 'I'm lonely still.'
>
> Then...God thought and thought,
> Till he thought: I'll make me a man!
>
> Up from the bed of the river
> God scooped the clay;
> And by the bank of the river
> He kneeled him down;
> And there the great God Almighty
> Who lit the sun and fixed it in the sky,
> Who flung the stars to the most far corner of the night,
> Who rounded the earth in the middle of his hand;
> This Great God,
> Like a mammy bending over her baby,
> Kneeled down in the dust
> Toiling over a lump of clay
> Till he shaped it in his own image;
>
> Then into it he blew the breath of life,
> And man became a living soul.
> Amen. Amen. [44]

Amen, indeed! This Great God loves me like a baby, and breathes life into me. As expressed in a wonderful phrase from Reynolds Price, Genesis gives us a creation account of our "origin-in-love."[45]

This is not just a story about the dim and distant beginnings of humanity; it is about us. We tend to read the name Adam as if it is the proper name, with a capital A, of the first individual man: "Mr. Adam." This name is much more profound than that, however. The Hebrew word *adamah* is the term for "ground." The Hebrew term *adam* is derived

---

[44] Johnson, *God's Trombones*, pp. 17, 19, 20.
[45] Price, *A Palpable God*, p. 22.

from this word for ground and basically means "of the ground:" "Then the Lord God formed *adam* from the dust of the *adamah* and breathed into his nostrils the breath of life. Thus *adam* became a living creature" (Gen. 2:7). Rather than being the name of the first individual man, *adam* is the name of all humankind and identifies our tie to the earth. (In the next chapter of Genesis, *adam* does become a proper name, but its original use is clearly in a generic sense meaning "humankind.") Hence, this is not just a myth of pre-historical beginnings; it is the story of all of our beginnings:

> Since this Genesis text is not just about how things got started but how things are going right now, it might be more accurate to replace the 'in general' translation of *adam* as 'the human' or 'the human being' with personal pronouns: we, you, us. [46]

An essential element of the story appears immediately: humankind's creaturely, dependent status. God is Creator, we are creature. As the psalmist has said, "Know that the Lord is God; he has made us and we are his own" (Ps. 100:3). Our immediate and direct dependence upon God is the one essential aspect of human existence. God has made us, breathed life into us, and set us free in a creation so vibrant and productive that it can only be described as a garden. The only condition of our freedom is our dependent status as creature. Rather than denying human freedom, however, the command of God's limitation on us acknowledges our freedom to obey or disobey. God has designed us for relationship, which is not possible with robots or automatons pre-programmed for automatic response. Freedom is necessary for true selfhood, but God intends that our selfhood is to be defined by God, not by us.

Yet, we want to define freedom for ourselves, and we spend our lives for the most part trying to define ourselves apart from God. We want the lead role in our life story; and God can either play a supporting role in our story or be written completely out of our story. As we will see shortly, there is plenty of this kind of story in the Bible. In fact, the Bible is not only a love story; but for the most part it is a story of unrequited love. God loves us, but we fail to return that love because we have focused it all on ourselves. But, as we shall also see shortly, the story can go only one of two ways. We can either love God, which is our God-created destiny, or we can leave God out and go it alone, defining and claiming the destiny of our own creation.

---

[46] Eugene Peterson, *Christ Plays in Ten Thousand Places*, p. 76.

What we are slow in learning is that we are free *for* relationship with God, but not free *from* relationship with God. The freedom to be human is inextricably bound up in our relationship with God. Our selfhood is designed to be of a kind in which God, not self, is sovereign. Rather than acknowledging this sovereign role of God, however, we pride ourselves on being "self-made." We are big on self esteem and self actualization. Especially in America, we promote the notion that everyone can make something of himself or herself, as if we are the prime creator of our existence. Somewhere I read someone's observation that to make an apple pie "from scratch," one must first create a universe. I would borrow this to say, anyone who wishes to be a self-made person, must first create a universe. As long as we acknowledge this component of dependency and live within our nature, we will co-habit with God in a common sphere of existence—one of unity, harmony, fellowship, peace—where the Lord God walks with us in the garden which God intends as our home (Gen. 3:8). This is the basic meaning of the idyllic Garden of Eden portion of the story.

The plot of the back-story thickens rather quickly, however, as newly created humankind denies this creaturely status, refusing to accept the constraints established by the Creator (Gen. 3). In the entire range of the world's writing, it would be difficult to find any passage so brief which has had such immense influence upon human thought as Genesis 3:1-13. The whole history of Christianity has lived within a structure of thought with its foundation in this passage. Here, in the part of the back-story commonly called "The Fall," we have a parable of human sinfulness—in Adam, in Eve, in all of us. As Sam Keen notes, this part of the story,

> represents the moment when the story begins to develop in a manner not intended by the Storyteller…. Historical existence (the time between 'once upon a time' and 'someday') is the time of conflicting themes during which the Storyteller is forced to improvise, making use of the dialogue and action created by his recalcitrant characters, to salvage the story he intended to tell. [47]

(Sidebar: If I may mix my metaphors for a moment, I like to think of human history as a kind of improvisational jazz, where every note we sound is taken by God and worked into a new thematic line that keeps the music alive and vibrant, with God taking even our dissonant notes and making new music out of them. Or, in the words of John Claypool,

---

[47] Keen, *To a Dancing God*, p. 92.

taking "the most destructive things of which we free creatures are capable and [transmuting] them into occasions of positive growth and blessing."[48])

The basic statement of God's sovereignty and the dependent nature of humanity's freedom is contained in the prohibition of the fruit of the tree. Unwilling to live within this constraint, however, humankind defies God's authority and seeks the position of self-dominance, setting self up as its own master. Having been created in the image of God, we have decided to worship the image of God (ourselves) instead of God. The temptation is "to be like God" (Gen. 3:5), and the temptation is too great to resist. It all comes in the form of a rather innocent sounding question: "Is it true that God has forbidden you?" (Gen. 3:1). It is with this question that the basic attitude of the creature towards the Creator is changed. As Dietrich Bonhoeffer has expressed it, with that question, "Man is expected to be the judge of God's word instead of simply hearing and doing it"[49] With that question, Adam and the whole of humankind begin to place self over God, "to be like God."

Adam is everyone, and his experience is the universal experience. The beings have supplanted Being, the creatures have replaced the Creator, humanity has taken the place of divinity. The story of the Fall refers less to some calamity in the pre-historic past than to a dimension of human experience which is always present—namely our tendency to reject God and idolize ourselves. We can't blame the snake. We can't blame Adam (or Eve). We are guilty because of our own yielding to the timeless temptation. The words of Genesis 11:4 are universal and echo throughout human history: "Come, let us make a name for ourselves." Despite the common notion that the temptation associated with the fall has to do with sex, William Sloane Coffin has correctly identified the nature of the temptation as having nothing to do with sex and everything to do with power:

> [Adam and Eve] wanted power; they wanted to know more, to have more, to be more. 'You will be like God'…tempted the serpent, and they jumped at the chance, as to this day does the Adam and Eve in almost every one of us. (If not literally true, the story is eternally true). [50]

We have gotten way off center by placing ourselves in the center. This is the very essence of sin, to put ourselves where God ought to

[48] Claypool, *God the Ingenious Alchemist*, p. 4.
[49] Bonhoeffer, *Creation and Fall*, p. 67.
[50] Coffin, *A Passion for the Possible*, p. 21.

be—at the center of our existence. Instead of centering our lives on God, we have chosen to put ourselves in the center. And, since there can only be one center, we end up sharply divided from one another, competing with each other for the center, for the title role in the story. Someone has said that Carl Jung described our proud trust in ourselves as our "Godalmightiness." We commonly call it pride. The Bible simply calls it sin. In fact, human pride in self-sufficiency is the original sin, because it is the initial sin, the initiating sin, the *origin*-al sin. It is the root from which all other sins spring forth. Robert Short sums it up well when he says "we all have the birth defect of lacking the one thing needful—faith in our creator."[51]

This rebellious spirit was addressed centuries later by Israel's prophets:

> Ages ago you broke your yoke and snapped your traces, crying, 'I will not be your slave.' [52]

> You thought in your own mind...I will rise above the cloud-banks and make myself like the Most High. [53]

God instructed Ezekiel to say to the prince of Tyre words that could apply to all of us:

> In your arrogance you say, "I am a god; I sit throned like a god on the high seas.' Though you are a man and no god, you try to think the thoughts of a god. [54]

This rebellious, self-exalting action results in alienation—alienation from our own selfhood, alienation from other persons, alienation from the order of nature, and alienation from God. The God-human relationship is severed, and we become separated from our very life source (Gen. 3:24; See also Is. 59:2a). It is as if our spiritual "umbilical cord" has been cut: "the godless man's life-thread breaks off" (Job 8:13).

The result is chaos, disorder, and disharmony. Our pride, our "Godalmightiness," is the essence of all our troubles, of the dissension and strife that characterize the human predicament, socially as well as individually. The primeval back-story of our history makes clear that all corruption, all confusion in the world, comes from the sin of wanting to

---

[51] Short, *The Gospel According to Peanuts*, p. 43.
[52] Jeremiah 2:20a; see also Jeremiah 18:12.
[53] Isaiah, 14:13-14; see also Isaiah 29:16.
[54] Ezekiel 28:2b.

be at the center. What existence might have been under God, it now is not. This is the significance of the remainder of the first eleven chapters of Genesis which describe the results of our sinful drive to be the center of creation. These are stories of conflict in the person/self, person/person, person/nature, and person/God relationships. In short, we have lost our intended state of existence; our "wrongdoing has upset nature's order..." (Jer. 5:25). In searching for a center of meaning other than God, we have simply and tragically lost our way.

This same theme appears much later in Paul's writings:

> Knowing God, they have refused to honour him as God, or render him thanks. Hence, all their thinking has ended in futility, and their misguided minds are plunged in darkness. They boast of their wisdom, but they have made fools of themselves.... Their wits are beclouded, they are strangers to the life that is in God. [55]

For Paul, life "in Adam" instead of "in Christ," is a primary metaphor for the human condition, life separated from God and estranged from one another. "In Adam," we no longer walk with God in the garden in the cool of the evening. As Colin Morris has pointed out, this is "no biblical fairy story. It is a recurrent nightmare of what has been irretrievably lost."[56] We find ourselves in a far country of loneliness, degradation and despair. We have become the universal Prodigal Son:

> Oh, rebel sons! Says the Lord,
> You make plans, but not of my devising,
> You weave schemes, but not inspired by me,
> piling sin upon sin. [57]

But our plans are destined for frustration and failure:

> The Lord brings the plans of the nations to nothing;
> he frustrates the counsel of the peoples. [58]

As Harvey Cox observes, Adam's "obsessive need to run everything led, according to the old biblical story, to exile, sorrow and fratricide. It

---

[55] Romans 1:21-22, Ephesians 4:18a; see also Romans 1:28-32.
[56] Morris, *The Hammer of the Lord*, p. 33.
[57] Isaiah 30:1; see also Jeremiah 2:29.
[58] Psalm 33:10; see also Psalm 127:1.

still does."[59] Once again, the primeval story in Genesis is our story. In Leonard Sweet's words, "We are our new idols. Every age has its golden calves, and ours is ourselves…. Postmodern culture is a sucker for the serpent's lie: 'You will be like God.'"[60]

At the end of Genesis 3, the man and woman are outside the gate, the gate is shut and guarded, and it is posted with a "Do Not Enter" sign. We stand there alongside Adam and Eve—no, we *are* Adam and Eve—looking back toward Eden and mourning what we have lost. The next several chapters of Genesis are sad tales of death and destruction, with a recurring pattern of arrogant disobedience and violence that contradicts the goodness of God's creation and denies the role of human stewardship of that creation. God is still sovereign over creation, but that sovereignty has come under attack. These pre-history stories of Genesis end with the tale of the Tower of Babel—a tale of human self-exaltation and the resulting defeat and confusion (Gen. 11:1-9). In Colin Morris' words, "The God who destroys the Tower of Babel is pronouncing judgment on the refusal to accept [our] finiteness…. *Every* civilization is, in the eyes of God, a Tower of Babel."[61] It is as if God has built into us a basic self-destruct mechanism that becomes activated when we seek to promote ourselves into godhood.

The 'back-story" ends here, outside the garden. The deed is done. Eden is lost. The gate to paradise is guarded to keep us out. There is no good news in this back-story. Or, is there? What we come to understand much later in the story is that God will use our plight in a way that lets us know God's mercy. In the words of the Apostle Paul, "For in making all mankind prisoners to disobedience, God's purpose was to show mercy to all mankind" (Rom. 11:32). There are hints of the main story even within the back-story. Look, for instance, at Genesis 3:9: "But the Lord God called to the man and said to him, 'Where are you?'" God knows full well that Adam was not *seeking* God, but was seeking to *hide* from God. But here is the hint and promise of gospel, of good news: God took the initiative to find Adam, to find *us*! Indeed, these back-story tales of loss and separation tell us not only of the beginning of sin, but also of the beginning of the redemptive acts of God. In the words of Gerhard von Rad,

> [The] continually widening cleft between God and man is matched by a secret increasing power of grace. The stories of

---

[59] Cox, *The Seduction of the Spirit*, p. 64.
[60] Sweet, *Soul Tsunami*, p. 288.
[61] Morris, *The Hammer of the Lord*, p. 101, emphasis added.

the Fall, of Cain, and of Noah show God's forgiving and supporting acts of salvation. Only in the story of the Tower of Babel [Gen. 11:1-9], when the nations are scattered and the unity of mankind is lost, does the judgment of God seem to be the last word. But here primeval history dovetails with sacred history: Abraham is called from the multitude of nations, 'that in him all generations of the earth should be blessed.'[62]

These stories of God's preemptive, redemptive action anticipate Jesus' parable of the Prodigal Son (Luke 15:11-32). In that story, when the prodigal son became aware of the chaos and disorder of his own existence, his father was already awaiting and desiring his return. The father saw him at a distance and was already on his way to meet him and bring him home. Even more immediate in the biblical story, as noted above by von Rad, is the promise of God to Abraham in Genesis 12:3, "that in him all generations of the earth should be blessed." Walter Brueggemann asserts that "this promissory utterance that characterizes the biblical God as a future-generating, future-governing God is the core theme of the entire Bible."[63] For the apostle Paul, in the early church, this remarkable promise was nothing less than "the Gospel beforehand" (Gal. 3:8). During my seminary days, I often heard New Testament scholar Frank Stagg quote the words of C. A. Dinsmore, "…there was a cross in the heart of God before there was one planted on the green hill outside of Jerusalem."

The world that was, and was lost, still may yet be. Out of chaos, God brought creation. Out of God's creation, we have brought chaos. But, perhaps, out of our chaos, God may once again bring a new creation. Sam Keen sums it up for us: "to those who have ears to hear, there is a promise hidden in the confused tale of history: the Storyteller will regain control of his creation and bring it to its intended fulfillment."[64]

But, we are getting ahead of the story.

With great dispatch, the biblical back-story is brought to a close, and we begin the real story of God's acts of redemptive love. The back-story of creation has prepared the way for the "primal drama" of the Bible, namely, "the restoration and mending of a scarred, broken creation to the intent of the Creator."[65] The remainder of Genesis (after the first 11

---

[62] von Rad, *Genesis*, p. 24.

[63] Brueggemann, *An Introduction to the Old Testament*, p. 46.

[64] Keen, *To a Dancing God*, p. 92.

[65] Brueggemann, *An Introduction to the Old Testament* p. 33.

chapters) and the remainder of the Bible are now given over to the main plot: the storyline of searching, redemptive love. The plot centers on God's enduring love expressed in God's continuing efforts to redeem lost creation and restore humankind and all creation to God's intended purpose of relationship. The story is one of God's seeking, redeeming, saving, restoring work and Word.

*****

PART TWO: THE BIBLE AS AUTOBIOGRAPHY

I have found the concept of "autobiography" to be a useful metaphor for conveying the underlying nature of the Bible as story. Individuals and communities told the biblical story as they gave accounts of their lives in relationship with God. Individual autobiography is a first-person account of a person's struggle in which the speaker is saying, "This happened to *me*." Community autobiography is a kind of corporate storytelling of spiritually significant experiences shared in the collective life of a whole people, in which the community says, "This is what happened to *us*." Harvey Cox characterizes religion as the corporate autobiography of a people, their "*collective* remembrance, group consciousness and common hope."[1]

In writing autobiography, we do not simply *tell* the story of our life; we *construct* the story so as to make sense of our history. People usually write an autobiography in later life, after they have developed a sense of self-understanding and perspective about the important events and shaping experiences of their lives and their meaning. Therefore, an autobiography is usually developed around the key molding and shaping influences of an individual's life: home, schooling, friendships, profession, outstanding achievements, devastating experiences, loves won and loves lost, etc. Meaning in our life stories comes when we interpret the events of our lives. Life shapes us as we go, and sometimes we have to pause to examine the shape we are in. In Joan Chittister's

---

[1] Cox, *The Seduction of the Spirit*, p.117, emphasis in the original.

words, "The fact is that someplace along the line we all live life backward. We look back and we wonder."[2] We not only wonder, we reflect on what we have done and left undone, on who we have become and who we failed to become, on whether we have made a difference and what difference we have made. And we search for the outline of our life story. While the resulting life-stories are not arbitrary creations of pure fiction, they are nonetheless projections from within our deepest self; and they are selective in content so as to achieve a coherence that fits the "plot" of the story we wish to tell.

Although our lives begin at birth and unfold chronologically, our understandings of our lives can begin at multiple points of life and unfold with no regard to chronology. We "re-view" our past in the light of later life experiences and "re-member" our story accordingly. In this process our past and our present are in dialog with each other. And, as Frederick Buechner has observed, "The past is the place we view the present from as much as the other way around."[3] In fact, when we begin to comprehend and tell our life-story, we do a kind of "time travel," where past, present, and future blur into one another. Events that are recorded forward must often be read backwards—and even "sideways."

We must keep in mind all of these characteristics of autobiography when we approach the Old and New Testaments.[4] In the following pages, I want to consider the Old Testament as the national autobiography of ancient Israel, followed by considering the New Testament as the early church's autobiography. Then, I want to suggest the Bible can be understood as at least a partial autobiography of God, limited of course to God's relationship to the people of this planet—and specifically to the people of Israel and the church. Lastly, for this section, I want to pick up my earlier notion of placing our own stories in the biblical story and consider the Bible as our autobiography.

*****

---

[2] Chittister, *Welcome to the Wisdom of the World*, p. 42.

[3] Buechner, *Now and Then*, p. 57.

[4] For a more scholarly understanding of Jewish and Christian religious discourse as being autobiographical in nature, see an account that I have only recently discovered in the writings of Nicholas Lash, in the chapter entitled "Ideology, Metaphor, and Analogy," from his book, *Theology on the Way to Emmaeus*.

[When] God speaks to Moses, he speaks with historical
accent.
Bernhard Anderson [5]

The Hebrew Bible is ancient Israel's story (and stories) of her
relationship with God.
Marcus Borg [6]

To put it in a nutshell, the Old Testament is Israel's witness to
its encounter with God.
Bernhard Anderson [7]

[In] the opening lines of Israel's long, intimate story Israel
declares its faith that its story...is inseparably related to the
world's story; that the world and Israel's own role in it have
meaning only in the proposition that the earth and all who
dwell in it are Yahweh's; and that the stuff of chaos rendered
unchaotic by the creative powers of Yahweh alone
nevertheless resides in all, restrained only by the living God
and God's living Word.
Davie Napier [8]

The Bible is the story of the people of God, told by the people of
God and told in two "installments." As the story of ancient Israel, the
Hebrew Bible, or the Old Testament, is part one of the story. (Part two,
the New Testament, is the story told by the early church, which I will
come to next.) There is no history of the ancient Hebrew people as we
typically think of history today. All we have in the Old Testament is a
collection of documents strung together in a more or less connected
narrative, with bodies of law, prophetic writings, songs, and other
writings inserted at various points. This story has significant gaps, one of
the most notable being the absence of any accounts during the last four
hundred years before the time of Jesus.[9] Also, some portions of the
story are told more than once, with little or no effort to reconcile
differences in the accounts.

Furthermore, behind the earliest written accounts of the earliest of

---

[5] Anderson, *Understanding the Old Testament*, p. 50.
[6] Borg, *Reading the Bible Again for the First Time*, p. 48.
[7] Anderson, *ibid*, p. 8.
[8] Napier, *Song of the Vineyard*, p. 52.
[9] This gap is partially filled by some of the story as it is
contained in the Apocrypha.

Israel's narratives lies a long history of oral transmission through recitation, reinterpretation, and retelling the story for the passing generations. Some scholars place the earliest written extended narratives of the first five books of the Bible (known as the Pentateuch) as early as the 900s BCE, although some of the stories originated orally centuries earlier. Finally, even after the accounts were initially written, they continued to be edited in light of Israel's ongoing life in relationship with God. The immediate foreground of the collection and preservation of the final narrative in its present written form is the Babylonian Exile in the 500s BCE, with a possible date as late as Ezra in the 400s BCE.

From Israel's continued maturing experiences as a people, the writers and editors firmly established their basic views of life's meaning—not just for Israel, but for all of creation. Although the Old Testament begins with the stories of the creation, Israel's "autobiography" does not begin with those stories, or even with the stories from Abraham's time. Rather, Israel's autobiographical story has its real beginnings with its recollections of its birth experiences as a people of God—the exodus from Egypt, the wilderness wanderings, the covenant between God and Israel, and the possession of the land—events so decisive that everything else came to be seen in their light. In these events Israel formed its knowledge of God and its idea of itself. This autobiographical story is less important as historical reporting of events than as a statement of Israel's foundational confession of faith of its experience of God in those events.

The plot of Israel's founding story is built around the tension between the opposing powers of empire on the one side and of God on the other. One side is personified in the pharaoh of Egypt, sitting on the throne in the center of the greatest national power in that part of the world at that time. The other side is personified in Moses, a fugitive from that imperial power hiding as a sheep herder on the backside of the wilderness. One side is cast in the role of slaveholder; the other side is cast in the role of slave. The historians of the slaveholders evidently took little notice of the events that unfolded, since no sure record of the events can be found in Egypt's archives. But the historians of the slaves took note, because in these events God's heart was revealed to them. They were surprised by a God who took note of their plight and stepped into history on their side. And the ensuing events shaped forever their understanding of the character of this God: "The Lord said, 'I have indeed seen the misery of my people in Egypt. I have heard their outcry against their slave-masters. I have taken heed of their sufferings, and I have come down to rescue them from the power of Egypt....'" (Ex. 3:7-8a).

Israel's *God is a misery-seeing, cry-hearing, heed-taking, down-coming, rescuing*

God, who chose to side with them and who did not abandon them in their misery. Robert McAfee Brown gives a succinct summary of the opening chapters of the book of Exodus:

1. A class struggle is going on.
2. God is aware of the struggle.
3. God takes sides in the struggle.
4. God calls people to join in the struggle. [10]

The exodus story establishes the basic theme of God's deliverance that is woven throughout the rest of Israel's story. It provides the initial clue to their (and our) understanding of the nature of God and how God acts in history to deliver the downtrodden and oppressed. (As inheritors of Israel's faith, we Christians see in Jesus this same nature of God as *a misery-seeing, cry-hearing, heed-taking, down-coming, rescuing God.*)

From this perspective Israel viewed creation and prehistory (Gen. 1-11) as the stage on which its autobiography unfolded. Israel understood the beginning of its history as liberation from the meaninglessness of life under oppression. Just as God was at the center of the creation of the community of Israel out of the chaos and nothingness of slavery, so also was God at the center of Israel's faith stories of creation of the cosmos out of chaos and nothingness. In the words of Davie Napier, God "brings order out of chaos. It is the impingement of his life upon history which imparts meaning to the meaningless. This is the faith which ancient Israel proclaims in her story."[11] In other words, the creative nature of God was inferred from Israel's experience of creative redemption by God. Although these primal narratives of beginnings move sequentially from creation to exodus and seem to be recorded forward, they must be understood by reading backwards from the exodus narratives as the beginning of the story, with the creation narratives forming a sort of back-story.

God in relationship with Israel is the central reality of Israel's autobiography. The plot of the story was developed by generations of story-tellers and writers whose understandings and perspectives were shaped by several centuries of God's actions toward and through Israel. They wrote from within the "simplicity of a community which had screened out all uncertainties.... It is an affirmation in story form which asserts 'This is the most important story we know, and we have come to believe it is decisively about us.'"[12] Israel's understanding of God and its

---

[10] Brown, *Unexpected News,* p. 35.
[11] Napier, *Song of the Vineyard,* p. 89.
[12] Walter Brueggemann, *The Bible Makes Sense,* p. 46.

relationship with God is summarized in its fundamental confession of faith found in Deuteronomy 26:5-9:

> My father was a homeless Aramaean who went down to Egypt with a small company and lived there until they became a great, powerful, and numerous nation. But the Egyptians ill-treated us, humiliated us and imposed cruel slavery upon us. Then we cried to the Lord the God of our fathers for help, and he listened to us and saw our humiliation, our hardship and distress; and so the Lord brought us out of Egypt with a strong hand and outstretched arm, with terrifying deeds, and with signs and portents. He brought us to this place and gave us this land, a land flowing with milk and honey.

The theme of Israel's autobiography is its primary molding experience of the covenant relationship between God and God's people. This is the one story out of which all the others come, the "megamyth" that "serves as a framework for all others."[13]

*****

The New Testament as the Early Church's "Autobiography"

> We are apt to assume that the New Testament produced the Church, but the contrary is the case—the Church gave rise to the New Testament.
> Georgia Harkness [14]

> The New Testament is the early Christian movement's story (and stories) of her relationship with God as disclosed in Jesus.
> Marcus Borg [15]

> The gospel was originally a ... living storytelling tradition of messengers who told the good news of the victory of Jesus.
> Thomas E. Boomershine [16]

The New Testament, which is the early church's autobiography, is part two of the story of God and God's people as told in the Bible. This part of the story has its beginnings in telling of the life, death, and

---

[13] Howard Schwartz, *Reimagining the Bible*, p. 90.
[14] Harkness, *Toward Understanding the Bible*, pp. 81-82.
[15] Borg, *Reading the Bible Again for the First Time*, p. 48.
[16] Boomershine, *Story Journey*, p. 17.

resurrection of Jesus and the continuing powerful presence of his Spirit. The storytellers of the church retold stories that had first been told *by* Jesus (as they remembered them) and added their own stories *about* Jesus. The writers' understandings and perspectives were variously shaped by what they had known and heard about Jesus and the experiences of Jesus' followers years after his death. As New Testament scholar Archibald Hunter has expressed it, "Life always precedes literature, and the Good News about Christ was being preached long before a single scrap of Christian literature existed."[17] Before early Christians wrote their stories, they lived them, and many suffered and died for the message of their stories. Their own life experiences and stories became part of a developing tradition and were woven into their stories of Jesus and of the communities of his followers. As such, the gospel stories are not bare historical accounts of Jesus' life but are proclamations of faith that Jesus is the one in whom God has come to live among God's people in a unique and life-giving way.

Since all of the authors (with the possible exception of Luke) of the New Testament books were Jews, it is to be expected that Israel's storytelling tradition as recorded in the Old Testament provided the background, context, and interpretative framework and background for their stories. Israel's images of God and God's relationship with the world shaped the New Testament storytellers' identity and sense of who they were, both as individuals and as communities of faith. In the same way that the story of the exodus is a story of salvation for Israel, the story told by the church is its experience of salvation through Jesus Christ on the cross and in the resurrection. Once again, God moves in the nothingness and chaos of death to create a new order of resurrection and life. The theme of the church's story is its experiences of God's saving purpose in a new covenant relationship between God and God's people through Jesus as Christ.

The story of the Bible, in both of its parts, might be summarized as the autobiographical accounts of people who had come to know the redemptive nature and work of God individually and collectively.

*****

---

[17] Hunter, *Bible and Gospel*, p. 27.

The Bible as God's (Partial) "Autobiography"

The word of God means 'God speaking,' God declaring
himself...God's self-disclosure.
Georgia Harkness [18]

We cannot know God himself unless he chooses to reveal
himself.
Bernhard Anderson [19]

[W*ho*] God is—God Himself must tell us in His Revelation.
Emil Brunner [20]

The Word of God is God's creative self-manifestation.
Paul Tillich [21]

[The] church takes Scripture as a gift from God and God's
own self-disclosure, even if humanly mediated. For that
reason the church, upon hearing Scripture, characteristically
responds, 'The Word of the Lord...thanks be to God.'
Walter Brueggemann [22]

Since the Bible is the record of God's self-revelation in history, then
I propose that it can be considered as at least a partial "autobiography"
of God. (Of course, God's realm of activity is not limited to just the
events recorded in the experiences of Israel and the church. For that
matter, God's self-revelatory activity is not even necessarily limited to
this world.) As I have noted, the Bible has come to us from human
authors, working in the contexts of worshiping communities, and has
been shaped by editors over a long period of time. For some believers
and would-be believers, this is potentially problematic, since it seems to
undermine the authority of the Bible. But I would suggest to the
contrary that this, in fact, underscores the notion of God as the ultimate
author—not of the words, but of their meaning.

This is God's story of God at work in human history, the story of
the acts of God. God's self-revelation is not given as directly
communicated knowledge, "but through events occurring in the
historical experience of mankind, events which are apprehended by faith

---

[18] Harkness, *Toward Understanding the Bible*, p. 21.
[19] Anderson, *The Unfolding Drama of the Bible*, p. 38.
[20] Brunner, *Our Faith*, p. 6, emphasis in the original.
[21] Tillich, *Biblical Religion*, p. 78.
[22] Brueggemann, *An Introduction to the Old Testament*,
p. 397.

as the 'mighty acts' of God."[23] As Bernhard Anderson has expressed it, the biblical story "has its beginning and end in the purpose of God. History is *His*-Story."[24]

Viewed as God's autobiography, the Bible is seen once again to center on the primary experience of relationship between God and humankind as revealed to and through Israel and the church.

*****

The Bible as Our "Autobiography"

The Christian faith may be expressed in many forms, but in the last analysis there is no substitute for retelling what Christians call 'the story of our life.'
Bernhard Anderson [25]

Our lives are story journeys. The events of our lives connect with many other stories. But at the deepest and most profound level, the stories of our lives are empowered and given meaning by being connected to God's story.
Thomas E. Boomershine [26]

The fatal error is to read the Bible as a spectator rather than a participant.
Robert McAfee Brown [27]

Until you can read the story of Adam and Eve, of Abraham and Sarah, of David and Bathsheba, as your own story…you have not really understood it. The Bible…is a book finally about ourselves.
Frederick Buechner [28]

The Bible is inherently the live Word of God that addresses us concerning the character and will of the gospel-giving God, empowering us to an alternative life in the world.
Walter Brueggemann [29]

---

[23] John Baillie, *The Idea of Revelation*, p. 62.
[24] Anderson, *The Unfolding Drama of the Bible*, p.28, emphasis in the original.
[25] Anderson, *Understanding the Old Testament*, p. 2.
[26] Boomershine, *Story Journey*, p. 16.
[27] Brown, *The Bible Speaks to You*, p. 21
[28] Buechner, *Now and Then*, p.21.
[29] Brueggemann, "Biblical Authority", *Struggling with Scripture*, p. 11.

> The Bible tells a story…of which our life is a part. It is not that stories are a part of the human life, but that human life is part of a story.
> Leslie Newbigin [30]

> We become ourselves the important Scripture beyond Scripture that may well be the Bible's foremost purpose.
> John Durham [31]

The stories of the Bible are not just accounts of the divine-human relationships of the past. If that were the case, we would be interested in its stories only as historians, seeking understanding of past events as an archeologist sifts through the dust of ancient peoples' lives to understand how they lived. In so doing, we might find some artifacts of interest, some collectibles of antiquity. We might even see in their lives some precedent of relevance for today, object lessons that can be used for instruction in how to live. But the best of the artifacts would likely be put in museums, and the rest would end up in our attics or on eBay. The best of the stories would be taught in history classrooms or bound into history books that few would read. Some of them would become sermon illustrations or bedtime stories read from well-illustrated children's books. Or, even worse, they might be reduced to mere homilies and aphorisms that become throw-away lines in our daily lives: "She has the patience of Job." "Well, that's just the cross I have to bear." "He is such a Doubting Thomas."

Whatever the biblical stories may tell us about various peoples' ancient past, "they tell us infinitely more about our own living present. They describe *us*…. We are not reading ancient history. We are reading 'our' story put in pictorial form."[32] The drama of the biblical story requires our participation in the story if it is to be understood. As I noted earlier, John Durham, in *The Biblical Rembrandt*, writes about Rembrandt's use of many of his paintings of biblical scenes as an opportunity for self-portrait, painting himself into these scenes as a statement of his involvement in the story the scene portrays. For Rembrandt, the Bible was a story he *experienced*, a story "that was real to him because he read it as a book about himself…. In a way, the Bible became for Rembrandt a kind of diary, an account of moments in his

---

[30] Newbigin, *Open Secret*, quoted on http://sermonquotes.wordpress.com/category/stories, accessed May 9, 2008.
[31] Durham, *The Biblical Rembrandt*, p. 233.
[32] Robert McAfee Brown, *The Bible Speaks to You*, p. 169, emphasis in the original.

own life."[33]

The Bible is a universal story, not that it is about all humankind but that it is about each one of us as individuals. I can affirm Sam Keen's assertion that, "If I am to discover the holy, it must be in my biography and not in the history of Israel."[34] The biblical story, which is God's story of divine self-disclosure, is also "a story that invites, more, *insists* on, our participation."[35] As J. A. Sanders has pointed out, "Most biblical texts must be read, not by looking in them for models of morality, but by looking in them for mirrors of identity." He then goes on to caution, "Whenever our reading of a biblical passage makes us feel self-righteous, we can be confident that we have misread it."[36] In the biblical story, we must find our own story. Only when we find ourselves *in* the biblical story can we truly understand the Bible and come to know who we truly are. I suggest that the biblical story is not just the story of those who inhabit its pages, or my story, but *our* story as humankind. We read there the stories of individuals like us. In its collective stories of ancient families and communities, we find our shared story that is common to all of us as human beings. This is the meta-narrative for all of creation, and it contains the threads of each of our individual personal stories.

A few years ago, I read an account of a meeting between representatives of a native community and officials of the British Columbia government to discuss ownership of contested land. The government was claiming rights to land that the native community had long occupied. One of the native elders asked: "If this is your land, where are your stories?" He knew that it is our stories that give "meaning and value to the place we call home."[37] By way of analogy I suggest that we might also say something similar about the meaning and value of our faith: "If this is your faith, where are your stories?" For me, my stories are found in the biblical stories. The biblical story *is* my story. What follows in the remainder of this book is my confessional understanding of the biblical story and some of its meaning for how we are to live with the Word of God. I invite you to join me in looking at this story in the hopes that you will find yourself there and it will become your story as well.

---

[33] Durham, *The Biblical Rembrandt*, pp. 49, 60.

[34] Keen, *To a Dancing God*, p. 99.

[35] Eugene Peterson, *Christ Plays in Ten Thousand Places*, p. 182, emphasis in the original.

[36] Sanders, "Hermeneutics," *The Interpreter's Dictionary of the Bible, Supplementary Volume*, Keith Crim, ed., pp. 406, 407.

[37] Century Marks: "Stories About Home," *The Christian Century*, January 25, 2005, p. 6.

PART THREE: THE STORY AS WORD

God's Word does not *tell* the redemptive story of love for humankind; God's Word *is* the story. In common usage today, the "Word of God" almost always refers to the Bible, not just in the sense that the Bible *contains* the Word of God, but that the Bible itself, as a book, *is* the Word of God. Such an understanding is far too restrictive, however, because the "Word of God" is much more than a book, as we shall see. The significance of the Word of God has been foundational for my faith from the beginnings of the outline of my thoughts in the early 1970s that have led up to this book. It is by means of God's Word that life is created and sustained: "One does not live by bread alone, but by every word that comes from the mouth of God" (Matt. 4:4). God's Word does not sustain just my life; it sustains the existence of life itself. In this section I will explore the various ways in which this life-giving Word has been and is being expressed, followed by the inferences and implications of what this Word means for me.

*****

The Word of God

According to biblical religion, all divine manifestations are manifestations through the word.
Paul Tillich [1]

Language, spoken and written, is the primary means for

---

[1] Tillich, *Biblical Religion*, p. 36.

getting us in on what *is*, on what God is and is doing.... [The] Apocalypse of St. John presents the risen and present Jesus, under the aspect of words, of speech.... [The] risen Jesus Christ ... identifies himself to John alphabetically, 'I am Alpha and Omega'—he is the alphabet, all the letters from A to Z, that is, the stuff, the vowels and consonants out of which all words are made.

Eugene Peterson [2]

Although many concepts and images are required in the attempt to express God's self-disclosure, nature and purpose, the essential mode whereby God acts within history and reveals the divine will to humanity may well be expressed for my purposes within the concept of "word." Eugene Peterson argues, "Language is sacred. All words are holy." And he goes on to assert that when words are torn out of the story that God speaks and are used apart from the "syntax of the God story," language is desecrated.[3] Words separated from the story become like leaves which lose their life when they are plucked from the tree. They become merely leaf-shaped dead things. Similarly, when words are plucked out of God's story, they lose their life and become merely word-shaped dead things. So looking at the biblical meaning of "word" will help keep our words alive.

"Word" in the Old Testament is usually the English translation of the Hebrew word *dabar*, and in the New Testament it is commonly the translation of the Greek word *logos*. *Logos*, in turn, is used both as "word" in the writings of the New Testament and in the Greek translations of *dabar* in the Old Testament. Although there is scholarly disagreement and uncertainty about the root of the word *dabar*, some scholars connect it to a root meaning "to be behind." "Accordingly, 'a dynamic motion forward from that which is behind' is thought to be the idea lying behind [*dabar*]."[4] In this usage, one must seek the historical background of a topic or event in order to understand the underlying concept. A word is expressive of what lies behind and before its utterance, therefore what *is* must be understood as the expression of what already *was*.

It is not until a thing is named, that is, given its *dabar*, that it becomes subject to thought. The true nature of the thing itself comes to light

---

[2] Peterson, *Eat This Book*, pp. 3, 61, emphasis in the original.

[3] Peterson, *Tell It Slant*, pp. 264-265.

[4] W. H. Schmidt, *Theological Dictionary of the Old Testament*, Volume III, Botterweck and Ringgren, eds., p. 94.

only when its *dabar* clearly communicates the thing that is named. The narration of the events of history provides the understanding of those events. In fact, the most important characteristic of *dabar* is the truthfulness of its relationship to the event or thing it names. This characteristic of truthfulness gives *dabar* moral significance, because in every spoken word, "there should be a relation of truth between word and thing, and a relation of fidelity between the one who speaks and the one who hears."[5] This linkage of integrity between the one who utters the word, the word that is uttered, and the one who receives the word is foundational to understanding the character of the Word of God in all of its expression. Oliver Sachs, in his fascinating book *The Man Who Mistook His Wife for a Hat*, asserts that natural speech does not consist of words or propositions alone: "It consists of utterance—an uttering-forth of one's whole meaning with one's whole being—the understanding of which involves infinitely more than mere word-recognition."[6] This characteristic of utterance is especially true of God's self expressions. God's Word is not just words from God or about God; it is God's uttering forth God's own self.

A second foundational aspect of *dabar* is its dynamic nature. In ancient Israel as elsewhere in the ancient Orient, the concept of the word, especially the Word of God, was not understood primarily as an expression of thought but as a powerful and dynamic force. The Hebrew *dabar* has a "material concept with its energy felt so vitally in the verbal concept that the word appears as a material force which is always present and at work, which runs and has the power to make alive."[7] As the writer of Hebrews asserted, God's Word is a living, dynamic force in creation and history (Heb. 4:12a). God's activity through the Word recalls familiar expressions like, "No sooner said than done," and "You have only to say the word, and (whatever is desired) is accomplished." For the biblical writers, the divine *dabar* is not just a spoken utterance, it is itself "an action or an event…. God speaks and it is done."[8] God doesn't speak *about* an event; God's Word *is* the event. God's Word has God's power.

As we will see shortly, the universe was brought into being by the power of God's speaking. This is obviously a Word to be reckoned with! God's Word, as God-breathed self-disclosure, is less noun than verb.

---

[5] O. Procksch, *Theological Dictionary of the New Testament*, Volume IV, G. Kittel, ed., p. 93.
[6] Sachs, *The Man Who Mistook His Wife for a Hat*, p. 81, emphasis in the original.
[7] Procksch, *ibid*, p. 93.
[8] John Baillie, *The Idea of Revelation*, p. 81.

For the God of Abraham—the God who speaks to make the divine self known—speaking and doing are inseparable. This reflects the Hebrew conception of God as dynamic action, in contrast to the Greek concept of the divine nature as static being. For the Hebrews, God is the God who does things, not just a god who is. The Hebrew understanding of God was continually challenged by the ongoing activity of a living God who was involved in Israel's life.

In the New Testament, the "Word" of God is usually expressed as the "*logos*" of God, with the word "*logos*" appearing more than 300 times. Its essential meaning is the linguistic and functional equivalent of *dabar* in the Old Testament, although it was sometimes used in a larger sense to mean the preaching of Jesus (as in Luke 5:1: "and the people crowded upon him to listen to the *logos* of God.") and to represent the whole Christian message of the gospel (as in Acts 13:44: "On the following Sabbath almost the whole city gathered to hear the *logos* of God."). In the prologue of John's gospel (see John 1:1, 14), *logos* finds its highest meaning as the eternal divine Word which is incarnated in the person of Jesus Christ (although in the rest of John's gospel, *logos* is used in the more ordinary sense).

The incarnation takes the Hebrew concept of an active and present God to a new level. One of my favorite expressions regarding the meaning of the life of Jesus is found in Peter's sermon in Acts 10, where he said of Jesus, "He went about doing good" (Acts 10:38). I like that as a summary of Jesus' life and purpose, but for the current point, I want to stop the quotation two words earlier: "He went about...." That in itself is an astounding claim regarding the nature of God. God is a good God, and we know that best not because God declares that to us from on high, but because God reveals it to us by going about in our world. The chief characteristic of the living God is activity, not absence. God is not the "Unmoved Mover" of Aristotle, but the powerful presence of one who "came to dwell among us" (John 1:14).

In addition to bearing the meaning of *dabar*, *logos* added an understanding derived from Greek philosophy which declared *logos*, understood as "reason," put sense and reason into the world and into mankind. For the writers of the New Testament, *logos* was the mind of a God who created a world of order and not of chaos. This made it easy for John to apply the term to Jesus, who *was* the incarnate mind of God.[9] Dorothy Sayers links the concept of Jesus as the mind of God with my earlier notion of God's autobiography: "Christian doctrine...affirms that

---

[9] See William Barclay, "Logos," *More New Testament Words*, pp. 115-117.

the Mind of the Maker was…incarnate personally and uniquely [in Jesus]…. [We] might say that [in Jesus] God wrote His own autobiography."[10]

In the following pages, we will briefly look at the Word as the powerful self-disclosure of God as expressed in creation, in the Torah, in the prophets, in the incarnation in Jesus, in the church, and in the book (the Bible).

*****

The Word in Creation

'Let there *be*' the Word comes, and then there *is*, Creation *is*. Something *is* where before there was nothing and the morning stars sing together and all the Sons of God shout for joy because sequence has begun, time has begun, a story has begun.
Frederick Buechner [11]

Before there was light and order, before there were stars or animals, before there was a human race, 'God said'; and therefore 'In the beginning the Word already was.'
Jaroslav Pelikan [12]

God speaks…the concrete thing itself…. The essential point is therefore not that the Word has 'effects' but that God's Word is itself the work…. [The] word of command and the event [are indissolubly one]…. With God the imperative is the indicative. The latter does not follow the former. The indicative is not the effect of the imperative; it *is* the imperative.
Dietrich Bonhoeffer [13]

In Genesis 1, the whole story begins with the creative Word of God. Eight times in the story of the six days of creation, God spoke and the universe was born: "God said…and there was." This creative Word of God is not a static expression of thought about creating but an active expression of power where the utterance *is* the creative event. The biblical writers in both the Old and New Testaments understood this:

---

[10] Sayers, *The Mind of the Maker*, p. 87.
[11] Buechner, *A Room Called Remember*, p. 86, emphasis in the original.
[12] Pelikan, *Whose Bible Is It?*, p. 25.
[13] Bonhoeffer, *Creation and Fall*, p. 23.

"The Lord's word made the heavens.... For he spoke, and it was; he commanded, and it stood firm."[14] I like the way Peter Pitzele has addressed this aspect of God's creative Word:

> Language is the instrument for creation *and* for its transmission to us. In this myth of the beginning, language is lifted from history and made to precede it.... The word becomes the holy medium for imagining God. Before the life of the world, there are the words of life. An impulse stirs in the divine Imagination; it comes into divine speech and is immediately realized. Between the conception and the act no shadow falls. [15]

Further, God's Word doesn't just initiate creation; it sustains it by the endless expression of God's creative will over against the relentless forces of chaos that would return creation to non-being. The process of creation becomes the process of preservation. As Dietrich Bonhoeffer has put it, "*Creation* means the wresting out of non-being; *preservation* means confirmation of being."[16] It is worth noting in the first creation account (Genesis 1), that there is no end to the seventh day. It still continues; it might well be said that we are living in the seventh day of God's continuing acts of creation. God's rest after the six days of creation is not a rest of inactivity but a different kind of activity, one of sustaining creation.

The thirteenth century Flemish mystic, Jan van Ruysbroeck, said, "God creates the world anew in each moment."[17] In the more whimsical words of G. K. Chesterton, "It is possible that God says every morning, 'Do it again' to the sun; and every evening, 'Do it again to the moon.'"[18] More seriously, if God's Word of creation should be withdrawn, creation itself would revert into the primeval chaos from which it was created. As expressed by Marcus Borg, "If God ceased to vibrate [that is, speak] the universe (and us) into existence, it (and we) would cease to exist."[19] The testimony of the biblical writer of old is that our life is

---

[14] Psalm 33:6, 9; See also Psalm 147:15-18; Psalm 148:6; Hebrews 11:3.

[15] Pitzele, *Our Fathers' Wells*, p. 12, emphasis in the original.

[16] Dietrich Bonhoeffer, *Creation and Fall*, p. 26, emphasis in the original.

[17] Quoted in *Reader's Digest*, December 1977, p. 159.

[18] Chesterton, *Orthodoxy*, p. 55.

[19] Borg, *Reading the Bible Again for the First Time*, p. 72.

dependent upon "every word that comes from the mouth of the Lord" (Deut. 8:3b). This concept is expressed also in the New Testament: "The Son sustains the universe by his word of power" (Heb. 1:3a).

This concept of our dependence on the sustaining Word of God has given me both the title and the organizing principle for this book: "Man cannot live by bread alone; he lives on every word that God utters" (Matt. 4:4). In *The Message*, Eugene Peterson's paraphrase of this passage from Matthew reads even more pointedly: "It takes more than bread to stay alive. It takes a steady stream of words from God's mouth." In short, if God ceases to speak, we cease to exist: "If the Word is not there, the world plunges into the bottomless abyss."[20]

*****

The Word Revealed in Torah

The God who gives is the God who command
Walter Brueggemann [21]

The first five books of the Bible (sometimes referred to as the Pentateuch) constitute the Torah of Judaism. In Christian usage, the term "Torah" is often mistranslated as "law," which overlooks the fact that the Torah largely consists of narrative. Further, the commands of "Torah" are better understood as "instruction," in the sense of giving guidance. It is true that the Torah does contain a large body of commandments, but seeing it only as law misses the communal and covenantal context of the commands that reflect a Creator-creature relationship of protective sovereignty and grateful dependency. The dismissive attitude of so many Christians toward Old Testament law does not reflect a proper understanding of the nature of God's commands in the life of Israel. The Enlightenment has influenced our modern understanding of freedom as autonomy rather than covenant. But for ancient Israel God's commands were the basis of community and their sense of identity as the people of God. As Walter Brueggemann points out, God's commands are

---

[20] Dietrich Bonhoeffer, *Creation and Fall*, p. 22.
[21] Brueggemann, A*n Introduction to the Old Testament*, p. 24.

"intentional and self-conscious acts of discipline whereby this community at risk may sustain itself in its wonder and gratitude, in its particular identity as a people living from a miracle."[22]

Worth noting is that the obligations of the Ten Commandments were prefaced with an historical account of God's saving action on behalf of the people: "I am the Lord your God who brought you out of Egypt, out of the land of slavery" (Ex. 20:2). As Bernhard Anderson had noted, "the law was preceded by Israel's gospel—the 'good news' of what God had done."[23]

Israel's appreciation for the blessing of the life-sustaining freedom enabled by God's commands of Torah is expressed later by the psalmist:

> I will walk in freedom wherever I will,
> because I have studied thy precepts....
> Thy word is a lamp unto my feet
> and a light on my path. [24]

God is not planning for these people to move from being Pharaoh's slaves to being God's slaves. Rather, they are to become God's special possession, a people bound together in a covenant community with God and with one another (Ex. 19: 4-5). God's law is not one of controlling power but of the power of love.

The primary and normative revelation of the Word of God given as instruction in the Torah is found in the Ten Commandments—The Decalogue—that is, the "Ten Words:" "God spoke, and these were his words" (Ex. 20:1-17). The ten commands given in this passage underlie the divine covenant with Israel; and all subsequent commands of God to Israel can be characterized as interpretations of these ten foundational commands. Throughout the narratives of the Torah, God is shown speaking the Word in covenant promise and command to the people:

> Moses came and told the people all the words of the Lord, all his laws. [25]

> Moses wrote down the words of the covenant, the Ten

---

[22] Brueggemann, An *Introduction to the Old Testament* p. 24.
[23] Anderson, *Understanding the Old Testament*, p. 91.
[24] Psalm 119: 45, 105.
[25] Exodus 24:3.

Words.... [26]

The Lord 'announced the terms of his covenant to you, bidding you observe the Ten Words.' [27]

[The] Lord wrote down the Ten Words. [28]

Biblical scholars widely agree that the Torah reached its current form at the time of the Babylonian exile of 587 BCE or shortly thereafter. The experience of the exile had made Israel feel at risk as a people without a place to validate their community identity. To a considerable degree, Israel's sense of identity was tied to its sense of place, the land Yahweh had given them. Consequently, the loss of place created a deep identity crisis for Israel. In this setting, Israel experienced God's Word of Torah as a blessing because, even in exile, it was accessible to those who would put it in their hearts.

> The commandment that I lay on you this day is not too difficult for you, it is not too remote. It is not in heaven, that you should say, 'Who will go up to heaven for us to fetch it and tell it to us, so that we can keep it?' Nor is it beyond the sea, that you should say, 'Who will cross the sea for us to fetch it and tell it to us, so that we can keep it?' It is a thing very near to you, upon your lips and in your heart ready to be kept. [29]

In the midst of life-denying exile, Torah became the creative, life-giving Word of God for Israel:

> Moses finished speaking to all of Israel, and then he said, 'Take to heart all these warnings which I solemnly give you this day: command your children to be careful to observe all the words of this law. For you they are no empty words; *they are your very life.* [30]

As with the divine Word of creation, God's word of Torah command carried with it the power of performance. The Word of Torah was alive with the creative and life-sustaining power of God, and it was later described by the early church as "the living utterances of God" (See

---

[26] Exodus 34:28.
[27] Deuteronomy 4:13.
[28] Deuteronomy 10:4.
[29] Deuteronomy 30:11-14.
[30] Deuteronomy 32:45-47, emphasis added.

89

Acts 7:38). The Word of Torah had the power to shape Israel's life differently from the dominant culture of exile that would hold life captive. Rather than being primarily restrictive, Torah commands provided freedom for the people of Israel within the sovereignty of God, regardless of where they might find themselves.

*****

The Word Revealed Through the Prophets

> I will raise up for them a prophet...and I will put my words
> into his mouth.
> Deuteronomy 18:15, 17-18

The Word that God spoke in creation and Torah is also the Word spoken to and through the prophets of Israel to bring about God's purpose in history. In the life of Israel, the prophets were agents of divine revelation of God's plan that would be realized in history. According to some accountings, the phrase "the word of the Lord" appears nearly 400 times in the Old Testament, and in about 250 of those times it is used in reference to the prophets of Israel. God spoke to and through the prophets in such a way that they served as the "mouthpiece" of God, receiving and transmitting God's Word as a single action. Yet, as Abraham Heschel has pointed out, the Word of God was translated and transmitted through the life circumstances and personalities of the prophets:

> [The] prophet is a person, not a microphone. He is endowed
> with a mission, with the power of a word not his own that
> accounts for his greatness—but also with temperament,
> concern, character, and individuality.... The word of God
> reverberated in the voice of man. The prophet's task is to
> convey a divine view, yet as a person he *is* a point of view. He
> speaks from the perspective of God *as perceived from the
> perspective of his own situation.* [31]

God did not ignore the prophets' personalities but used them to reflect and convey the divine personality. This association with the divine presence intensified all aspects of the various prophets' personalities. Quite simply, they were inspired (literally "in-breathed") by

---

[31] Heschel, *The Prophets*, Volume I, p. x, emphasis added.

God. As Marcus Borg has noted, the prophets "were speaking from their knowledge *of* God—not from their knowledge *about* God, but from their *knowing* God."[32] The prophetic experience helps us understand how "history" can become "revelation." The "actual event" *plus* the prophetic interpretation become revelation, the Word of God uttered in history. An uninterpreted event is not revelation; it merely happens. On the other hand, without the event, the prophet would remain mute, with nothing to say. Prophets cannot exist in a vacuum, because their words are drawn from their experiences of God in the covenant life of the community and in the particular circumstances of the community life. Not only were the prophets and their words rooted in Israel's history, Israel's history was also rooted in the messages of the prophets. The events of Israel's history not only influenced the Word of God to them, God's Word in turn influenced Israel's history. Time and again Israel's history was transformed by the interpreted events of the prophets.

Throughout the books of the prophets, there are repeated instances of God's Word being delivered through the prophets as fulfillment of God's promise to raise up and commission a prophet to speak what God commands:

> Then the Lord stretched out his hand and touched my mouth, and said to me, 'I put my words into your mouth.' [33]

> But the Lord took me as I followed the flock and said to me, 'Go and prophesy to my people Israel.' So now listen to the word of the Lord. [34]

We have the familiar formula (repeated 123 times, by some accounting): "The word of the Lord came to"… Samuel, Ezekiel, Jeremiah, Isaiah, Jonah, Micah, Zephaniah, Hosea, etc.[35] Significantly, this phrase always occurs with the use of the definite article, "*the* word of the Lord," and never just "*a* word." The words given to and through the prophets were always the Word of God for a specific context of time and place. These words were neither random ramblings unrelated to immediate circumstances nor universal truths that could be applicable to all circumstances. They were never a generalized word that the prophets were free to apply to events as they may have picked and chosen (or as

---

[32] Borg, *Reading the Bible Again for the First Time*, p. 125, emphasis in the original.
[33] Jeremiah 1:9.
[34] Amos 7:15-16.
[35] See for example: Hos. 1:1, Mic. 1:1, Zeph. 1:1, Jer. 1:2.

we may pick and choose, although we may well profit from the study and hearing of God's Word in those times and circumstances as they speak to our time and place).

There was such a dynamic element to the Word that, even when the prophet called of God was reluctant to speak, the Word could not be contained. Once the prophet accepted the call to speak God's utterances, there was a power in God's Word that could not be stopped by the prophet. And once given by God to the prophet, the Word had to be delivered to God's people: "The Lord God has spoken; who will not prophesy?" (Amos 3:8). Jeremiah gives poignant testimony to the pressure of the prophetic Word. Clearly, this Word did not originate within Jeremiah; the Lord placed it within him. But, having received God's Word, Jeremiah could not keep it contained within himself, despite the social mockery and shame that came from his preaching:

> I am reproached and mocked all the time
> for uttering the word of the Lord.
> Whenever I said, 'I will call him to mind no more,
> nor speak his name again',
> then his word was imprisoned in my body,
> like a fire blazing in my heart,
> and I was weary with holding it under,
> and could endure it no more. [36]

Jeremiah identified the divine Word proclaimed through him with the God of creation: "These are the words of the Lord, who gave the sun for a light by day and the moon and stars by night" (Jer. 31:35). In like manner, for Ezekiel the breath of God's life-giving utterances in creation (in Gen. 1) was the same life-giving breath of the Word he was to speak to Israel:

> This is the word of the Lord God to these bones:
> 'I will put breath into you, and you shall live....'
> And as I prophesied there was a rustling sound....
> Breath came into them; they came to life. [37]

As in creation, the Word given the prophets was dynamic and powerful, with God's own power for creation and destruction: "I put my words into your mouth. This day I give you authority over nations and over kingdoms, to pull down and to uproot, to destroy and to demolish, to

---

[36] Jeremiah 20:8b-9.
[37] Ezekiel 37:1-14.

build and to plant" (Jer. 1:9-10). Nature itself, created by the Word, will someday pass away, "but the word of our God endures for evermore" (Isa. 40:8).

The Word delivered through the prophets has the same characteristic "no sooner said than done" aspect of the other modes of God's utterances. The Word and the event function as a unit; speaking and acting are two sides of the same coin:

> Say to them, these are the words of the Lord God.... I, the Lord, will say what I will, and it shall be done... I will speak, I will act. This is the very word of the Lord God. [38]

Therefore, God's Word carries within it the power to accomplish God's purpose. True prophecy carries its fulfillment within itself. It will not return to God unfulfilled:

> [The] word which comes from my mouth [shall] prevail;
> it shall not return to me fruitless
> without accomplishing my purpose
> or succeeding in the task I gave it. [39]

Whenever the true prophet speaks, things take place.

Since God's Word will not go unfulfilled, the words of God's prophets can be taken with confidence, provided that their words were not invented by the prophets themselves. There was always a temptation for the prophets to become false prophets, sometimes becoming prophets for hire, concerned more with the "profit motive" than the "prophet motive." There was the danger that these false prophets would speak lies, not the Word of God, as Jeremiah warned:

> These are the words of the Lord of Hosts:
> 'Do not listen to what the prophets say,
> who buoy you up with false hopes;
> the vision they report springs from their own imagination,
> it is not from the mouth of the Lord.' [40]

The word of the false prophet can be identified in that it will not come true. Unfortunately, the truth of the prophecy can be known only after the fact:

---

[38] Ezekiel 12:23-25.
[39] Isaiah 55:11.
[40] Jeremiah 23:16.

If you ask yourselves, 'How shall we recognize a word that the Lord has not uttered?', this is the answer: When the word spoken by the prophet in the name of the Lord is not fulfilled and does not come true, it is not a word spoken by the Lord.... [When] his words come true it will be known that the Lord has sent him. [41]

The Word of revelation through the prophet can be both blessing and judgment, but it is always a life-giving force whose simple withdrawal means the loss of God's grace. God's silence can be every bit as life threatening as God's words of judgment:

The time is coming, says the Lord God,
when I will send famine on the land,
not hunger for bread or thirst for water,
but for hearing the word of the Lord. [42]

In other words, "Man shall not live by bread alone."

*****

The Word Becomes Flesh: Jesus Christ

When St. John rewrote Genesis, emphasizing the primacy of the language (Word and words) in the very being-ness of God and the way God works, he went on to make the truly astonishing statement that 'the Word became flesh and lived among us...' (John 1:14 NRSV). With that statement St. John launched his detailed witness of Jesus as that Word....
Eugene Peterson [43]

The whole life and ministry and death of Jesus is in a way a figure of speech for God, a metaphor for the love that was in him.... And of course metaphors are, God knows, all we any of us have of him.
Frederick Buechner [44]

Jesus Christ is God Himself coming. In him, the 'Word became flesh.' That means, in him *is* present that which these

---

[41] Deuteronomy 18:21-22; Jeremiah 28:9.

[42] Amos 8:11.

[43] Peterson, *Eat This Book*, p. 137.

[44] Buechner, *A Room Called Remember*, p. 95.

Prophets and Apostles were not, but of which they could only
speak.
Emil Brunner [45]

[The] divine Logos, expressive Being, has found its fullest
expression in him.
John Macquarrie [46]

All the revealed words of God are partial manifestations of the
Word, Who is the splendor of God's truth.
Thomas Merton [47]

If a word is to be valid, the one concerned ratifies it with an
Amen.
O. Procksch [48]

With Jesus, we have not only one who *spoke* the Word of God, but
one who *is* the living Word. The opening verses of the Gospel of John
declare Jesus as the divine Word who has come to dwell among us: "So
the Word [*logos*] became flesh; he came to dwell among us" (John 1:14;
see all of John 1:1-14). John's account makes this most lyrical
pronouncement of the Word made flesh; but Paul, writing some 30 plus
years before John, first declared it to be so: "For in [Jesus] the complete
being of God, by God's own choice, came to dwell" (Col. 1:19).

Two thousand years of Christian history have all but made many of
us immune to this astonishing claim. Sure, countless people simply find
it incredible and summarily dismiss it. That is easily understood, because
it flies into the face of common sense and reason. It is not surprising,
then, that unbelievers reject this claim. Rather it is dismaying that
believers no longer think it is surprising. What could be more unusual
than to claim that a child born to poor parents in a backwater country
would be the defining utterance of God's Word? John and Paul were
saying that the *Creator*, the one who is the creative cause of the very
existence of the universe, has come to live among the *created* as one of *us!*
This challenges our rationalist tendencies to place the "First Cause" of
creation majestically, and safely, outside space and time.

Christianity has always had to address this "scandal of particularity,"
its claim that the ultimate disclosure of universal reality occurred in a

---

[45] Brunner, *Our Faith*, p. 9, emphasis in the original.
[46] Macquarrie, *Principles of Christian Theology*, p. 305.
[47] Merton, *Bread in the Wilderness*, p. 69.
[48] Procksch, *Theological Dictionary of the New
Testament*, Volume IV, G. Kittel, ed., p. 93.

particular series of historical events centered in the life of one person. This certainly is foolishness to the rational Greeks, and understandably offensive to the religious Jews (1 Cor. 1:23). As Sarah Hinlicky Wilson has put it, for the rationalist, it's like saying "'the circle became square' or 'infinity became zero;'" and for the holiness of the religious, it's like saying, "'Purity became filth and dwelt among us.' It's not only absurd; it's offensive."[49] But that is what Christians believe. It is what I believe; but I am still amazed.

Robert McAfee Brown has provided a very provocative phrase for the strange and unexpected ways in which God is at work in the world. He refers to them as the "pseudonyms of God." He then goes on to say:

> Jesus himself is the grand pseudonym, the supreme instance
> of God acting in ways contrary to our expectation, the point at
> which we are offered the criterion in terms of which the action
> of God elsewhere can be measured. [50]

In other words, we don't start with God's other utterances in order to define Jesus. We start with Jesus to understand all of God's other expressions of the Word. It is a sweet irony that we have very few of Jesus' words. There is no evidence that he ever wrote a word, except maybe for a few scribbles in the sand (See John 8:6). We certainly have no written word of Jesus that was ever preserved. And, while his sayings quoted in the Gospels may be repeated more than any other words in history, everything the New Testament quotes him as saying can be spoken aloud in two hours. We treasure the words of Jesus, but it is even more important to treasure Jesus as the Word—made flesh, coming to dwell among us.

At about the same time that John was writing his gospel witness to the Word made flesh, the writer of the letter to the Hebrews asserted that in Jesus was the fullness of all previous expressions of the Word:

> When in former times God spoke to our forefathers, he spoke
> in fragmentary and varied fashion through the prophets. But
> in this the final age he has spoken to us in the Son. [51]

Unlike with the prophets, "strictly speaking, the word of God did not come to Jesus, who was himself the Word of God in person and in the

---

[49] Wilson, "Plato Was Wrong," *Christian Century*, December 28, 2004, p. 16.
[50] Brown, *The Pseudonyms of God*, p. 87.
[51] Hebrews 1:1-2.

flesh."[52] However fragmentary those earlier manifestations of the Word may have been, Jesus himself made clear that he did not come to replace either the Word of Torah command or the Word spoken by the prophets. Rather, he came to complete both of those expressions of God's Word:

> Do not suppose that I have come to abolish the law and the prophets; I did not come to abolish, but to complete.... You have heard it said...but I say.... [53]

As with the Word of the true prophet, the Word present in Jesus is authoritative and true because it comes from God: "[The] word you hear is not mine, it is the word of the Father who sent me" (John 14:24). The Apostle Paul wrote that Jesus is the affirmation of God's Word in all of its previous utterances: "He is the Yes pronounced upon God's promises, every one of them" (2 Cor. 1:20a). And the writer of the book of Revelation proclaimed that Jesus is nothing less than God's "Amen," which ratifies Jesus as God's Word: "These are the words of the Amen, the faithful and true witness, the prime source of God's creation" (Rev. 3:14).

As "the prime source of God's creation," it was through this Word that creation itself was spoken into being:

> When all things began the Word already was. The Word dwelt with God, and what God was, the Word was. The Word, then, was with God at the beginning, and through him all things came to be; no single thing was created without him.[54]

I like the way that Frederick Buechner expresses the power of the claim made by this passage:

> At that point where everything was nothing or nothing everything, before the Big Bang banged or the Steady State was stated, when there was no up and no down, no life and no death, no here and no there, at the very beginning, John says, there was this Word which was God and through which all things were made. [55]

This powerful and creative Word is exhibited in the words of Jesus, showing his mastery over creation as he

---

[52] Jaroslav Pelikan, *Whose Bible Is It?*, p. 12.
[53] See Matthew 5:17-28.
[54] John 1:1-3.
[55] Buechner, *A Room Called Remember*, pp. 85-86.

... drove the spirits out with a word and healed all who were sick. [56]

> ... stood up and rebuked the wind and the sea and there was dead calm. The men were astonished at what had happened, and exclaimed, 'What sort of man is this? Even the wind and the sea obey him?' [57]

The Word of God revealed in the Son is not only the Word of creation's beginning but also the sustaining Word of creation (Heb. 1:3a) and the sustaining Word of eternal life (John 6:68).

This is a Word worth hearing. We shall explore the message and meaning of the Word in greater detail in Parts Four, Five and Six.

*****

The Church Becomes the Bearer of the Word

> The Church...is old in the sense that it is a continuation of the life of Israel, the People of God. It is new in the sense that it is founded on the revelation made through Jesus Christ of God's final purpose for mankind.
> R. Newton Flew [58]

The God of the Bible is a strange God indeed when it comes to communicating. As we have seen, the biblical story of God's interaction with humanity begins with God's response to the cries of a group of slaves in Egypt who became God's chosen people, not because they were worthy, but simply because they were needy and God loved them. In Jesus, God's communication was given to us in the life of the son of an insignificant carpenter living under the rule of an occupying power in a minor part of the Roman Empire. And then we see Jesus entrusting the Word into the hands of a motley crowd of underdogs whom he called out to follow him and who became the church. Strange indeed, but true.

The Word was given of Christ to a small group of devoted followers shortly before his death was to take him from them. As with God's choosing Israel, Jesus' disciples were not chosen because they were

---

[56] Matthew 8:16.

[57] Matthew 8:26-27.

[58] Flew, in *Jesus and His Church*, cited by Robert McAfee Brown, *The Significance of the Church*, p. 33.

worthy, but simply because he loved them. In the words of his prayer for the disciples not long before his arrest, Jesus entrusted them into God's care and then entrusted the Word of God into their care:

> And now I am coming to thee; but while I am still in the world I speak these words.... I have delivered thy words to them....thy word is truth. As thou hast sent me into the world, I have sent them into the world.[59]

The church was formed to be the body of Christ and commissioned to continue to live out God's Word in God's world.

Significantly, Jesus did not anoint or appoint some*one* to be his successor. Rather, he anointed and appointed a *community*, the church. It takes the whole church to be the "body of Christ" because the church is made up of *individuals* in *community*. The very essence of the church, of being "Christian," is the social relationship of individuals. As Robert McAfee Brown has stated, "Christ does not just leave 'changed individuals,' he leaves a community, the Church."[60] The notion of an "individual Christian" is a contradiction in terms, an oxymoron. From the very beginning of the church, the Christian life was a life "in common" (Acts 2:42). As I noted earlier, this is not the first time that God formed a community to be the bearer of the divine Word. At Sinai, God formed a Torah community out of the motley group of people who were rescued out of Egyptian bondage (Ex. 19:4-5). God does call individuals, but they are always individuals in a community. God's Word of relationship simply cannot be lived out in isolation.

Not long after Jesus' resurrection and departure from the midst of his followers, the power of God's Word filled their lives with the coming of the Holy Spirit, and the first thing they did was to speak God's Word: "And they were all filled by the Holy Spirit and began to talk in other tongues, as the Spirit gave them power" (Acts 2:4). The New Testament book of Acts gives the story of the emerging church of the first century and its ministry of the Word:

> [We] devote ourselves to prayer and to the ministry of the Word.[61]

> [They] went through the country preaching the Word.[62]

---

[59] John 17:13-19.
[60] Brown, *The Significance of the Church*, p. 47.
[61] Acts 6:4.
[62] Acts 8:4.

The church's expression of the Word was powerful: "When we brought you the Gospel, we brought it not in mere words but in the power of the Holy Spirit..." (Thess. 1:5). It was, in fact, so powerful that those who preached it were characterized as "turning the world upside down" (Acts 17:6, NRSV). And this was not said of them by their admirers.

Not only was it an active and powerful Word the church delivered, it also required active response on the part of the hearer: "Only be sure that you act on the message and do not merely listen" (Jas. 1:22). It was the same life-giving Word of the God who first created life through the utterance of the Word: "You have been born anew...through the living and enduring word of God" (1 Pet.1:23). From its beginning, the role of the church has been to continue the creative work of the Word of calling persons into fullness of being and into reconciliation with God: "From first to last this has been the work of God. He has reconciled us men to himself through Christ, and he has enlisted us in this service of reconciliation" (2 Cor. 5:18). The church is to embody the love of God that was revealed in Christ. It is to be a fellowship of love.

The ongoing work of the church through the ages has been to continue the interpretive process that keeps the Word delivered of God in the past relevant to life in each succeeding generation. It is, in fact, not possible to read the biblical text in meaningful ways that reveal to us the Word of God without interpreting its words anew in our own context. The challenge and responsibility for the church is that it always be faithful and intentional about this interpretive process, being faithful to the Word as delivered and interpreted in days past while at the same time being intentional in seeking the fresh Word of God that speaks to us today. "Interpretive issues concern not only the reiteration of old meanings, important as they are, but also attentiveness to new meanings that arise in careful, diligent study."[64] In Part Six, I will address some of the implications for the church as the Body of Christ charged to speak and be the Word in our day and time and place.

So, with that, we move to the book of the Word.

*****

---

[63] Acts 12:24.

[64] Walter Brueggemann, *An Introduction to the Old Testament*, p. 395.

The Written Word

[There] was a Word of God before there was a written Bible
of any kind.
Jaroslav Pelikan [65]

We open this book and find that page after page it takes us off
guard, surprises us, and draws us into its reality, pulls us into
participation with God on *his* terms.... In our reading of this
book we come to realize that what we need is not primarily
informational, telling us about God and ourselves, but
formational, shaping us into our true being.
Eugene Peterson [66]

Because [Scripture] is God-given...the book endlessly
summons, requires, demands, and surprises with fresh
readings. The only way to turn the book into a fixed idol is to
imagine that the final interpretation has been given, an act of
imagination that is a deep act of disobedience to the lively
God who indwells this text. The only way to avoid such
idolatry is to know that the lively God of the text has not
given any final interpretation of the book.
Walter Brueggemann [67]

The fact that a statement is found in the Bible does not make
it true. What makes it true is that it comes from God, and our
best knowledge of whether or not it is of the mind of God is
whether it accords with the life, the words, the mind of Christ.
Georgia Harkness [68]

[We] are fed by the Word of God.... In the Scriptures, the
Word is incarnate not in flesh but in human words. But man
lives by every word that proceeds from the mouth of God....
The word of God is full of the Word of God.
Thomas Merton [69]

Think of the difference between a corpse and a living,
breathing body, and you'll understand the difference between

---

[65] Pelikan, *Whose Bible Is It?*, p. 9.
[66] Peterson, *Eat This Book*, pp. 6, 23-24, emphasis in the
original.
[67] Brueggemann, *An Introduction to the Old Testament*,
p. 13.
[68] Harkness, *Toward Understanding the Bible*, p. 25.
[69] Merton, *Bread in the Wilderness*, pp. 4, 75.

a bunch of words and words vitalized by God's breath.
Brian McLaren [70]

God himself 'comes alive,' and speaks to us, as we take the Bible
seriously. It is for this reason that Christians speak of the Bible
as 'the Word of God.'
Robert McAfee Brown [71]

It may come as a surprise to some that the Bible never calls itself the
"Word of God." But it should not be surprising because, as we have
seen, the Bible is not exclusively *the* Word, since the Word of God is
much more than a book, even for those of us who would claim for the
Bible a unique status as *the* book. The Bible is, perhaps, more accurately
understood as conveying the Word of God, or as the written *record* of the
Word—the record of the creative, regulative, and redemptive
work/Word of God in a particular history. Further, it is through the
Word as Bible that the living Word who is Jesus becomes known to us
today and can become a living Word for us, in us, and through us.

In keeping with the full, active, powerful nature of the Word, the
Bible *becomes* the Word of God anew today when the Holy Spirit moves
through its words in such a way that God speaks a personal, life-
changing Word to us as individuals. This process, which Walter
Brueggemann calls "imaginative remembering," does not intend to stay
with the "old happenings" of the Bible, "but intends to recreate a
rooted, lively world of meaning that is marked by both coherence and
surprise in which the listening generation, time after time, can situate its
life."[72] This kind of reading of the Bible is an act of faith on the part of
the reader, done with a spirit of openness and responsiveness of will.

This understanding of the Bible may suggest that the task for us is
not so much that we "get back to the Bible" as that we let the biblical
message get through to us, by speaking fresh and new in our own lives
today. "Only as the Word is proclaimed and uttered in the radicality of
each new situation does it become a dynamic Word."[73] This dynamic
power of the Word present in the Bible is evidenced time and again in
the lives of people who find in its pages that God is revealed in life-
changing ways, not because of the words of the Bible but because of the
living presence of the Word in the Bible. Witness, for example, the

---

[70] McLaren, *A Generous Orthodoxy*, p. 161.
[71] Brown, *The Bible Speaks to You*, p.17, emphasis in the
original.
[72] Brueggemann, *An Introduction to the Old* Testament,
p. 8.
[73] Karl Donfried, *The Dynamic Word*, p. 18.

countless testimonies shared by the Gideons of people for whom God has come alive in the reading of the Bibles the Gideons have placed in hotel rooms around the world. Though my own testimony is far less dramatic than theirs, I have experienced the exciting, living presence of God in study of the Bible when the words on the page have become the Word that God speaks in my heart. In short, what we call the Bible's "inspiration" is properly understood as "its capacity to be the vehicle of the Holy Spirit."[74] The Bible that I have come to know can be described in words that I borrow from Barbara Brown Taylor:

> [The Bible is] the scripture that none of us knows until we have taken the words inside ourselves, entering into the live risks, mysteries, decisions and relationships that they require of us.... Holy words are not meant to stay on the pages. They are meant to happen to us, to fly off the pages into our own bodies, and through us to animate the world of God's own imagining. [75]

The story has been told of Paul Tillich's response to a fundamentalist who waved a Bible in his face and asked, "Do you believe this is the Word of God?" Tillich is said to have replied, "It is if it has a hold on you as tight as your hold on it."

This is not to deny that the writers of the Bible were inspired, "that God's own purpose, will, and presence have been 'breathed' through these texts."[76] Rather, in a very real sense the inspiration of the Scripture may have less to do with the work of the Holy Spirit in its writing than with the work of the Holy Spirit in our reading of it. As someone has said, "The Word without the Holy Spirit is about as useful as a sundial by moonlight." A proper reading of the Bible lets us find there the Word of God, or more properly put, lets the Word of God find us. But the biblical words themselves are never *the* Word. Elton Trueblood has cautioned against biblical literalism as a test for the truth of the Bible; and he points out that biblical literalism "was not even a possible [test of truth] in the early Church because many of the books, to which adherence is now required, had not yet been written."[77] We must guard against the idolatry both of the words and of the book that contains

---

[74] Rowan Williams, "What is the Church? In God's Company", *Christian Century*, June 12, 2007, p. 26.

[75] Taylor, "Stand and Deliver," *Christian Century*, May 2, 2004, p. 37.

[76] Walter Brueggemann, *An Introduction to the Old Testament*, p. 11.

[77] Trueblood, *The Company of the* Committed, p. 93.

them.

The tendency to treat the words and the book as idols can be made clear by just two illustrations. In 1978, an individual wrote a letter to the editor of his religious denomination's state paper, protesting a proposed change from using the King James Version of the Bible as the primary source in all of the denominational Sunday school literature and replacing it with a variety of versions. He wrote that he had also sent a request to the denomination's national publishing house that they reinstate the King James Version, explaining his "concern about the inherent danger involved in tampering with God's word, regardless of our high and lofty motives."[78] A friend recently commented that his mother will only trust the King James Version because it is the only "Authorized" version. She apparently mistakes King James' authorization for God's.

It is even worse when we believe that *our* word about the Bible is the last word about the Word. The role of perspective that affects all of our understanding also distorts our reading of the Bible. As Robert McAfee Brown cautions,

> It is clear that there are some selective lenses by means of which we read scripture, and that those lenses need to be torn from our eyes. One reason we can read Scripture complacently is that we approach it selectively. We read what we can bear to read, we hear what is tolerable to hear, and we evade (or 'spiritualize') those parts which leave us uncomfortable, if not outraged. What we *bring to* Scripture, in other words, conditions what we *draw from* scripture.[79]

And as David James Duncan warns, some readers of the Bible

> share a conviction that their causes and agendas are approved of, and directly inspired, by no less a being than God. This enviable conviction is…arrived at by accepting on faith, hence as 'higher-than-fact,' that the Christian Bible pared down into American TV English is God's 'word' to humankind, that this same Bible is His only word to humankind, and that [their] selective slant is the one true slant. [80]

The Word in the Bible is alive with the life of God; and as with

---

[78] *The Baptist Standard*, Volume 90, Number 48, p. 2.
[79] Robert McAfee Brown, *Theology in a New Key*, p. 81, emphasis in the original.
[80] Duncan, *God Laughs and Plays*, p. 44.

other living things, the Bible does not do well when it is cut off from its roots and prevented from bearing new fruit. No one ever has the last word on God, because as Brian K. Blount points out, God "is a God of the living, not the dead, but a last word is necessarily a dead word.... *Nothing that is living is ever last.* A living word is always a beginning word."[81] We must never allow our words about our experience of the Word to become a substitute for the Word. And we must never mistake our latest experience of the Word as the last word from the Word.

*****

---

[81] Blount, "Biblical Authority," *Struggling with Scripture*, pp. 56, 57, emphasis in the original.

PART FOUR: THE MESSAGE OF THE WORD—
THE STORY UNFOLDS

[Listen] to the words I am to speak. I will tell you a story with a meaning.[1]

Let me hear the words of the Lord.[2]

We are not 'trapped' in an unfriendly and hostile universe. Rather, God has a plan and a direction for it. It follows that our main task is to try to discover that plan and make our lives fall into line with it, so that we are working with the creator God rather than against him.
Robert McAfee Brown [3]

*****

The Void in God's Heart: Part Two

Throughout the Bible we meet a God who longs for fellowship with us; a God who wants a community, a people, a child. It begins with the choosing of Abraham, who would father a nation who would be God's people and who would be a blessing to all nations (Gen. 12: 1-2). It

---

[1] Psalm 78:1b-2a.
[2] Psalm 85:8.
[3] Brown, *The Bible Speaks to You*, p. 59.

continues with the calling of Israel to be God's people, God's "son." This is Moses' message to both pharaoh and Israel: "tell Pharaoh that these are the words of the Lord: Israel is my first-born son.... Say therefore to the Israelites, 'I am the Lord.... I will adopt you as my people, and I will be your God" (Ex. 4:22; 6:6-7). God chooses Israel and covenants with them:

> If only you will listen to me and keep my covenant, then out
> of all the peoples you shall become my special
> possession...for you are a people holy to the Lord your God;
> the Lord your God chose you out of all the nations on earth
> to be his special possession. [4]

God's covenant with Israel is not just for the benefit of Israel, however: "It is in its end function of universal import. It is Word and people—and world."[5] It is God's intention that Israel would be "a light to the nations," so that God's salvation might reach "earth's farthest bounds" (Is. 49:6).

But the biblical record is full of accounts of the failures of God's people to be true to God. Recall the Garden of Eden experience (Gen. 3) and God's summary statement before the flood: "[Man] had done much evil on earth" (Gen. 6:5). Israel's story is one of repeated failures. Consider just a sampling of the biblical record:

> Then the Israelites did what was wrong in the eyes of the
> Lord.... They forsook the Lord, their fathers' God who had
> brought them out of Egypt, and went after other gods.... The
> Lord set judges over them, who rescued them.... Yet they did
> not listen even to these judges.... They did not obey the
> Lord.... The Lord would relent as often as he heard them
> groaning under oppression and ill-treatment.... But they
> would relapse into deeper corruption.... They gave up none
> of their evil practices and their willful ways...and every man
> did what was right in his own eyes.
>
> [What] David had done was wrong in the eyes of the Lord.
>
> [Solomon] did what was wrong in the eyes of the Lord. [6]

Like society today, the Israelites wanted a God whose nature and

---

[4] Exodus 18:5; Deuteronomy 7:6.
[5] Davie Napier, *Song of the Vineyard*, p. 65.
[6] Judges 2:11-19, 25; 2 Samuel 11:27; 1 Kings 11:6.

expectations were more compatible with the prevailing culture and who required less of them. While Moses was still on Mt. Sinai receiving the foundational commandments of the covenant relationship, the people of Israel were already taking the God issue into their own hands, creating a golden calf statue and attributing to it the role of the God who had brought them up from Egypt (Ex. 32:1-6). This may have been the first time that Israel sought a God more in keeping with their desires, but it certainly was not the last. Throughout their years in the promised land of Canaan, Israel constantly wrestled with the challenge of adjusting to the agricultural ways of the land and the related conflict of religious loyalties.

This behavior was not just the stuff of Israel's history and story; it was also the subject of sermons, especially in times of Israel's distress. For example, hear the words of Nehemiah: "And thou didst see the misery of our forefathers in Egypt and didst hear their cry for help at the Red Sea, and …Thou didst tear the sea apart before them so that they went through in the middle of it on dry ground." And then follows a lengthy listing of all that the Lord had done for the people, interspersed with accounts of the peoples' unfaithfulness and grateful acknowledgment of God's graciousness and compassion.[7] The psalmist summarized it all: "The Lord looks down from heaven on all mankind to see if any act wisely, if any seek out God. But all are disloyal" (Ps.14:2-3).

We are no exception to this kind of behavior. In commenting on Israel's struggle between faith and culture, Bernhard Anderson draws the parallel between their experience and ours:

> It is not surprising…that the Israelites, unaccustomed to the ways of agriculture, turned to the gods of the land. They did not mean to turn away from Yahweh, the God of the Exodus and the Sinai covenant. To Yahweh they would look in times of military crisis; and to Baal they would turn for success in agriculture. Thus they would serve Yahweh and Baal side by side. Like many modern people who keep religion and science in separate compartments, they would acknowledge that each was lord in his own sphere. [8]

Eugene Peterson in his recent book, *Tell It Slant*, makes it clear that this desire for a controllable god has been a regular feature in human history; and Peterson is very direct in his assertion of our national resemblance

---

[7] See Nehemiah 9:9-38.
[8] Anderson, *Understanding the Old Testament*, p. 144.

to these early Israelites, charging, "America leads the world at present in golden-calf production."[9] If we are honest, we must confess our own unfaithfulness and plead no exception to Paul's assertion: "For there is no distinction to be made anywhere; everyone has sinned; everyone falls short of the beauty of God's plan" (Rom. 3:23; Phillips Translation).

God seems to find such unfaithfulness on the part of Israel hard to believe:

> He said, 'Surely they are my people, my sons who will not play
> me false'; and he became their deliverer in all their troubles....
> [He] himself ransomed them by his love.... Yet they rebelled
> and grieved his holy spirit. [10]

The prophets, especially, convey a deep sense of the divine pathos that results from the brokenness and loss between what is in hand and what is promised. In the words of Geddes MacGregor, "For a creature to withdraw from God as we creatures do must surely be infinite agony for him who is the God of love."[11] To recall my earlier image of the void in God's heart, it is safe to say that the "Israel void" in God's heart was filled with pain. God's words to the prophets of Israel express the divine wistfulness and heartbreak of God:

> I am the Lord your God
> who brought you up from Egypt.
> But my people did not listen to my words
> and Israel would have none of me. [12]

> I have sons whom I reared and brought up,
> but they have rebelled against me.
> ...Israel, my own people,
> has no knowledge, no discernment. [13]

> I was there to be sought by a people who did not ask, to be
> found by men who did not seek me. I said, 'Here am I, here
> am I', to a nation that did not invoke me by name. [14]

> I said, how gladly would I treat you as a son...
> I said, you shall call me Father

---

[9] Peterson, *Tell It Slant*, p. 151.
[10] Isaiah 63:8-9, 10.
[11] MacGregor, *He Who Lets Us Be*, p. 149.
[12] Psalm 81:10-11a.
[13] Isaiah 1:2.
[14] Isaiah 65:1-2.

and never cease from following after me.
But like a woman who is unfaithful to her lover,
so you, Israel, were unfaithful to me.
This is the very word of the Lord....
Come back to me, wayward sons;
I will heal your apostasy. [15]

These passages bring to my mind a story told by Raymond E. Balcomb of a little boy who was playing hide-and-seek with a friend. The little boy hid himself and waited for his playmate to come find him. He waited and waited for a long time, but no one came. Finally he came out of hiding, only to discover that his friend had left. In fact, his playmate had not been looking for him at all. Tearfully, he ran to his father, crying, "I hide, but no one wants to seek me."[16] The evidence in the testimony of the prophets is that God knows well this feeling of abandonment, not because God has been hiding, but because no one has been seeking. The evidence is there as far back as the story of the Garden, where God was doing the seeking and the people were doing the hiding. God might well have lamented, "I seek, but no one wants to be found."

*****

God's Righteous Anger

If we are going to be true to the biblical record, we have to acknowledge that it reveals not only God's wistfulness about human unfaithfulness, but it also reveals plenty of testimony to God's righteous anger, especially in the writings of the prophets. The prophets were clear that God's commands must be obeyed in order for Israel to survive, much less prosper. Much of the prophecy of the Old Testament relates to the threat of disaster as punishment for Israel's disobedience. However, the barrier between Israel and God was not raised by God's initiative, but by Israel's iniquities: "because of your sins he has hidden his face" (Isa.59:2).

God's righteous anger seems to be reserved for those who are closest and dearest to God, which should always be a caution for those who believe themselves to be chosen as God's special treasure. The

---

[15] Jeremiah 3:19-20, 22. See also Jeremiah 7:25-26; 11:7-8.

[16] Balcomb, *Try Reading the Bible This Way*, p. 163.

writer of Ecclesiastes cautions, "Go carefully when you visit the house of God" (Eccles. 5:1). The prophet Amos specifically links God's judgment to the unfaithfulness of the people whom God had chosen for the special relationship of covenant love. After listing the transgressions of the people in the first two chapters, Amos delivers God's Word of judgment:

> Listen, Israelites, to these words that the Lord addresses to you, to the whole nation which he brought up from Egypt:
> 'For you alone have I cared
> among all the nations of the world;
> *therefore will I punish you*
> for all your iniquities.' [17]

Throughout the Bible there is what H. J. Cadbury has labeled "the Principle of Proportionate Duty" (referring to Luke 12: 35-48). Referring to this same passage, Frank Stagg has stated, "Responsibility is measured by opportunity. The more one is given, the more is required of him."[18] Jesus clearly articulated this principle, according to Matthew's Gospel:

> Then he spoke of the towns in which most of his miracles had been performed, and denounced them for their impenitence. 'Alas for you, Chorazin!' he said; 'alas for you, Bethsaida! If the miracles that were performed in you had been performed in Tyre and Sidon, they would have repented long ago in sackcloth and ashes. But it will be more bearable, I tell you, for Tyre and Sidon on the day of judgement than for you. And as for you, Capernaum, will you be exalted to the skies? No, brought down to the depths! For if the miracles had been performed in Sodom which were performed in you, Sodom would be standing to this day. But it will be more bearable, I tell you, for the land of Sodom on the day of judgement than for you.' [19]

Yes indeed, "go carefully when you visit the house of the Lord." To know much is to be accountable for much. To be near to God and to be indifferent or to turn away bears dire consequences. Without a doubt, God is entirely capable of uttering forth a word of punishment: "[With] a word he shall slay the wicked" (Is. 11:4). And the wicked can include

---

[17] Amos 3:1-2, emphasis added.
[18] Stagg, *Studies in Luke's Gospel*, p. 92.
[19] Matthew 11:20-24.

those who are dearest to God's heart.

*****

Love Divine, All Loves Excelling [20]

> The cross is the ultimate symbol of a broken heart.
> Leonard Sweet[21]

The reality of divine wrath is undeniable and inescapable, but wrath is not the center of God's nature. It may be the heat of God's nature, but it is not the heart of God's nature: "It was not to judge the world that God sent his Son into the world, but that through him the world might be saved" (John 3:17). Despite our unfaithfulness, God still loves. As someone has expressed it, God chastens people, but God doesn't forsake them. No one expressed better the unfailing love of God than the prophet Hosea. Even when Hosea was warning the people of the dire consequences of their unfaithfulness to God, he revealed the brokenness of God's heart for love of Israel:

> When Israel was a boy, I loved him;
> I called my son out of Egypt;
> but the more I called, the further they went away from me....
> It was I who taught Ephraim how to walk,
> I who had taken them in my arms;
> but they did not know that I harnessed them in leading-strings
> and led them with bonds of love—
> that I had lifted them like a little child to my cheek....
> How can I give you up, Ephraim,
> how surrender you, Israel? [22]

I think the reason I like that imagery from Hosea is that I have held my own children (and grandchildren) to my cheek and have supported them while they learned to walk. One of my favorite metaphors for the security of being God's child is that of a father walking along holding the hand of a child just learning to walk. The safety and security of the child are not dependent upon the child's walking ability but on the sureness of the father's grasp of the child's hand. The child has only to reach up to the father's hand to avoid falling. The danger of falling comes only when the child pulls away from the father. I am reminded of

---

[20] Title of a hymn by Charles Wesley.
[21] Sweet, *The Three Hardest Words*, p. 114.
[22] Hosea 11:1-2a, 3-4, 8a.

113

two Psalms: "Though he may fall [or stumble, as it is sometimes translated], he will not go headlong, for the Lord grasps him by the hand" (Ps. 37:24). "My foot had almost slipped, my foothold had all but given way...yet I am always with thee, thou holdest my right hand" (Ps. 73:2, 23).

I know nothing more tenderly precious than loving a little child. I can easily imagine the heartbreak that would result from later rejection by that child after he or she has grown up. I have been greatly blessed by never having to experience that in my own life with my children. But, if my children had turned away from me, as Israel turned away from God, I know that my heart would never forget the tenderness of nuzzling the cheek and holding the chubby little hand to hold up the chunky little body. Neither does God's heart. As Brian McLaren has put it,

> God is a brokenhearted Parent when we squander our
> birthright and leave our spiritual house. God is full of joy
> when the prodigal daughters and sons come home and rejoin
> the family and reenter the family story. [23]

The loving faithfulness of God in spite of the faithlessness of God's own children is the main theme of the Bible. The Bible also has a lot to say about the final judgment, and I confess that I don't have a clear understanding of how that is going to work. The Bible is pretty clear that judgment is inescapable, but I don't believe judgment is the final Word; redemption is the final Word.

In our common usage of the word, to "redeem" something is to buy back something that was once ours. It is in this sense that God seeks to "redeem" us, to buy or win us back into fellowship:

> Have no fear; for I have paid your ransom;
> I have called you by my name and you are my own.
> When you pass through deep waters, I am with you,
> ...I am the Lord your God,
> the Holy One of Israel, your deliverer. [24]

Robert McAfee Brown notes that redemption is thus a hopeful word: "It says that God has not forsaken us, even when we have forsaken him, but that he seeks us constantly.... A redeeming God, then, is *a seeking*

---

[23] McLaren, *A Generous Orthodoxy*, p. 283.
[24] Isaiah 43:1, 3. It is worth noting that God declares that the ransom has been paid long before Christ's death on the cross. Ransom and redemption are not late additions to the nature and heart of God.

114

God, willing to restore fellowship because of his deep love."[25] For Carlyle Marney, this aspect of the nature of God is the very source of our human nature: "Man is what man is because God is in history, our history, as a Father, looking for children estranged and strayed, as one who cares utterly.... The result is a way, a life, a being-made-whole."[26]

The prophecy of Isaiah has another poignant passage that brings God's love down to us in very human terms. Through Isaiah's prophetic words, God reminded Israel that when they chose to worship idols, Israel had to *carry the idols*, which then became "a burden for weary creatures." In contrast, *God carried Israel.* Israel was a load on God from its beginning, even from the womb; but God remained faithful, even into old age: "[Even] when white hairs come, I will carry you still; *I have made you and I will bear the burden, I will carry you and bring you to safety*" (Isa. 46: 3-4, emphasis added). Surely, these are some of the most precious words ever spoken to sinful people. Even with a heavy heart, God still bears the burden of carrying us. The biblical record is full of God's Word of forgiveness and love:

> I have dearly loved you from of old, and I still maintain my unfailing care for you. [27]

> Man, say to the Israelites, You complain, 'We are burdened by our sins and offences; we are pining away because of them; we despair of life.' So tell them: As I live, says the Lord God, I have no desire for the death of the wicked. I would rather that a wicked man should mend his ways and live. Give up your evil ways, give them up; O Israelites, why should you die? [28]

> Let the wicked abandon their ways
> and evil men their thoughts;
> let them return to the Lord, who will have pity on them,
> return to our God, for he will freely forgive. [29]

God has not given up on Israel, and God has not given up on us. God still longs for the completion of God's plan for creation and for us. God still longs to walk with us in the garden in the cool of the evening. In the New Testament, we see the continuation of God's tender, loving

---

[25] Brown, *The Bible Speaks to You*, pp. 66, 67, emphasis in the original.
[26] Marney, *Priests to Each Other*, p. 46.
[27] Jeremiah 31:3b.
[28] Ezekiel 33:11.
[29] Isaiah 55:7.

care, which is poured out for us even in face of our waywardness and rejection:

> [He] is very patient with you, because it is not his will for any to be lost. [30]

> God loved the world so much that he gave us his only Son, that everyone who has faith in him may not die but have eternal life. It was not to judge the world that God sent his Son into the world, but that through him the world might be saved. [31]

> Father, forgive them. [32]

> For at the very time we were still powerless, then Christ died for the wicked.... Christ died for us while we were yet sinners, and that is God's own proof of his love towards us. [33]

> [I] am convinced that there is ...nothing in all creation that can separate us from the love of God in Christ Jesus our Lord. [34]

God still seeks to save us from our "lostness." God still comes seeking us long after the Garden has been lost. This theme lies at the heart of God in relating not just to Israel of old, but to all of humankind at all times. When we feel that God is lost from us, the problem is not God, but us. God continues to take the initiative of seeking and finding us, even in the dark and cloudy days of our souls:

> For these are the words of the Lord God: Now I myself will ask after my sheep and go in search of them. As a shepherd goes in search of his sheep when his flock is dispersed all around him, so I will go in search of my sheep and rescue them, no matter where they are scattered in dark and cloudy days. I will bring them out from every nation, gather them in from other lands, and lead them home to their own soil.... I myself will tend my flock, I myself pen them in their fold, says the Lord God. I will search for the lost, recover the straggler, bandage the hurt, strengthen the sick, leave the healthy and

---

[30] 2 Peter 3:9.
[31] John 3:16-17.
[32] Jesus' first prayer from the cross, Luke 23:34.
[33] Romans 5:6, 8.
[34] Romans 8:38a, 39.

strong to play, and give them their proper food. [35]

[The] Son of Man has come to seek and save what is lost. [36]

God remains faithful to the divine task of redemption and reconciliation. Words said long ago to Israel and to the church are God's Word for all of us today:

> I will rescue them from all their sinful backsliding and purify them. Thus they shall become my people, and I will become their God... It shall no longer be said, 'They are not my people', they shall be called Sons of the Living God. [37]

> You are now people of God, who were once not his people. [38]

Because the universe was created for the children of God, all of creation itself joins in God's longing for reconciliation: "[The] created universe waits with eager expectation for God's sons to be revealed" (Rom. 8:19).

The entire universe is eagerly waiting for us. God is eagerly awaiting us. The scorned lover is waiting for the unfaithful beloved. The scorned parent is still seeking the lost child. So far, the story is one of unrequited love. How will it end?

*****

The End Is in the Beginning

> The Bible begins with the fact that God spoke and it was done. The second period, which deals with God's journey with this one man and with this one people, begins with the word spoken by God to this one man. And when this second period is brought to an end there is a new beginning: the Word became flesh. It is God's word that binds world history as a whole, according to the testimony of the Bible.... From the word comes history.
> Claus Westermann [39]

---

[35] Ezekiel 34:11-13a, 15-16.
[36] Luke 19:10.
[37] Ezekiel 37:23; Hosea 1:10.
[38] 1 Peter 2:10.
[39] Westermann, *A Thousand Years and a Day*, p. 22.

117

God is in the beginning and he will be in the end.
Dietrich Bonhoeffer [40]

God's love story—the tale of 'I love you'—has a future face.
Leonard Sweet[41]

If I stake my life on one field, one wild force, one sentence
issuing from Sinai it is this one: *There is no goal beyond love.*
David James Duncan [42]

We have an understandable tendency to treat creation only as the
acts of God that took place "in the beginning," prior to the existence of
the world and as the means by which the world began. This is certainly
true, but it is only part of the truth of creation. God continues the
sustaining work of creation that keeps the universe going. God does not
simply linger behind us in the primeval past as the divine "originator."
God is also God-with-us, an aspect of God's Being that is best
expressed in Christ, who is called Immanuel, meaning "God with us."
But that is not all of the truth of creation either. God is also God-ahead-
of-us, calling us to the future of being with God.

"Eschatology" is the theological term for the doctrine of the last
things, the end of history; and as Carl Braaten has proposed, "The
starting point of Christian theology is not at the beginning but at the
end." The real clue to the story is in the last chapter. This is a story
where it is helpful to read the end before we start at the beginning.
Braaten proposes an understanding of God who is prior to the creation
and who creates so that, from the beginning, creation is being drawn
forward from the power of its goal, its end. He then calls for an

> eschatology of creation that starts with Jesus' proclamation of
> the kingdom of God and its initial arrival (the firstfruits) in the
> new creation of the resurrection life.... The Creator God is
> the God of promise.... [And in the Christ-event] God as the
> power of the future has revealed himself as creative love. [43]

In this understanding of creation, the emphasis of creation's meaning is
derived by its intended end rather than its beginning. Jurgen Moltmann
adds that eschatology is not about "last things," as much as it is "the

---

[40] Bonhoeffer, *Creation and Fall*, p. 20.
[41] Sweet, *The Three Hardest Words*, p. 38.
[42] Duncan, *God Laughs and Plays*, p. 227, emphasis in
the original.
[43] Braaten, *The Future of God*, pp. 18, 103, 105.

medium of Christian faith as such."[44]

I am very much in agreement with the eschatological interpretation of creation, and I agree that it is most fully expressed and lived out in Jesus Christ. As I noted above, Jesus is nothing less than "God with us." But I also believe that Jesus didn't change the heart of God; rather, he fully revealed the heart of God that had been present in God's relationship with humanity from the beginning and that will be the fulfillment of that relationship in the end. As I noted earlier, redemption is not a recent addition to the heart of God. Braaten has made this same point: "Christian eschatology speaks of the future in *utterances of hope based on a history of promise.*"[45] Jesus does not reveal to us an unknown God; rather he reveals anew and in full expression the God of history. The future, the "not-yet," finds its content in God's identity as revealed in the past. Future tense is, in fact, God's very nature: "I will be what I will be" (Ex. 3:13, alternate reading). Creation came from the uttering forth of the Word, the creative Word that God continues to utter.

Our primary posture toward the future can be one of hope instead of anxiety only in the strength of a past in which the God of the future has been revealed as a God of history and hope. The transcendent reality described in the biblical traditions is not so much the God who stands above us, but *"the God who goes ahead of us*, opening the way for the greater fulfillment on the road to the future."[46] Christian hope is rooted in a living memory, recalling the past history in which promises for the future were heard and in which the new creation began to dawn. Out of that memory of the past emerges a promise of what is to come. The past is no longer seen as completed facts but as a real anticipation of a new future. "The Christian looks back through the community of faith not in order to extrapolate but in order to anticipate."[47]

Scripture makes clear that God has a plan and a purpose in creation that are enduring and unstoppable: "Mark this; I have spoken, and I will bring it about, I have a plan to carry out, and carry it out I will" (Isa. 46:11b). Furthermore, God has not abandoned the plan: "'Shall I bring to the point of birth and not deliver?' the Lord says; 'shall I who deliver close the womb?'" (Isa. 66:9). As the psalmist has stated, "The Lord's

---

[44] Moltmann, *Theology of Hope*, p. 16.
[45] Braaten, "Toward a Theology of Hope," *Theology Today*, XXIV, July, 1967, p. 216, emphasis added.
[46] Richard Shaull, "Theology and the Transformation of Society," *Theology Today*, XXV (April, 1968), p. 27, emphasis in the original.
[47] David. O. Woodyard, *Beyond Cynicism: The Practice of Hope*, p. 52.

own plans shall stand for ever" (Ps. 33:11a). God continues the work of creation, working to achieve the divine intention for creation, which is not yet fully accomplished.

Even creation itself joins in God's creative work to bring creation to fulfillment of God's purpose: "Up to the present, we know, the whole universe groans in all its parts as if in the pangs of childbirth" (Rom. 8:22). And when God's Word has accomplished this creative work and completed God's creative task, nature itself will join in the celebration: "Before you mountains and hills shall break into cries of joy, and all the trees of the wild shall clap their hands" (Isa. 55:12). This is direct reversal of the effect of humanity's sinful rebellion on the creative fruitfulness of nature: "[Accursed] shall be the ground on your account.... It will grow thorns and thistles for you, none but wild plants for you to eat" (Gen. 3:17-18).

So we find clues to the meaning of history in the past actions of God, but God's plan for our future reveals the deepest meaning of history—history both past and present. What does God's future plan for us hold? What is God's desire for creation, for us? What is God's eternal and abiding purpose? The apostle Paul answered this question with joyous confidence: "He has made known to us his hidden purpose...namely, that the universe, all in heaven and on earth, might be brought into a unity.... *From first to last this has been the work of God. He has reconciled us...to himself*" (Eph. 2:16; 2 Cor. 5:18, emphasis added). In short, God is still at work to reconcile lost creation and to reunite us, God's rebel children, with God's own Self in the unity of love—bringing life where there has been death: "It was there from the beginning; we have heard it; we have seen it with our own eyes; we looked upon it, and felt it with our own hands; and it is of this we tell. Our theme is the word of life" (1 John 1:1). And this reconciliation is not only the restoration of relationship with God's Self, but also with each other: "This was his purpose, to reconcile the two into a single body of God..." (Eph. 2:16). What humankind has split asunder, God will join together.

God's abiding purpose for unity, reconciliation, harmony, and relationship is going to be realized in a new creation, a re-creation, which will restore all creation to its intended state of existence present in the beginning (symbolized in the garden of Eden stories), which was lost through our sinful waywardness. God's intended end is the restoration of God's created beginning:

> Men will say that this same land which was waste has become like a Garden of Eden.... Now at last God has his dwelling among men....

I will be his God and he shall be my son....
I am the beginning and the end. [48]

What lies ahead at the consummation of God's purpose not even Paul could imagine, but in the words of Scripture he stated, it will be "Things beyond our seeing, things beyond our hearing, things beyond our imagining, all prepared by God for those who love him" (1 Cor. 2:9). Paul could see only "puzzling reflections in a mirror," but in God's planned future, he knew, "we shall see face to face" (1 Cor. 13:12). Paul didn't know; we don't know, but even the "puzzling reflections" in the Bible portray for us at least the mood of God's intention. Ezekiel's ecstatic and poetic vision helps us catch a glimpse:

> I will make a covenant with them to ensure prosperity; I will rid the land of wild beasts, and men shall live in peace of mind on open pastures and sleep in the woods. I will settle them in the neighborhood of my hill and send them rain in due season, blessed rain. Trees in the countryside shall bear fruit, the land shall yield its produce, and men shall live in peace of mind on their own soil... I [will] break the bars of their yokes and rescue them from those who have enslaved them. They shall never be ravaged by the nations again nor shall wild beasts devour them; they shall live in peace of mind, with no one to alarm them. I will give prosperity to their plantations; they shall never again be victims of famine in the land nor any longer bear the taunts of the nations. They shall know that I, the Lord their God, am with them, and that they are my people Israel, says the Lord God. You are my flock, my people, the flock I feed, and I am your God. This is the very word of the Lord God. [49]

Other passages from the prophets give us some of God's Word that reveals the predominant characteristics of that future state:

- *Peace*, where weapons of war will be turned into tools of domestic production, and no nation will ever again train for war (Mic. 4:3b; see also Isa. 2:4b).

- *Freedom* from burdens and the yoke of slavery (Isa. 10:27).

- *Safety* and *harmony*, where the wolf and sheep will lie down

---

[48] Ezekiel 36:35; Revelation 21:3b, 7, 6a.
[49] Ezekiel 34:25-31. Contrast with Genesis 3.

121

together, children will lead lions, and the bear and cow will be friends; hurt and destruction shall be no more, and weapons of war will be swept away so all living creatures may lie down without fear (Isa. 11:6-9; Hos. 2:18; see also Isa. 65:25; Jer. 31: 23b-24).

- *Fruition* and *plenty* characterized by long life, enjoying the fruits of one's labor, blessed childrearing, and God's answering even before we call (Isa. 65:19-24; Mic. 4:4a).

In short, the Word of God delivered through the prophets speaks of nothing less than a new creation: "For behold, I create new heavens and a new earth" (Isa. 65 17a). The consistent message of the prophets is that in "that day" God will no longer remember our transgressions: "Former things shall no more be remembered nor shall they be called to mind. Rejoice and be filled with delight, you boundless realms which I create" (Isa. 65:17-18a). Hosea presents an image of this new creation as one where we will be linked with God in the intimacy of marriage: "I will betroth you to myself for ever, betroth you in lawful wedlock and unfailing devotion and love; I will betroth you to myself to have and to hold, and you shall know the Lord" (Hos. 2:19).

In the New Testament, several hundred years after the visions of the prophets of Israel, their vision of a new heaven and a new earth was given new expression by John the Seer. His concluding vision in the book of Revelation is of a "new heaven and a new earth, for the first heaven and the first earth had vanished" (Rev. 21:1). The most common interpretation of this vision is that John is talking about something other than this earth, which seems indeed to be what the text says, because the "first earth" will vanish. But what does it mean that the "first heaven" will also pass away? That one is a little harder to comprehend. Maybe what will pass away is the *distinction* and *separation* between the first heaven and the first earth. Heaven is not a place but a circumstance where God's reign is fully realized and God's will is fully accomplished. John Macquarrie suggests that heaven is the symbol (or metaphor) that stands for fullness of being: "Heaven is not a reward that gets added on to the life of faith, hope, and love, but it is simply the end of that life...the working out of the life that is oriented by these principles [of faith, hope, and love]."[50]

If the end is truly the realization of God's original intention, which is expressed in the creation vision in Genesis as some form of existence

---

[50] Macquarrie, *Principles of Christian Theology*, p. 365.

where God "walks with us in the garden," then maybe Marcus Borg is on the right track when he says that this last vision of John "is perhaps best understood as the 'dream of God'—God's dream for humankind. Throughout the Bible, God's dream is a dream for *this* earth, and not for *another* world."[51] It is for this dream that Jesus taught us to pray "on earth as in heaven." It is this dream that Jesus outlined for us in the Sermon on the Mount. For John, as Borg notes, it is the only dream worth living:

> I heard a loud voice proclaiming from the throne: 'Now at last God has his dwelling among men! He shall dwell among them and they shall be his people, and God himself will be with them. He will wipe away every tear from their eyes; there shall be an end to death, and to mourning and crying and pain; for the old order has passed away!' Then he who sat on the throne said, 'Behold! I am making all things new!' …A draught from the water-springs of life will be my free gift to the thirsty. All this is the victor's heritage; and I will be his God and he shall be my son.' [52]

As in the garden in Eden, there will once again be free access to the tree of life, which was lost as a result of our rebellion (Gen. 3:24); and there will be not just one tree of life, but two: "Then he showed me the river of the water of life, sparkling like crystal, flowing from the throne of God and of the Lamb down the middle of the city's street. On either side of the river stood a tree of life" (Rev. 22: 1-2a).

This is the how the story ends. The end is like the beginning, only better!

But the story has not yet ended. Eugene Peterson has pointed out a parallel between God's finishing the work of speaking creation into existence (Gen. 2:1-2) and John's account of the Word's accomplishment of the salvation of creation in Jesus' declaration "It is finished" (John 19:30).[53] God declared the initiating act of creation was finished, but God's sustaining activity of creation continues. In like manner, Jesus declared the initiating act of salvation has been finished, but God's redeeming activity of salvation continues. The initiating work of the story of creation and salvation has been accomplished, but living the story continues.

It is as if we have jumped ahead to the final pages of the story and skipped all of the parts in between now and then. But this we cannot do,

---

[51] Borg, *Reading the Bible Again for the First Time*, p. 291, emphasis added.
[52] Revelation 21:3-7.
[53] Peterson, *Tell It Slant*, pp. 258-259.

because we are still living the story. We know something of the future that lies ahead in God's plan, but we still seek understanding of how it will come about for *us* in the living of *our days* in the meantime. We certainly have the clues to the plot of the story and we have its outcome in broad stroke, but we have a lot of living left to do. Our individual plot lines are still developing. Therefore, for the present moment, the story ends not with a period (or, more appropriately, an exclamation point) but with an ellipsis....

*****

PART FIVE: TO BE CONTINUED...

Every new generation through the centuries and millennia is challenged...again to face the secret of God's dealings with our world in matters both great and small.
Claus Westermann [1]

[When] our/my story is connected appropriately with the story of God, there is revelation.... Through the words of the story, the Word of God becomes present. In that moment, it becomes a sacred story through which God speaks.
Thomas E. Boomershine [2]

We are well warned: it is not enough to understand the Bible, or admire it. God has spoken; now it's our move.
Eugene Peterson [3]

*****

The New Creation

God's story isn't over. Our story isn't over. My story isn't over. As I look back on my faith journey, it has been a long and at times challenging path. Many times I have paused along the way, sometimes for reflection, sometimes out of fatigue, and (in honesty) sometimes out of reluctance to continue. Sometimes I have wandered from the path.

---

[1] Westermann, *A Thousand Years and a Day*, p. 274.
[2] Boomershine, *Story Journey*, p. 21.
[3] Peterson, *Eat This Book*, p. 109.

But every time I have paused or wandered, I have heard the soft call of the voice saying, "Follow me." So, here I am, still on the journey, sometimes still pausing, sometimes still wandering. It is not the pillar of smoke by day or the pillar of fire by night that guides my wandering; it is the voice of my traveling companion.

How will the human story go from here? How will God go about accomplishing God's purpose for redeeming this lost creation? The plan began long ago in the heart of God. The prophet Isaiah foresaw it:

> The people who walked in darkness have seen a great light;
> light has dawned upon them, dwellers in a land as dark as
> death....for a boy has been born to us...and he shall be called
> in purpose wonderful...Prince of Peace. [4]

The prophet foresaw it, and John and Paul declared its accomplishment:

> God loved the world so much that he gave his only Son, that
> everyone who has faith in him may not die but have eternal
> life....that through him the world might be saved.... For it is
> my Father's will that everyone who looks upon the Son and
> puts his faith in him shall possess eternal life.... [5]

> He has reconciled us ... to himself through Christ... that the
> universe, all in heaven and on earth might be brought into a
> unity in Christ. [6]

As I have already indicated, the redemptive nature of God's love has been constant through the generations. I frankly do not know how God's plan looks for everyone. But I can testify, as one who knows God in Christ, how the plan looks for me. It is in the incarnation of God's Word and love in Jesus that I see most clearly the plan and purpose of God in creation. In the words of Dorothy Sayers, "By incarnation, the creator says in effect: 'See! this is what my eternal Idea looks like in terms of my own creation.'"[7] And what does that eternal Idea look like? David James Duncan has expressed it well. Jesus spent the bulk of his life "demonstrating in word and deed that there is no goal beyond the experience and expression of love."[8]

More particularly, it is in Christ's death that this miracle of grace and

---

[4] Isaiah 9:2-7.
[5] John 3:16-17; 6:40a.
[6] 2 Corinthians 5:18; Ephesians 1:10.
[7] Sayers, *The Mind of the Maker*, p. 90.
[8] Duncan, *God Laughs and Plays*, p. 95.

reconciliation is accomplished. Consider how the early evangelists told the story. Jesus lived 33 years; his public ministry lasted three years; the events of the passion took place in a week. Yet the accounts of that week make up a quarter of Matthew's gospel, a third of Mark's, one fifth of Luke's, and nearly half of John's. Eugene Peterson sums it up rather succinctly: "Jesus suffered and died. This is the plot that provides the structure of the gospel story.... It was to tell this story, Jesus' suffering and death, that each evangelist wrote his Gospel."[9] It was about this story as well that Paul wrote in his letters: "through the cross, [Jesus] killed the enmity.... Through him God chose to reconcile the whole universe to himself, making peace through the shedding of his blood upon the cross—to reconcile all things" (Eph. 2:16; Col. 1:13-27).

With the incarnation, the future has broken in on history in a new and powerful way. The new heaven has already opened to us, and the new earth is already available. "When anyone is united to Christ there is a new world; the old order has gone, and *a new order has already begun*" (2 Cor. 5:17, emphasis added). And we find that love and compassion are at the center of this new creation. The redemption of God's creation comes about through God's love that was expressed in Christ's compassion. In the words of Matthew Fox, "The Christ story redeems creativity by setting it in the context of compassion.... The result of Christ's compassion is a 'New Creation' and a new relationship to creation wherein we are reunited with the whole."[10] I find that this passage from John Macquarrie expresses well the core of my faith and understanding of God's incarnation in Jesus Christ:

> [Is] this not all that we need to know about the historical Jesus? To know that he was one who taught that in the face of the end men are called to radical self-giving love, and that he himself lived this way even to the point where he gave himself up to death. [11]

Jesus' life and death are of a single piece. As I will set forth later, his way of life brought about his death; his death has no meaning apart from his life. But his life did not end in his death. The resurrection affirms both Jesus' life and death as being uniquely of God. As I have already noted, God is revealed throughout the Bible as the God of history, and as Jurgen Moltmann has noted, the resurrection of Christ in history is the ultimate "history-making event from which all other

---

[9] Peterson, *Christ Plays in Ten Thousand Places*, p. 142.
[10] Fox, *Creativity*, p. 95.
[11] Macquarrie, *Principles of Christian Theology*, p. 277.

history is enlightened, questioned, and transformed.... In remembering this one, unique event, we remember the hope for the future of all world history."[12] Christian hope is grounded in Christ's death and resurrection, and Jesus is the representative in whom God and humanity exchange hope for each other. Because of Jesus' cross, God has reason to hope for humanity, and because of Jesus' resurrection, we have reason to hope in God. As expressed by John Topol, "Through his death, humankind remains faithful to God; through his resurrection, God remains faithful to humankind."[13] Resurrection hope is the kind of hope that points us ahead to "something we do not yet see" and enables us in the meantime to "overflow with hope" (Rom. 8:25; 15:13).

Christian hope must never be confused with secular optimism, for mere optimism must eventually stumble over the threshold of death. Knowing we have to die, we human beings nevertheless wish to hope. But all too often human hoping becomes merely wishful thinking, with no basis for our optimism or our hope other than that we wish it to be so. The truth is that we cannot escape or neutralize the reality of death by either ignoring it or by trying to find security for our soul in a doctrine of immortality. We cannot deny death's reality and finality by counting on some deathless, immortal element innate within us. Christian faith and hope affirm the deadliness and inescapability of death. Death is real and dead is dead. But death is not the end of our story. As Christians, we anticipate a new beginning.

Therefore, the story continues with all who receive God's Word in Christ. Walter Brueggemann calls God's action in Jesus Christ nothing less than "God's gift of *power to become the children of God*' (John 1:13)."[14] As God revealed God's self *to* Jesus as "Abba! Father!," so God's self is revealed *through* Jesus, in such manner that the Spirit of the Son enables us to cry in our own hearts, "Abba! Father!" (Gal. 4:6). In the language of Exodus, we are no longer slaves; we have been adopted as God's children. As expressed by John in the Prologue to his Gospel, "For all who did receive him, to those who have yielded him their allegiance, he gave the right to become the children of God...the offspring of God himself" (John 1:12-13). I am reminded of the words of one of my favorite hymns: "No more a stranger; nor a guest, But like a child at home."[15]

---

[12] Jurgen Moltmann, *Theology of Hope*, p. 180.

[13] Topol, *The Way to Peace*, p. 148.

[14] Walter Brueggemann, *The Bible Makes Sense*, p. 124, emphasis in the original.

[15] Isaac Watts, "My Shepherd Will Supply My Need," *The Baptist Hymnal*, Wesley L. Forbis, ed.

It has often been said that all politics is local. Dominic Crossan proposes also that all incarnation is local: "It is, in other words, about history.... [Jesus] is always both dated in the there-and-then...and also updated to here-and-now for new times and new places, new needs and new communities."[16] God's presence in the beginning of creation was quite local, "in the garden." Whatever that back-story image fully means, it at least means this: God was with God's people in the midst of God's good creation. God's Word of presence was then incarnated in the descendants of Abraham and in the people whom God rescued out of Egypt—the people God stayed with in the wilderness, and led into a land, a home, a place. God's Word was later uttered by the prophets into specific moments in time and in specific circumstances of life. God's Word was supremely incarnated in the life, death, and resurrection of Jesus. This was the final incarnation in the sense that it was the definitive incarnation, but it was not final in the sense of being the last. God's Word is to be incarnated anew in Christ's body today—the church.

In short, God's story is an ongoing saga of God's incarnated love, which brings us to today, and to here, and to us. "God is love" will be only an abstract proposition for today unless it is once again, time after time, incarnated anew in the lives of God's people in the midst of the stuff of this present place and time. To paraphrase G. K. Chesterton, "You cannot admire love in general, because the essence of love is that it is particular."[17]

If incarnation is the mode and if Jesus is the model, we're going to have to take Jesus' incarnation seriously. As I noted above, it was in the cross of Christ that God's reconciling purpose was accomplished, and the cross would have no meaning apart from the resurrection; but it is also true that the cross would have had no meaning apart from the life of Jesus. God was present in Jesus' life as well as at his death. It took the *whole* life of Jesus, including its ending on a cross, to get God's *whole* Word across. The writer of the letter to the Hebrews made clear the point that it took the whole of Jesus' life to express fully the splendor of God's being (Heb. 1:1-3a, 2:3a).

All who would be Christian know that we *must* take *Jesus* seriously. What I am now suggesting is that we must also take *incarnation* seriously. From very ancient times in some non-biblical cultures, there has been a dualistic understanding of human beings that separates body from soul,

---

[16] Crossan, *A Long Way from Tipperary*, p. 149.
[17] Chesterton was speaking of the nature of "will" in his book, *Orthodoxy*, p. 34.

assigning our fleshly existence to a secondary status in determining what it means to be human. In this concept, flesh and history take a back seat to spirit and eternity. But God—Israel's God, the church's God, and my God—is the God of creation who comes to us in our history, not as a generalization, but in particular times and places, in particular people and communities. This is a radical departure from the philosophical and religious concepts of God as being aloof and uninvolved in history. So we must not rush past the understanding of God's choice of incarnation as the means of divine self-revelation.

But, after having tried to absorb that concept, there is still another puzzler. Why did God choose Jesus, a first century Palestinian Jew of humble birth, to be the one to incarnate supremely God's very being? The simple truth is, I don't know. But I believe there is an element of consistency in God's choosing at this point. If we consider God's other choices, we can see the outline of a pattern. Remember, God began this work of reconciliation by choosing Abraham, a poor, wandering Aramaean to father a great nation who would be God's chosen people. God later chose Moses, a fugitive murderer hiding out as a shepherd on the back side of the wilderness, to lead a ragtag crowd of slaves out of Egypt to become God's special treasure. Through the centuries, God chose a mishmash of prophets to utter forth the divine Word both to the unfaithful and against their oppressors. God entrusted that Word of creative, saving, redeeming love into the hearts, hands and mouths of a small group of Jesus' disciples that became God's church. God has put that Word into *my* life and added me to the family. It boggles the mind to consider that I am part of God's strategy for communicating God's presence in the world. Carlyle Marney goes even further to declare, "*Every* self is an incarnation, in prospect."[18] And, as Leonard Sweet has put it, "We aren't called to be Mother Teresas. [And we probably say "Thank goodness; who could live up to her?" Don't relax yet, though, because Sweet isn't through.] But *we* are called to be *Jesus*."[19] Face it. This is a very unusual kind of God.

That God is a personal, active, self-revealing God is a constant theme of the Bible. When it comes to knowing God, the initiative is always entirely God's. Only God can reveal God's self to us, and God's mode of revelation has to be at least potentially comprehensible by us. A fairly obvious, yet often overlooked, truth is that God knows how to describe God's self much better than we do—because God alone knows fully both God's self and us. Earlier, I briefly mentioned Christianity's

---

[18] Marney, *Priests to Each Other*, p. 30, emphasis added.
[19] Sweet, *Soul Salsa*, p. 116, emphasis added.

"scandal of particularity," which claims that in Jesus we have the ultimate expression of the infinite. Once we accept the fact that history is the stage of God's self-revelation, we may expect that such self-revelation will always be localized in specific historical events. Universality is always lived out in particularity. History itself is made up of the particularities of real life and real lives. Further, once we understand that God is personal, it becomes entirely reasonable to propose a personal model as the most appropriate and adequate way of communicating God's self-expression—that is, what God has to say about God's self. As I have tried to make clear, the primary mode of God's self expression is God's Word, in all of its utterances; and the fullest utterance of that Word is the One who *is* the Word.

Any adequate model of personal communication must involve an "I-Thou" intercourse, in which there is both expression and response. Although we usually think of God's Word as coming to us in a one-way communication, this communication is not just a divine monolog. Rather, it is a dialog in which we are expected to take an active part. As Harvey Cox has observed, this dialogical communication is the essence of the incarnation:

> God speaks, but man also speaks back. The Creator makes
> man a responding creature and constantly calls him to respond
> to the Creator and to his fellow man, hopefully in love, but
> always in freedom. The thrust of the idea of the Incarnation is
> that God intentionally makes Himself fully vulnerable to
> whatever response man makes.... God allows Himself to be
> one who is willing to risk the most dangerous consequences of
> dialogue in order to make His message known.[20]

People have argued endlessly about the question of whether a tree that falls in the forest makes any sound when no one is around to hear it. Obviously, sound waves are generated regardless of whether there is anyone present, but it may be argued that sound *waves* do not actually become *sound* unless there is some type of auditory device that is activated in response to the waves. In a similar way, personal communication presupposes a two-party relationship of sender and receiver, or revealer and responder, or I and Thou. Perfect communication would require perfect revelation and perfect response, which is impossible unless the revealer and responder are in perfect unity—that is, one. And this is exactly what the New Testament writers concluded had occurred in Jesus Christ, based on Jesus' own testimony:

---

[20] Cox, *The Seduction of the Spirit*, pp. 308-309.

131

> I am not here on my own, but he who sent me is true.... I
> came from God and now am here. I have not come on my
> own; but he sent me.... *Anyone who has seen me has seen the*
> *Father....* Don't you believe that I am in the Father, and that
> *the Father is in me?* The words I say to you are not just my own.
> Rather, it is the Father, living in me, who is doing his work. [21]

In logical development, we move from the relatively known to the relatively unknown. Therefore, we do not begin with God to understand Christ. Rather, we begin with Christ, who is God-with-us, to understand God. As William Sloane Coffin has stated, "What is finally important is not that Jesus is Godlike, but that God is Christ-like. God is like Christ. That's what we need to know."[22] And, once again, the apostle Paul got the message early on: "He is the image of the invisible God, the firstborn over all creation.... For God was pleased to have all his fullness dwell in him..." (Col. 1:15, 19).

Going a step further, in the incarnation Jesus revealed not only the face of God, but also God's intended face for humankind. In this regard, I can affirm these words from Bishop Spong as the witness that I would also give:

> I can only bear witness to what I believe the Christ event is.
> Jesus is the point in the human enterprise where, for me, the
> divine and the human flow together perfectly, revealing God
> as the Source of love, the Source of life, and the Ground of
> Being. Jesus is human being where the essence of the divine
> life breaks forth with a peculiar [and I would add, unique]
> intensity. [23]

Seen in this way, Jesus Christ revealed not only God (as revealer) but also God's intention for humanity (as responder). Indeed, the incarnation becomes the definitive model for this communication, because the incarnation is God's own Self informing human life with God's creative and purposive presence. It is at one and the same time both the perfect revelation of God to humanity and the perfect response of humanity to God. The self-expressive Word of God is present in Jesus Christ, revealing the truth about both God and humanity.

Acceptance of the concept of incarnation means we must begin

---

[21] John 7:28; 8:42; 14:9-10, emphasis added.

[22] Coffin, *Credo*, p. 12.

[23] Spong, *Rescuing the Bible from Fundamentalism*, p. 243.

there for our understanding of God's nature, judging all other manifestations of God in light of the incarnation. At the same time, we must also begin there for our understanding of humanity, judging all other estimates of human nature accordingly. To let preconceptions of either theology or anthropology sit in judgment on the incarnation is gross error. Rather, for Christians, the Truth of God in Christ judges our understanding of all other truths. In short, *Jesus is essential to the definition of both God and humanity*. Jesus is a window through which we may see God and a mirror in which we see ourselves, not as we are, but as we are intended to be—the perfectly created response to God's perfect expression of creative purpose.

*****

Jesus: One Like Us

Before moving on, we need to grasp some of the implications of Jesus' humanity. There is ample New Testament witness to the humanity of Jesus:

> The Word became flesh and made his dwelling among us... taking the very nature of a servant, being made in human likeness... Since the children have flesh and blood, he too shared in their humanity... For this reason he had to be made like his brothers in every way... Because he himself suffered when he was tempted, he is able to help those who are being tempted... [24]

That Jesus was fully human means the baby born in the Bethlehem stable was a normal, human baby. In whatever way we may respond to the concept of virgin birth, we must not construe it to mean that this baby had some unique advantage that made him anatomically or automatically divine. As Carl Braaten expressed it in his book *The Future of God*,

> Jesus had to earn his right to be the representative of mankind.... It was not all part of a plot decreed in advance, so that Jesus had only to follow a flawless script. His unity with God was perfect, but not automatic. [25]

---

[24] John 1:14; Philippians 2:7 Hebrews 2:14; and many other passages too numerous to mention.
[25] Braaten, *The Future of God*, p. 89.

I noted earlier that, in creation, God has given us freedom because God has designed us for relationship with one another and with God, which is not possible with robots or automatons pre-programmed for automatic response. What holds true for all of humanity must also hold true for Jesus if incarnation is to have any meaning for us. A belief in an "automatic Jesus" would make Jesus other than fully human, a kind of superhero God-in-a-man-suit. Not only does this contradict the testimony of Scripture, it makes a mockery of the whole idea that God can relate to humanity as One who came among us. The humanity of Jesus means this fully human baby had to grow to maturity just like every other human being; and once again that is the witness of the New Testament, which portrays Jesus as growing in understanding: "And Jesus grew in wisdom and stature" (Luke 2:52); having normal human needs for food: "The next day as they were leaving Bethany, Jesus was hungry" (Mark 11:12); "The Son of Man came eating and drinking." (Matt. 11:19); having normal human emotions: "Jesus wept" (John 11: 35); and dealing with real human temptations: "he began to be deeply distressed and troubled…. He said to them, My soul is overwhelmed with sorrow to the point of death…. Going a little farther, he fell to the ground and prayed that if possible the hour might pass from him" (Mark 14:33-35).

The Gospel accounts portray a *person* who had to withdraw in prayer for understanding, guidance, and strength. He had to *learn* obedience: "Although he was a son, he learned obedience" (Heb. 5:8), and could do nothing without God: "I tell you the truth, the Son can do nothing by himself; he can do only what he sees his Father doing" (John 5:19). Jesus' humanity, just like *Adam*, meant that he was free to respond to God in obedience or disobedience; otherwise, he lacked the human freedom granted by God to all of us, and his temptations were mere charades. In whatever way we would define Jesus' divinity, we must not be allowed to presuppose his perfect response to the Father's will. Rather, *his divinity resulted from his perfection of obedience*, and he was declared Son of God by God's confirming act of resurrection (Rom. 1:3-4) at the culmination of his life and growth in perfect obedience: "Although he was a son, he learned obedience from what he suffered and, *once made perfect*, he became the source of eternal salvation for all who obey him" (Heb. 5:8-9, emphasis added). We must preserve Jesus' full humanity, including his freedom to reject God's purpose. If Jesus had rejected God's purpose, he would not have been recognized as God's Son; and we would probably have never heard of him. As expressed by John Webster, "Without the movement of God's unrestricted love and self-giving, without the Son's eternal obedience to the Father, there is no history of Jesus."[26] Therefore, we must conclude that Jesus' *obedient response was essential for his Sonship, not merely derived from it.*

But, on the other hand, what if Jesus was *born* the Son of God, as a literal reading of the biblical writers requires? What if the divine nature was his to lose through unfaithfulness? In this view, rather than starting as a kind of neutral being—a kind of child-of-God-in-potential—and then *becoming* Son of God through his faithfulness, what if he *started* as Son of God and through constant faithfulness *remained* Son of God and was affirmed as such after his resurrection? In this view then, by extension, what if each of us, who are created in the image of God, is actually *born* as a Child of God and this nature is ours to lose, rather than ours to gain? In this case we are not born sinful; we *become* sinful in our unfaithfulness. This seems to fit well with the notion that we are created in God's image, only to fall away from it, rather than being born sinful from the first breath of life God breathes into us. However this may be, the end result remains that "all have sinned and fall short," so we are still in need of God's redemptive love toward us. And, as noted above, in whatever way we define Jesus' divinity, it must not negate his humanity.

*****

Jesus: Son of God

What, then, of Jesus' divinity? The key to our understanding of Jesus' divinity has already been alluded to above in the sketch of the incarnation as the perfect focusing of God's self-expression, and it is supported by some of the New Testament references that affirm that God was in Christ. Let us now trace the implications of his divinity as we did for his humanity. A fully divine Jesus means that there was never a time when the human will of Jesus was other than the perfect expression of God's will; not because of some divine magic that pre-empted the human will, but because each step of Jesus' growing understanding was matched with his obedient response. This, I think, is the significance of Jesus' prayer life that brought him into such intimate communion with God that he recognized God as the source of his very being: "I came from God and now am here. I have not come on my own; but he sent me" (John 8:42). Jesus was *declared* Son of God because he lived out the full implications of his understanding of God as Father, through his life, death, and resurrection.

---

[26] Quoted by Jason Byassee and Mike Allen in "Being constructive: An interview with John Webster," *Christian Century*, June 3, 2008, p. 32.

It is in Jesus' life that we find the Father revealed. Earlier, I asserted that God knows best how to reveal God's self, and now we find that God chose a relational model of Father and Son[27] to communicate God's essential nature as Love: God is Love—reconciling, self-giving, undying Love. The total self-giving of Jesus Christ in making himself vulnerable to the worst that humanity could do enabled him to be declared Son of God. In the cross God is made known most fully. In the cross God suffers the worst we can do and still comes to us as Love; inviting us to respond by yielding to this love. And, in turn, we come to understand most clearly that we are intended to live in God's love. In the words of Scripture, in God we live and move and have our existence (Acts 17:27); God is the Source, Guide, and Goal of all that is (Rom. 11:36); and God is Love (1 John 4:9). Everyone who loves is a child of God, and one who dwells in love is dwelling in God; and God is dwelling in her/him (see 1 John 4:7-17).

*****

The Medium Is the Message

So, incarnation as God's mode of communication seems quite reasonable as an abstract concept, but the incarnation in Jesus as *the defining expression of God's self-revelation* is still unexpected. We may no longer be surprised at the incongruity of God's choice of person, time, and place, because for us it has become a standard of the faith, a truism perhaps more than a truth. Robert McAfee Brown attempted to help us be surprised by God's incarnation in Jesus by putting it into a more contemporary setting. If it were to happen today, he suggested that it would be more like this:

> A child would be born into a backward South African tribe, the child of poor parents with almost no education. He would grow up under a government that would not acknowledge his right to citizenship. During his entire lifetime he would travel no more than about fifty miles from the village of his birth, and would spend most of that lifetime simply following his father's trade—a hunter, perhaps, or a primitive farmer. Toward the end he would begin to gather a few followers together, talking about things that sounded so dangerous to

---

[27] I follow the common biblical usage of Father and Son, not at all intending it to represent gender on God's part or special status for the male of the human species.

the authorities that the police would finally move in and arrest him, at which point his following would collapse and his friends would fade back into their former jobs and situations. After a short time in prison and a rigged trial he would be shot by the prison guards as an enemy of the state. [28]

That's certainly not how *we* would do it, but it is how *God* did it; and I'm willing to bet that God had good reasons, so it is worth giving our fullest attention to Jesus' incarnation. If Marshall McLuhan is correct that the medium is the message, then we must seek some understanding of this medium.

It is the nature of incarnation that it is restricted to a particular time and place, and this is true of Jesus' incarnation. Georgia Harkness has stated,

> When God chose to incarnate himself in human form and Jesus accepted his God-given mission, this incarnation occurred within the stream of a particular history, the history of the Jewish people. Indeed, there could have been no incarnation in an abstraction, for incarnation means concrete embodiment, and concrete embodiment is always historical. The incarnate Lord had to live within a particular time and place, and the time and place of Jesus, with all the past that was focused there, gave the framework for what Jesus was and what he taught. [29]

If we are going to seek understanding of his incarnation, we need to consider the implications of its time and place. In the words of a Jewish New Testament scholar, "If one takes the incarnation—that is, the claim that the 'Word became flesh and lived among us' (John 1:14)—seriously, then one should take seriously the time when, the place where, and the people among whom this event occurred." [30]

In their book *The Jesus Movement*, Ekkehard W. and Wolfgang Stegemann have provided a comprehensive look at the context of the life of Jesus and the struggle for identity of the social movement set under way by him in its first century in Palestine. [31] Ancient Palestinian society fell into two broad

---

[28] Brown, *The Pseudonyms of God*, p. 85.
[29] Harkness, *Christian Ethics*, p. 51.
[30] Amy-Jill Levine, *The Misunderstood Jew*, p. 7.
[31] Much of the following account of Jesus' social context and its meaning for understanding Jesus is derived from this source.

groups: the upper stratum (the elite) and the lower stratum (the masses). The upper stratum lived generally in the cities and accounted for about 1-5 percent of the population. The groups making up the upper stratum were, in descending order of rank and wealth:

- the "Roman imperial aristocracy,"
- the "rich" (without leading political office), and
- the "retainers" (free individuals, freed slaves, and slaves who assumed duties for their masters in prominent political positions or performed important administrative tasks in the private sphere).

The wealthy stood out from the rest of the populace through their opulent eating habits and clothing. (Read the parable in Luke 16:19-31 of the rich man and Lazarus in this context. The rich man was dressed elegantly and was gorged; Lazarus had no clothes worth mentioning and was starving to death.)

The lower stratum was comprised of people who had to earn a living for themselves and their families through their own work. Some, the "relatively prosperous" poor, were artisans who might own their own businesses in the cities. In the villages various kinds of artisans, such as carpenters, cobblers, and blacksmiths, were sometimes able to earn money in nearby cities. Others, the "relatively poor," were free farmers who might own a piece of land in the country. Both of these groups could at least provide adequate sustenance for themselves and their families. Below them were the "absolute poor," the wage earners, employees, day laborers, and slaves who lived at or below the poverty level of minimum existence. Jesus and most of his early followers came from the lower stratum of the predominantly Jewish Palestinian society, which consisted mostly of agricultural day laborers who worked on land they didn't own. Only a relative few managed, not always by honorable means, to accumulate property.

The lower stratum had little to eat and little to wear. The vast majority of the rural population lived in chronic hunger, on the delicate balance between starvation on the one hand and subsistence on the other. Through a complex web of circumstances beyond their control, they were always at risk of falling off that balance on the side of starvation: "Especially the simple rural people—that is, the great majority of the population as a whole—apparently lived with constant concern about achieving the means of survival."[32] This very real life situation served as the context for Jesus' familiar message in Matthew 6:25-34 about being anxious about food, drink and clothing. The poor were fortunate to have even two garments; and the poorest of the poor had no outer garment at all, wearing only rags or going naked.

The overwhelming majority of Jesus' early following came from the rural lower stratum, some coming from the subgroup of the absolute poor. In light of this, it is impressive that an artisan like Joseph managed to feed his family, which included five boys and several girls (according to Mark 6:3). As the Stegemanns note,

> Even a trained artisan in a small place like Nazareth in Galilee seldom earned more than a day laborer. Even with 400 denarii a year [which was twice as much as the estimated 200 denarii per year for a day laborer], Jesus' family probably still lacked what it needed. Yet in this respect they were no different from their neighbors in the country. [33]

Judea was ruled by a priestly aristocracy based in the Jerusalem temple who were assigned the responsibility for maintaining order and making timely delivery of tribute (taxes) to the Roman authorities. Naturally enough, whenever conflicts arose between the locals and their Roman masters, the priests sided with Rome. Theirs was a delicate situation, which made them sensitive to criticism of both them and "their" temple. Anyone bold enough to challenge the legitimacy of their rule faced the possibility of execution. When Jesus entered Jerusalem, he was walking into the midst of an explosive political environment which had a short fuse.

It is worth pausing here to note, in anticipation of what will come later, that "kingdom" itself is a political word. All too often we spiritualize the expression, "the kingdom of God," so that it applies primarily or exclusively to the future and to life in heaven, not to the present and to life here in the midst of earthly claims of competing kingdoms. Although Jesus did not coin this phrase himself, he used it as a major theme in his teaching. In so doing, he intentionally placed the kingdom of God in opposition to the ruling power structures of that day, and of every day since.

To the extent that Jesus subverted higher-order norms like

---

[32] Stegemann and Stegemann, *The Jesus Movement*, p. 51.
[33] Stegemann and Stegemann, *ibid*, p. 90.

Torah obedience, as interpreted by the Pharisees, support of the temple's sacrificial system, and the need to send tithes to the temple, he posed a serious threat to the leaders in Jerusalem whose base of power resided in the temple and was buttressed by their control over the interpretation of the Torah. [34]

Because of the religious implications of Jesus' critiques of the Pharisees and of the political relevance of Jesus' rejection of the power of the sword, both the Sanhedrin and the Procurator had to take Jesus' life in the names of both their religious and secular forms of political responsibility and in the interests of their own safety and well being.

*****

Jesus Was a Jew

For Christians to ignore the fact that Jesus was a Jew is not uncommon. Even when we acknowledge it, we often want to minimize it as if it were incidental to who he was and what he was about. But to take this attitude is to deny the reality and relevance of incarnation. If Jesus' time, place, and position in society were not relevant to God's message, God would have chosen either someone else or some other medium of revelation. The particularity of Jesus' incarnation means that, like it or not, Jesus is best understood as thoroughly Jewish. As Bart D. Ehrman has rightly noted, "Jesus of Nazareth cannot be understood apart from his Jewish context. Whatever else we may say about Jesus, he was totally Jewish."[35] Ehrman goes on to make four points in support of this:

·   First, he took his stand *in* the Old Testament, not *against* it.
·   Second, Jesus followed the Jewish custom of Sabbath observance and keeping the Jewish festivals.
·   Third, Jesus' followers were drawn from the predominantly Jewish society of Palestine.
·   Fourth, Jesus' controversies all had to do with Jewish opponents over interpretations of the will and law of the God of the Jews.

---

[34] William R. Herzog II, *Prophet and Teacher*, p. 82.
[35] Ehrman, from The Teaching Company, "From Jesus to Constantine," Lecture 6: "Jesus as a Jew."

In sum, "He was an interpreter of the Jewish Scriptures, he kept Jewish custom, and he had Jewish followers. The burden of his message was a Jewish, prophetic message."[36] So not only was he Jewish, he followed in the tracks of a long line of "*Jewish teachers and prophets.*"[37] The Jews perceived Jesus to be a prophet, and, as such, they expected him to interpret the Torah and mediate between God and the people. In the same manner of the Jewish prophets before him from Amos to Zechariah, Jesus appealed to the Torah as the foundation for his critiques of the ruling elites and of the abuses of the temple.

Jesus also took his ethical stand within the Jewish scriptures, not against them. Many of his teachings are paralleled in the Old Testament and other Jewish writings of Jesus' day. As Levine points out, "Jesus's connections to the basic Jewish teachings were right on target…. Jesus does not have to be unique in all cases to be profound."[38] Levine is right that Jesus' Word was not a brand new Word from God, but I propose that it *was* a brand new expression of that Word. Jesus' message had its root and most of its fruit in God's character and God's previous utterances of the Word throughout Jewish history, but it is also true that he brought a new standard for interpreting the Scriptures and understanding the Word. Leonard Sweet illustrates this quite well, using the Lord's Prayer:

> Want to talk about the originality of the Lord's Prayer? You can find almost exact parallels to each of its six petitions in some Jewish source. The originality of the Lord's Prayer is not in Jesus' choice of words but in the order, brevity, and synthesis of its design. The originality of Jesus was in the way the teachings of his ancestors lived and evolved in him. Jesus lived those teachings and reworked them for the first-century world. [39]

Also commenting on the Lord's Prayer, Levine concludes, "it is an ideal prayer for a first century Jew."[40]

Jesus not only was selective in the passages he chose from the Torah and prophets, he also gave new interpretations and emphases to the Scriptures he selected. For example, numerous times in the Sermon on

---

[36] Ehrman, from The Teaching Company, "From Jesus to Constantine," Lecture 6: "Jesus as a Jew."

[37] Amy-Jill Levine, *The Misunderstood Jew*, p. 20, emphasis in the original.

[38] Levine, *ibid*, pp. 21, 23.

[39] Sweet, *Soul Salsa,* p. 70.

[40] Levine, *The Misunderstood Jew*, p. 51.

the Mount Jesus reminded his hearers of what they have been told in the past and then asserts a new interpretation.[41] Jesus judged the Scriptures by what he knew of the mind and heart of God, rather than letting the Scriptures define God. Jesus always emphasized moral relationships of the life of the people of God, not the cultic institution and requirements of the temple. He consistently wove together humanitarian rather than cultic understandings of Scriptures. Accordingly, he rejected all priestly interpretations that made Torah a burden to the people. And Jesus not only brought new understanding of Scripture, he also brought a new energy to that understanding. Those who heard him teach declared that they had never heard anyone teach like that. Even his enemies are reported to have said, "No man ever spoke as this man speaks" (John 7:46).

*****

Blindsided By the Word

Jesus' inaugural appearance as teacher came in his home town of Nazareth. Read Luke's account (in Luke 4):

> So he came to Nazareth, where he had been brought up, and went to synagogue on the Sabbath day as he regularly did. He stood up to read the lesson and was handed the scroll of the prophet Isaiah. He opened the scroll and found the passage which says,
> 'The spirit of the Lord is upon me because he has anointed me;
> he has sent me to announce good news to the poor,
> to proclaim release for prisoners and recovery of sight for the blind; to let the broken victims go free,
> to proclaim the year of the Lord's favour.' [42]

So far, so good. After all, these were words from the prophet Isaiah. Words from a long time ago. Safe words. Then Jesus pushed ahead: "He rolled up the scroll, gave it back to the attendant, and sat down; and all eyes in the synagogue were fixed on him" (v. 20). He had them right where he wanted them. They had heard the reading; they were waiting for the interpretation and application. "He began to speak: 'Today', he said, 'in your very hearing this text has come true'" (v. 21).

---

[41] See Matthew 5: 31-34, 38-39, 43-44.
[42] Luke 4:16-19.

This statement was unexpected. These weren't words from Isaiah; these were new words, and the people weren't sure what to make of them. They were impressed and amazed; they asked each other, "Wait a minute, isn't this the carpenter's son, Joseph's boy? Who would have thought he'd turn out so good?" They were expressing hometown pride in the local boy who made good, perhaps taking some of the credit for how well he'd turned out. But this admiration was also mixed with the assumption that the fulfillment of Isaiah's prophecy was good news for them. If this was the local boy, after all, then the blessings of the prophecy that he declared to have come true must surely be meant for them.

Jesus saw clearly the congregation was missing the point, so he illustrated it for them, as all good teachers do. He called their attention to an exalted figure from the Scripture, the prophet Elijah, whom God sent to a widow (a "widow woman", as southerners of my childhood were apt to say, somewhat redundantly) who provided for him when there was famine in his home land, even though there were many perfectly fine local (read "Jewish") widows that God could have selected to help Elijah. She was a woman, a widow, and a foreigner. That gave her three marks against her on the social register. Those in Jesus' audience might have lived with the first two, but the third? No way! But, just in case they still hadn't caught on, Jesus gave them another example: Elisha, who didn't heal the many lepers in Israel, not a single one of them as Jesus made clear, but healed another foreigner.

Okay, then it was clear. The crowd finally got the point: the fulfillment of Isaiah's prophecy would not be good news for them *just because* they were Jews. And opinions of Jesus suddenly changed. This wasn't a local boy made good; this was a young squirt who was rising above his upbringing. These weren't good words at all, or safe words; they were fighting words. So in a mob fury they rose up and dragged him out of town, intending to throw him over a cliff. But he moved through the mob and *went on his way*. [That phrase, "on his way," is important for us. What was Jesus' way? Hold that question.]

When I read this account in Luke, I am inclined (and I suspect that we are all so inclined) to take offense not at Jesus but at those who turned against him. When we do this, we are subconsciously and sinfully casting ourselves in the role of Jesus and not among the good, faithful, "church going" people of Nazareth. But that kind of reading is a mistake because it treats the text only as a dead account of a long past event. At the time of Jesus' birth, the Jews had been looking for a Messiah for centuries. They had a whole collection of mental images of what the Messiah would be—individual images and collective images. Apparently Jesus didn't conform closely enough to the prevalent images to be recognized as Messiah by most of the Jews. They looked at their mental images and then looked at Jesus, and they preferred their own mental images. It is more than ironic that, having been forbidden to create a graven image, they had created mental images which they substituted for Jesus. But before we judge them, we must ask, do we not do the same? Do we not fail to recognize when God is made manifest in our midst and in our lives because the manifestation doesn't conform to our idolatrous mental images? If we are honest, we must confess that we more often than not miss God's presence.

It is not until we read this story of long ago as part of *our* story today that we get at the real point of the story. When we read it as our story, humility and honesty should make us hesitate to cast ourselves as Jesus. So if we are in this story at all, and if we are not in the role of Jesus, we must be part of the congregation-turned-mob. Robert McAfee Brown helps make this kind of reading clear:

> We hear that (a) the gospel message is initially addressed not to us but to the poor and oppressed, (b) their liberation makes things risky for us since the nonpoor cannot anticipate gentle responses from the poor once the latter are free, (c) being 'religious' (or whatever is for us the equivalent of going to the synagogue) is not a guarantee whatever that the future will fall happily for us, and (d) God may look upon rank 'outsiders'...with more favor than on us.[43]

Now, we must listen to the story as Jesus tells *us* that he will take his blessings, not to us *just because* we claim to be Christians, or claim to be in the church, but to those outside the church, to foreigners, even to our enemies. As James A. Sanders notes, that "is not the sort of message any congregation wants to hear, especially today, whether conservative or liberal. What is the use of being a member of the in-group if, when God intervenes to sort everything out, he takes his blessings to sinners, to outsiders?"[44]

As I have already noted a couple of times, the artist Rembrandt frequently painted a self-portrait in the midst of a biblical scene which he was painting, well aware of the importance of placing himself in the biblical story to make it his own story. If we were to portray the scene in this passage from Luke's gospel, and if we could paint with the talent and integrity of Rembrandt, we would have to portray ourselves as

---

[43] Brown, *Theology in a New Key*, p. 95.
[44] Sanders, "Hermeneutics," *The Interpreter's Dictionary of the Bible*, Supplementary Volume, p. 407.

participants in the angry mob rather than painting our face on Jesus.

As Brown goes on to say, "A message like that—who needs it? Over the cliff with him."[45]

*****

The Imitation of Christ

> Jesus didn't offer the world a new belief system. He offered the
> world a new heart—a new heart for God, a new heart for
> yourself, a new heart for truth, a new heart for life, a new heart
> for others.
> Leonard Sweet[46]

Jesus' teachings had much in common with the Messianic dogma of Judaism of his day, but he was not dogmatic in his manner and method of teaching. Jesus formulated no doctrine or system of ethical principles and rules that can be extracted, isolated, collated, and then used as a checklist of holiness. Since Jesus didn't resort to a checklist for defining what it means to be a follower, then we certainly should not presume to do so. If I may borrow a phrase from Leonard Sweet (who was using it in reference to himself) and apply it to Jesus, Jesus was more interested "in relational prepositions than in doctrinal propositions." Sweet then goes on to explain the difference:

> Relational prepositions are words that draw people
> into/within/among/between/amidst into a divine connection.
> Doctrinal propositions separate people into categories and
> camps and positions. It's the difference between faith as a set
> of ideas about Christ to be believed or a relationship with
> Christ that is lived.[47]

This in itself is a clue that Jesus' teaching cannot be reduced to principles and checklists of right behavior—no matter how much we are prone to do this.

The "checklist" approach to Jesus' teaching is further hampered by the fact that we don't even have a record of everything that Jesus said. Moreover, what we do have was filtered through the memories, interests, and concerns (and, perhaps, even biases and prejudices) of first-century

---

[45] Brown, *Theology in a New Key*, p. 95.
[46] Sweet, *The Three Hardest Words*, p. 42.
[47] Sweet, *Soul Salsa*, p. 107.

Christians. Moreover, we have to make allowances for Jesus' use of paradox, hyperbole, poetry, story, metaphor, and parable. As many have suggested, we cannot always take Jesus literally, though we must always take him seriously. Finally, as I stressed earlier in the Introduction, our own biases and presuppositions significantly influence our interpretations, including the way we interpret Jesus' teachings and their importance for us.

Jesus' teaching was unsystematic, a composite of various elements concentrating upon actions and attitudes, filled with illustrations and stories, using parables instead of principles. While this teaching method sometimes makes it difficult to nail down precise meanings, it keeps his teaching alive and relevant to every age and every human situation. As noted earlier, Jesus did not ignore the law; but he went behind the law to the One who gave the law. He sifted through biblical traditions and interpretations to set forth their original meanings. He did not argue (or argue logically, anyway) to convince people to agree so much as he persuaded them by appealing to the heart. His teaching, rather than being abstract, scholarly, and systematic, was direct, spontaneous, and relevant to the moment at hand. It was aimed at the individual conscience as the immediate occasion demanded. As Amy Jill Levine has noted,

> In fact, there is no indication that Jesus had a *systematic* interpretation of the Torah. He did not, as did the rabbis, discuss the various distinctions of tort law with other rabbinic scholars. Rather, the Gospels suggest that he responded to questions that were posed to him, either by circumstances ('Can one heal on the Sabbath?') or posed by those seeking either to learn from him or to test him ('What is the greatest commandment?'). [48]

Consequently, Jesus didn't combine ethics and religion as if they were two separate things. For him, religion was faith in the Father—the God of love—and ethics was faithfulness to the value the Father places on all children and all of creation. For Jesus, God's truth was not concepts and doctrines to be delivered and believed but a way of love to be lived. Jesus taught and modeled incarnational love as the embodiment of God's will. He didn't come primarily to deliver words about God, because even he couldn't make language express the inexpressible. He didn't come so much to *speak* the Word, as to *be* the Word. *Truth* has to be incarnated,

---

[48] Levine, *The Misunderstood Jew*, p. 28, emphasis in the original.

146

not "in-languaged."

This life of incarnational love is the fulfillment of God's original intention in creation for all who are created in the divine image. For Jesus' ethics, what mattered was not just conduct alone but character from which conduct springs—not just the performance but the person behind the performance. Jesus demonstrated that life is to be lived in the imitation of the Father (John 17). The indicative (that which is) leads to the imperative (that which must be done). What God is, we must be (Matt. 5:48). "Man is what man is because God is in history, our history, as a Father, looking for children estranged and strayed, as one who cares utterly."[49] As children of God, our behavior is not governed by *having* to do the Father's will, but by *loving* to do the Father's will. This means loving the Father and loving those the Father loves, including even the enemies of the Father (Matt. 5:44) and those who persecute the Father's family (Matt. 5: 11-12).

Various metaphors allow us to go deeper into understanding Jesus' teachings, including "The Family of God and the Life of Sonship," "The Kingdom [or Reign] of God and the Life of Obedience," and "The Son of God and the Life of Imitation."[50] It is this third metaphor that I wish to explore. As R. E. O. White acknowledges, the idea of the "imitation of Christ" is open to over-simplification and misunderstanding. A recent example of this would be the wildly popular bracelets, bumper stickers, and tee shirts of a few years ago, bearing the letters WWJD, "What Would Jesus Do?" For that question to have real content, we must also ask WDJD? ("What *Did* Jesus Do?") and WDTMFUT? ("What Does That Mean For Us Today?").

Reynolds Price provides an appropriate word of caution for anyone seeking to imitate Christ:

> Above all, anyone who considers what Jesus might or might not do should first be firmly aware the he or she is *not* Jesus; and for many Christians, that's a hard mental feat.[51]

Jesus was Jesus and we are not. Jesus lived then and we live now. Jesus lived there and we live here. Turning to Jesus as our guide is not as simple as we would like it to be, which is why we are so regularly tempted to reduce Jesus to a set of rules. So it may be helpful to rephrase the

---

[49] Carlyle Marney, *Priests to Each Other*, p. 46.
[50] See R. E. O. White, *Biblical Ethics*.
[51] Price, *A Serious Way of Wondering*, pp. 50-51, emphasis in the original.

above questions as WWGDIJ ("What Was God Doing In Jesus?") and WWGDIM ("What Would God Do In Me?"). In any case, exploring the idea of the imitation of Christ does provide a convenient summary of one of Jesus' main areas of teaching. "The imitation of Christ is, in truth, the nearest principle in Christianity to a moral absolute.... *When all allowance is made for varying interpretation, the imitation of Christ remains the heart of the Christian ethic.*"[52]

The simplest and most familiar expression of the imitation theme is in Jesus' invitation, "Follow me," and in his pronouncement, "I am the way" (John 14:6). [Remember earlier, in the aftermath of Jesus' inaugural sermon, that Luke said Jesus "went on his way"? Be patient and hang in here with me. We're coming back to this.] Jesus simplified the Christian life into a single command: Love as I have loved *you*. Our love is not to be based on knowing *about* Jesus' love but on *knowing* Jesus' love through our experience of it in our own lives. "As the Father has loved me, I have also loved you. Dwell in my love....love one another as I have loved you.... Do you love me?... Follow me" (John 15:9, 10; 21:17, 19). Discipleship is not based on propositions about Jesus' love or presuppositions of Jesus' love but on the consequence of the experience of Jesus' love. The motivation is not admiration but gratitude: "[When] we feel Love's density, see its colors, feel its pulse, it's time to quit reasoning and cry: '*My God! Thanks!*'"[53] As stated by R. E. O. White, "Imitating, following, loving—such intimate language suggests naive piety rather than moral theory."[54]

Precisely because Jesus' ideal is expressed in personal character and not in a code, it is applicable in every situation in every culture in every generation. That is the relevance of incarnation for us. Here I want to be very careful. The incarnation in Jesus was unique; this was the all capitals "THE INCARNATION." But is not the whole idea of following him that we, in turn, become like him—in short, new incarnations? In the apostle Paul's understanding, the secret hidden through the ages and generations and now made known in Christ is this very thing: "Christ *in* you, the hope of a glory to come" (Col. 1:25c, emphasis added). Loving with the love of Jesus is the standard for Jesus' disciples, and we must not seek to universalize the characteristics of that standard by creating checklists of "right behavior" and divorcing them from their rootage in the life of Christ.

---

[52] White, *Biblical Ethics*, p. 109, emphasis in the original.
[53] David James Duncan, *God Laughs and Plays*, p. 227, emphasis in the original.
[54] White, *Biblical Ethics*, p. 115.

The best summary of Jesus' life of faith, which is to be lived in love, is the Sermon on the Mount (Matt. 5-7). If you don't have time for the whole sermon, you can spend your life on the Beatitudes (Matt. 5:3-12), which are in a sense the heart and core of the Sermon on the Mount. In this sermon Jesus set forth a clear pattern of the demands of the God-centered life, making clear what a life lived in obedient love would look like. In one sense the Sermon on the Mount is Jesus' own summary of what we see in Jesus' life. If we wish to understand Jesus, we can read this sermon. If we wish to understand this sermon, we have only to look at the life of Jesus.

We must be careful not to turn the Sermon on the Mount into a kind of "works righteousness" where we earn our righteousness by following a set of rules derived from the sermon. What we find in the sermon is not so much a "Christian ethic" of rules as a description of the lived faith of the Christian life. The Beatitudes are *descriptive of* the reign of God, not *prescriptive for* the reign of God. We don't have to "live up" to them in order to get into the kingdom of God; rather, when we have let our lives be defined by the reign of God, the Beatitudes are descriptive of what our lives will be like. The Sermon on the Mount portrays what it looks like to live the faith of God's children who belong in God's family and who live in thankfulness to God.

God doesn't deliver us because we are deserving. It has never worked that way. Israel's deliverance from Egyptian bondage did not depend on what *they* did, but on what *God* did. Israel's deliverance from Babylonian exile did not depend on what *they* did but on what *God* did. In like manner, our deliverance from sin's captivity does not depend on what *we* do but on what *God* does. "The beatitudes are not about high ideals but about God's gracious deliverance and our joyous participation."[55] We must always remember that we are not saved by rules; we are saved by grace, and we are to live by grace.

*****

---

[55] Glen Stassen, *Living the Sermon on the Mount*, p. 43.

> From then on Jesus began to point out to His disciples that He
> must go to Jerusalem and suffer many things from the elders,
> chief priests, and scribes, be killed, and be raised the third day.
> [56]

> You cannot know who Jesus is after the resurrection unless you
> have learned to follow Jesus during his life.... Only by learning
> to follow him to Jerusalem, where he becomes subject to the
> powers of this world, do we learn what the kingdom entails, as
> well as what kind of messiah this Jesus is.
> Stanley Hauerwas [57]

Jesus' life and teachings are summed up as "gospel," which may be
translated as "good news." Gospel is not just any ordinary, everyday good
news, however, but the kind of important public proclamation that
justifies sending a runner out ahead to announce its coming and then
celebrating its arrival when it is received. As I noted above, the Sermon
on the Mount is a verbal description and Jesus' life is a visual
representation of what life under the reign of God looks like. But, be
warned, if you are happy in the present kingdom, then the in-breaking of
a new reign is not good news for you.

There is a particularly interesting image of Jesus' journey to Jerusalem
in Mark's account:

> They were on the road, going up to Jerusalem, and Jesus was
> walking ahead of them; they were amazed, and those who
> followed were afraid. [58]

Do you remember the phrase, "went on his way," I called to your
attention earlier? Do you remember that other phrase, "follow me"?
Everywhere else I can think of in the Gospel stories of Jesus walking with
his disciples, they appeared to be walking together. This time, however,
Jesus was so far in front, the disciples were amazed—and afraid—as they
followed. There had been other times with Jesus when the disciples were

---

[56] Matthew 16:21. See also Matthew 20:18; Mark 10:32-
34; Luke 9:51; 18:31.
[57] Hauerwas, "Jesus and the Social Embodiment of the
Peaceable Kingdom," *The Hauerwas Reader*, Berkman
and Cartwright, eds., p. 119.
[58] Mark 10:32, NRSV.

confused, perhaps even uneasy, but this time was different: They were afraid. According to the Gospel accounts, it was not long before this at Caesarea Philippi that Jesus linked the life of self-denying love and the cross.[59] There Jesus began to make clear what lay ahead in Jerusalem; a cross was at the end of that road to Jerusalem. (Actually, the cross was not at the end of the road. There was a tomb beyond the cross. However, at the end of that road, it was an empty tomb. But that was way too much for the disciples to comprehend. Even with the advantage of knowing about the empty tomb, we still find it hard to comprehend.)

Mark begins and ends this section of his Gospel (10:32 and 10:52) with the phrase "on the road." The way to Jerusalem was literally uphill, but for Jesus going "up to Jerusalem" meant much more than going up an incline. He knew that in Jerusalem he would be given up to the authorities and lifted up on the cross. In Luke's account, as you will recall, Jesus' ministry began with the sermon that resulted in a mob that wanted to throw him off a cliff, but at that time Jesus "went on his way." In all of the Gospel accounts, the end of the way, the end of the road, resulted in the crucifixion. It seems quite clear that Jesus' way is risky. Jesus' is "the way" as John proclaims (John 14:6), but Jesus' way is not an easy way. Any reasonable person should hesitate when Jesus invites, "Follow me." The disciples had begun to glimpse what lay ahead; they were following, but they were lagging behind. They were afraid, but they followed.

In going to Jerusalem, Jesus was consciously confronting the power elite of religion, economics, and politics. One of the only ways to protest in a peasant society is public demonstration, which Jesus used in his triumphal entry into the city and his cleansing of the temple. Acting in his role as a social prophet, Jesus denounced the leadership of the nation and the temple for their failure to execute justice. This threat to law and order, and to the welfare of the political and religious leaders, simply could not be allowed. People like this had to be put in their place, and the power of empire had just the place for them: the cross. John Howard Yoder says,

> The shadow [of the cross] never lifts from the band on the
> road to Jerusalem.... The cross is not a detour or a hurdle on
> the way to the kingdom, nor is it even the way to the kingdom;
> it is the kingdom come. [60]

---

[59] Matthew 16:21-25; Mark 8:31-35; Luke 9:22-24.
[60] Yoder, *The Politics of Jesus*, pp. 46, 61.

The cross, with all that it symbolizes, permeates and gives meaning and unity to all the ethical teachings of Jesus. The cross also gives us our hope for the future:

> Jesus is the representative in whom God and man exchange
> hope for each other. Because of Jesus' cross God has reason to
> hope for man; on account of Jesus' resurrection man has a
> reason to hope in God. For Jesus' sake we do not give up on
> God, and he does not give up on us.[61]

In the incarnation and on the cross, we see God taking our flesh seriously and human flesh taking God seriously. And incarnation leads to a self-denying cross and a tomb. This is the Jesus way.

*****

The Thick Darkness

> In the beginning was silence.
> Before the word was chaos.
> And night.
>
> Then spirit moved across the waters.
> A word came forth.
> Meaning was given to form, direction to motion, order to
> chaos.
> A world emerged.
> The word bore one in its own likeness....
>
> And the word became words, and words, and words, and
> words, and words,
> And there was silence and chaos.
> And out of the silence came...?
> Sam Keen [62]

> In every man is the creative story. Since the first day of our
> beginning, the Spirit has brooded over the formless, dark void
> of our lives, calling us into existence....
> Elizabeth O'Connor [63]

---

[61] Carl E. Braaten, *The Future of God*, p. 91.
[62] Keen, *To a Dancing God*, pp. 108-109.
[63] O'Connor, *Eighth Day of Creation*, p. 17.

152

At Sinai God told Moses that God would come down upon the mountain in the sight of all the people. On the third day, which was to be the day of the Lord's coming to the people, there was thunder and lightning and a trumpet blast, and a thick cloud was on the mountain, for the Lord had descended upon it in fire. The people were afraid and stood at a distance, "while Moses drew near to the thick darkness where God was" (Ex 20:21). The image of God's presence as "thick darkness" appears again at the dedication of the temple by Solomon: "Then Solomon said, 'The Lord has said that he would reside in thick darkness'" (2 Chron 6:1), which refers to the cloud of the glory of the Lord which had earlier filled the house of God, even while the singers were affirming that the Lord "is good, for his steadfast love endures forever" (2 Chron 5:13-14).

I have long been intrigued with the notion of finding God in the "thick darkness." My own spiritual journey has had experiences of darkness, although I have been blessed in far greater measure. Nevertheless, it is reassuring to think of God's being present to meet us in the times and places of thick darkness in our lives. The classic testimony of Christian darkness is that of the Spanish mystic, St. John of the Cross, in his "Dark Night of the Soul." The more common expectation among Christians, however, is that God is found in light, not darkness. In fact, as Christians we don't generally do darkness very well. We are drawn too quickly to the light. Anticipating the resurrection, we rush past the darkness of Good Friday when God was present on another mountain in the crucifixion of Jesus. Yet in the very hour of darkness that came over the land in midday Jesus gave his spirit into the hands of the Father (Luke 23:44-46). And, as Colin Morris has observed, "The ultimate paradox is that the light by which the Christian walks issues from the darkness of a tomb."[64]

It is fitting, therefore, that we Christians celebrate Christmas, the coming of the Light, in the dead of winter when the hours of darkness are at their longest. Yet, in this season also, we rush through Advent, singing joyous hymns and carols of the lights of Christmas, when Advent is actually the time of darkness that precedes the Light. In the thick darkness of night, not even at the first light of day, Jesus was born. Advent is the celebration of God's coming in the darkness, the "season when we remember that darkness may be fruitful—the darkness of the soil where the hidden seed sleeps, or the darkness of the womb where

---

[64] Morris, *the Hammer of the Lord*, p. 51.

new life is created."[65] We are right to see Jesus as God's Light to the world, but we should not always experience darkness as the absence of God.

Isaiah presented the idea that we can choose to trust God in the darkness or try to walk in the light of our own creation. The Lord asked the question: "Which of you fears the Lord and obeys his servant's commands?" And then he answered it: "The man who walks in dark places with no light, yet trusts in the name of the Lord and leans on God." He then followed up with the judgment: "But you who kindle a fire and set fire-brands alight, go, walk into your own fire and among the firebrands you have set ablaze. This is your fate at my hands: you shall lie down in torment" (Isa 50: 10-11). The choice is up to us, and the consequences determine our fate: trust in the Lord even in the darkness or trust in the light we create in our attempts to overcome the darkness and end up in torment.

I like this verse from Minnie Louise Haskins:

> And I said to the man who stood at the gate of the year:
> 'Give me a light that I may tread safely into the unknown.'
> And he replied, 'Go into the darkness, and put your hand into
> the hand of God. That shall be to you better than light and
> safer than a known way. [66]

As Gordon Atkinson has expressed it, "Faith is measured breathing in the face of uncertainty. Faith is turning your heart to faithful living when your mind has reached the end of its rope. *Faith is the choice you make when you face the darkness.*"[67] Phyllis Tickle, speaking of "Everyday Spirituality" at a church in Memphis in 2002, described God as "that great luminous darkness that is complete light and complete joy."[68] Matthew Fox has called our attention to the beneficial and creative aspects of darkness:

> The darkness is a teacher.... Jesus taught people to 'enter the

---

[65] Mary Earle, "A Celtic Christmas,"
http://www.explorefaith.org/celtic/christmas.html,
accessed 9/07/08.
[66] Haskins, from "The Gate of the Year." Cited by Peter
Gomes, *Strength for the Journey*, p. 200.
[67] Atkinson, "Turtles All the Way Down,"
http://www.christiancentury.org/article.lasso?id=1037,
accessed 9/12/08, emphasis added.
[68] Tickle, "Everyday Spirituality,"
http://www.explorefaith.org/stepstones/everyday.html,
accessed 9/7/08.

dark.' He went off to Jerusalem, knowing that a call for his blood was in the air. He set off anyway. It's not that he didn't fear death, not that he didn't care to cling to life. It is just that he loved the quality of life he was teaching more than he feared death. His light overcame the darkness, even the darkness of the fear of death.... He showed us the way—by his teachings, by his life, *and* by his death. He showed us courage and how we can all enter the dark and not be lost there but actually be saved there. [69]

We need to take note of God's ordering of daylight and darkness in the first creation account in Genesis 1. There we find that "day" begins with sundown, not sunrise: "So evening came and morning came, the first day" (Gen. 1:5). This is the pattern for the remaining days—evening, then morning. There is a witness to faith in this pattern that the Jews have retained in their ordering of days, where the day begins at dusk. It is easy to believe in the coming of a new day at sunrise, when light is spreading over the world before our eyes. It takes faith to believe that a new day is beginning just as the world is going dark. Interestingly, in Zechariah's vision of the coming day of the Lord, "It shall be all one day... without distinction of day or night, and at evening-time there will be light" (Zech. 14:7). In the meantime, we have to have faith in the darkness.

The first account of creation in Genesis makes it clear that God's creative spirit moves in the darkness before God utters the creative Word that gives light:

> In the beginning of creation, when God made heaven and earth, the earth was without form and void, with darkness over the face of the abyss, and a mighty wind that swept [or, the spirit of God hovering] over the surface of the waters. God said, 'Let there be light.'[70]

The apostle Paul emphasized that God was in the pre-creation/pre-dawn darkness, and it is from the darkness that light came: "For it is God who said, 'Let light shine *out of* darkness'" (2 Cor. 4:6a, emphasis added). Later Paul added that we should not lose heart, because "we do not look at what can be seen but at what cannot be seen" (2 Cor. 4:18). In short, we have the light, but we do not live by sight that requires light. All we have to lead us into the future is the promise of God; but on this we have

---

[69] Fox, *Creativity*, pp. 169-170, emphasis in the original.
[70] Genesis 1:1-3a.

God's Word. And, as Carl Braaten says,

> If we want more security than the promise of God, we will
> have to exchange it for an idol that promises instant salvation.
> We live by hope or we live by sight, and there is no right way of
> synthesizing them.[71]

Seeing does not require faith. Walking in the light does not require faith.

But the Word of God, that same Word that brought light out of darkness in the beginning, gives us sufficient light in the moment to guide us in the darkness: "Thy word is a lamp to guide my feet and a light on my path" (Ps. 119:105). In speaking of this verse, Walter Brueggemann says, "It is a lamp and a light to fend off the darkness. It is for feet and path, *on the way* in venture. The darkness is real, and the light is for walking boldly, faithfully in the dark we do not and cannot control."[72] In the words of Carlyle Marney, "faith in the active voice is the demand for obedience to light I already have."[73] Robert McAfee Brown, picking up on the apostle Paul's metaphor in 1 Corinthians 13:12, says,

> We see through a glass darkly, but we *do* see—not everything,
> but enough.... Particularly, we see enough light shed on the
> mystery of Jesus Christ to know that he is the 'clue' to the
> meaning of life, not only showing us God as he is, but also
> showing us ourselves as we are meant to be.... 'We do not see
> everything ... but *we see Jesus.*' (Hebrews. 2: 8, 9)
> *And he is enough.* [74]

In Anne Lamott's words, "[Good Friday is] a sad day, of loss and cruelty, and all you have to go on is faith that the light shines in the darkness, and nothing...can overcome it."[75]

We must have faith to follow Jesus, even to the cross and into the tomb, and trust that we will encounter God there in the darkness, the thick darkness, the luminous darkness. Following Jesus "on the way" leads to a cross and the darkness of the tomb, but the way of the cross also leads home:

---

[71] Braaten, *The Future of* God, p. 130.
[72] Brueggemann, "Biblical Authority," *Struggling with Scripture*, p. 27, emphasis added.
[73] Marney, *Priests to Each Other*, p. 114.
[74] Brown, *The Bible Speaks to You*, pp. 308-309, emphasis added.
[75] Lamott, *Plan B: Further Thoughts on Faith*, p. 274.

I must needs go home by the way of the cross,
There's no other way but this;
I shall ne'er get sight of the gates of light,
If the way of the cross I miss.

I must needs go on in the blood-sprinkled way,
The path that the Savior trod,
If I ever climb to the heights sublime,
Where the soul is at home with God.

Then I bid farewell to the way of the world,
To walk in it nevermore;
For my Lord says, "Come," and I seek my home,
Where He waits at the open door.

The way of the cross leads home,
The way of the cross leads home;
It is sweet to know as I onward go,
The way of the cross leads home.[76]

*****

---

[76] Jessie B. Pounds, "The Way of the Cross Leads
Home," *The Hymnal for Worship and Celebration*, ed.
Tom Fettke.

PART SIX: LIVING BY THE WORD

Faith in Christ rests on two remarkable affirmations: Jesus
Christ reveals to us the face of God, which is love. And Jesus
Christ reveals to us the meaning of the human, which is love.
This double revelation is enough. I do not need to know that it
is the only true story on earth to affirm that it is worth giving
my heart to.
Diana Eck [1]

The final secret, I think, is this: that the words 'You shall love
the Lord your God' become in the end less a command than a
promise. And the promise is that, yes, on the weary feet of faith
and the fragile wings of hope, we will come to love him at last
as from the beginning he has loved us.
Frederick Buechner [2]

What Does This Mean for Us Today?

My spiritual journey is not over; I still have life ahead of me, at least
for the moment. If deathclock.com is a clue, I have almost another thirty
years. More seriously, I am alive today; and for each "today" that God
grants, I am called to follow. Like the disciples on the way to Jerusalem, I
may be afraid and I may lag behind, but I still would follow. So as I move
ahead one "today" at a time, what does all of this mean for how I should

---

[1] Eck, *Encountering God*, p. 89.
[2] Buechner, *A Room Called Remember*, p. 45.

live, for how we should live? Having answered the big question of life does not answer all of the little ones. The way of the cross leads home, but how do we live in this world in the meantime? What does it look like to follow Jesus on the way today? How do we live by the Word of God in these challenging and confusing times?

I remember reading in *Time* magazine back in the early 1970s a quote from Senator Patrick Moynihan that went something like this: "The fact that the United States is for peace in the world does not tell the Secretary of State what to do when he gets up in the morning." Similarly, the fact that I believe that God is Love, that God loves me, and that I am to love others with the love of God doesn't tell me what to do when I get up in the morning. This takes me back to the earlier question: WWGDIM, "What Would God Do In Me?"

"Today" is not just my challenge—it is our challenge; it is the church's challenge. In the pages that follow, I want to give my confessional understanding of some of the implications for being a Christian in the United States in the early 21ˢᵗ Century.

*****

Christus in Us

> With this in mind, then, I kneel in prayer to the Father, from whom every family in heaven and earth takes its name, that out of the treasures of his glory he may grant you strength and power through his Spirit in your inner being, that through faith Christ may dwell in your hearts in love. With deep roots and firm foundations, may you be strong to grasp, with all God's people, what is the breadth and length and height and depth of the love of Christ, and to know it, though it is beyond knowledge. So may you attain to fullness of being, the fullness of God himself.
> Paul the Apostle [3]

> Live your life as story.... Better yet, live your life as God's story.
> Leonard Sweet [4]

---

[3] Ephesians 3:14-19.
[4] Sweet, *Soul Salsa*, p. 160.

> Being Christian is a way of life; it's being part of God's story.

> Stanley Hauerwas [5]

Throughout Scripture, God rarely worked the same way twice. God's activity was always unique to the people with whom he was dealing and the time in which he was working. The universality of God is always expressed in the particularity of human lives. That is the essence of incarnational love, which means that the hope for accomplishing God's purpose in today's world lies with people who are alive today, people like us; actually, not with people *like* us, but with *us*. God's hope for the world lies *within* us—yet, not within *us*, but in *Christ* who is within us: "[What] we see in Christ is the destiny that God has set before humanity; Christ is the first fruits, but the Christian hope is that 'in Christ' God will bring all men to God-manhood."[6] Once again, we can turn to the writings of the apostle Paul:

> I became [the church's] servant by virtue of the task assigned to me for your benefit: to deliver his message in full; to announce the secret hidden for long ages and through many generations, but now disclosed to God's people.... The secret is this: *Christ in you, the hope of glory to come.*[7]

> [We] all reflect as in a mirror the splendour of the Lord; thus we are transfigured into his likeness, from splendour to splendour.... For the same God who said, 'Out of darkness let light shine', has caused his light to shine within us, to give the light of revelation—the revelation of the glory of God in the face of Jesus Christ. [8]

The promise of God in Christ is that God works within us to accomplish God's own purpose in and through our lives. We have only to be open to the power of God, rather than falling victim to our constant temptations to rely on ourselves and go it alone, thereby trying to assume God's own role, which was the human failing back in the beginning, not long (as the story goes) after God first spoke and said "out of darkness let light shine."

And how will this be known, that Christ is in us? We often tend to

---

[5] Hauerwas, "Christianity: It's not a Religion: It's an Adventure," *The Hauerwas Reader*, Berkman and Cartwright, eds., p. 522.
[6] John Macquarrie, *Principles of Christian Theology*, p. 303.
[7] Colossians 1:25-27, emphasis added.
[8] 2 Corinthians: 3:18b, 4:6.

think of the Golden Rule as our standard: "Always treat others as you would like them to treat you." That is indeed a high standard. Jesus said that this standard, plus loving God with all our being covers everything in the Law and the Prophets (Matt. 7:12). That definitely ranks it high on the behavior scale. However, as Leonard Sweet has suggested, for Jesus, "there was something beyond 'gold' status. Jesus demanded a 'platinum' discipleship. There is something beyond the Golden Rule, and it is 'the Platinum Rule.'"[9] Jesus left us a new commandment: "I give you a new commandment: love one another; *as I have loved you, so you are to love one another*" (John 13:34, emphasis added).

A true child is one who is motivated by the mother and/or father's spirit: "For all who are moved by the Spirit of God are sons of God" (Rom. 8:14). Augustine has said that we can discover the character of any community of people merely by observing what they love. If we are part of the community in Christ, "They'll know we are Christians by our love."[10] So,

> Dear friends, let us love one another, because love is from God. Everyone who loves is a child of God and knows God, but the unloving know nothing of God. For God is love.... God himself dwells in us if we love one another; his love is brought to perfection within us. [11]

Jesus approaches each of us today with the invitation of old: "Follow me" (Matt. 4:19; 9:9; 19:21; Mark. 1:17; 2:14; 10:21). The most distinctive element in Christian ethics is Jesus himself. Jesus doesn't give us laws. He gives us an invitation. Jesus' ethic is one of following the Leader. While I was typing this manuscript, whenever I would type the name of Eugene Peterson's book, *The Jesus Way*, Microsoft Word would attach a "Smart Tag" to the phrase "Jesus Way," offering several options for further action on my part, including a map and driving directions. My first thought was that it would be nice if it were that easy to find Jesus' way. But God's Word doesn't work like Microsoft Word. Jesus doesn't give us teachings in the form of a "Smart Tag" to provide us travel directions, a compass, a map, or a "triptik." The "Jesus Way" is that Jesus goes before us as a guide and traveling companion. Following Jesus doesn't require that we know the way, but that we follow the Way. This, in turn, requires that we are always to be on the move, from where we are at the moment to wherever Jesus'

---

[9] Sweet, *Soul Tsunami*, p. 174.
[10] Title of a hymn by Peter Scholtes, *Sing 'n' Celebrate!*, Charles F. Brown, editor, p. 44.
[11] 1 John 4:7-12.

leads us. As Henry Blackaby says, one thing is certain: "You cannot stay where you are and go with God at the same time."[12] Or, in the words of a church sign, "Do not ask the Lord to guide your footsteps if you're not willing to move your feet."

Sometimes Christians put the focus of salvation so much on heaven and the hereafter that we forget about God's earth and the here-and-now. Whatever may be said (or speculated) about the future life, it is clear that God saves us *in* this life. He doesn't save us *from* this life. The point of following Jesus is not to join him *there* (wherever or whatever "there" is), but to follow him *here*. Jesus' ethic is a kingdom of God ethic, but, as Jesus taught his disciples to pray, the realm of its activity is to be "on earth as it is in heaven." In the words of Colin Morris, "The kingdom of God does not come at the end of time; it is coming all the time."[13] As such, the reign of God always requires a response from us here and now. Rudolf Bultmann has said that in every moral decision the question must be decided anew: Do I choose to serve myself, or to serve God and my neighbor? Unless this question is decided, all of our talk about "values," "rules," "the situation," or even "love" is likely to be no more than a smoke screen behind which we maneuver so as to serve ourselves. Paul Tillich has made a similar point:

> Man is always put before a decision. He must decide for or against Yahweh, for or against the Christ, for or against the Kingdom of God.... [Every] decision is urgent; it has to be made now.... It is always an ultimate decision.... It decides man's destiny.... [The] decision against righteousness means self-destruction.[14]

The invitation to us is the same as to the first disciples: "follow me." That means that we too, like those disciples, are to walk in the way that Jesus walked; and probably like those disciples, we too will be amazed and afraid and lag behind. John Howard Yoder says that to be a disciple is to share in that style of life of which the cross is the culmination.

> The alternative to how the kings of the earth rule is not 'spirituality' but servanthood. [We cannot avoid] his call to an ethic marked by the cross, a cross identified by creating a new kind of community leading to a radically new kind of life.... Only at one point, only on one subject—but then consistently,

---

[12] Henry Blackaby and Claude V. King, *Experiencing God*, p. 234.
[13] Morris, *The Hammer of the Lord*, p. 36.
[14] Tillich, *Biblical Religion*, pp. 44, 45.

universally—is Jesus our example: in his cross.... The believer's cross must be, like his Lord's, the price of social nonconformity....the end of a path freely chosen after counting the cost. [15]

Jesus does not hide the cost of being his follower. This is not an ethic of "bait-and-switch." He says flat out, "If anyone wishes to be a follower of mine, he must leave self behind; he must take up his cross, and come with me" (Matt. 16:24). Following Jesus means we must travel lightly; we must leave behind all of our baggage, including especially our religious baggage—all of our idols that we still are trying to carry and that are burdens rather than blessings (Remember Isaiah 46:3-4?). We must put down *all* of our idols, including our images of our self. We must lose the very self that we have spent a lifetime putting together. Carlyle Marney rightly cautions us:

> It's a risk. I may lose my life. I may lose my image that holds my me. And, on the other hand: you may already have lost *your* life!... *Your* life is at stake on any of these issues: *sex, race, class, vocation, economics, nationalisms,* and *religion.* In any one of these, and add another one, *play,* a man can lose his life. [16]

It is a risk, but it seems to be an unavoidable risk. It seems that we almost inevitably lose our life to something or someone. Look at Marney's list above. If we pause for just a moment, we can add other items to the list of things that can lay claim or have already laid claim to our self.

We hear a lot today about self-fulfillment and self-esteem, but Jesus talked about self-sacrifice and self-denial. Believing we can hold onto our self may well be an illusion, or a delusion. When Jesus said that in order to follow him we must first deny self, he may not have been suggesting that the alternative is to hold on to our self. He may well have been saying that we have already given up our true self in order to follow some other lesser call on our life, and now we must reject that call and give up our self to God, as did Jesus, in order that we may be filled with God's life and God's love. Jurgen Moltmann has said, "To keep one's life means to hold onto oneself."[17] That may not only be impossible, it may not even be worth much if we could actually accomplish it. As William Sloane Coffin has observed, "Love measures our stature: the more we love, the bigger we are.

---

[15] Yoder, *The Politics of Jesus*, pp. 46, 63, 97.

[16] Marney, *Priests to Each Other*, pp. 77-78, emphasis in the original.

[17] Moltmann, *The Passion for* Life, p. 26.

There is no smaller package in all the world than that of a man all wrapped up in himself!"[18]

The cost of following Jesus is real, but so is the reward. Again in the words of Carlyle Marney, "What I lose is the product of my own image building. What I get back is the *me* that is created for immortality."[19] This is not Marney's promise, however; it is Jesus': "How blest are those who have suffered persecution for the cause of right; the kingdom of Heaven is theirs" (Matt. 5:10). There is undeniable tension between the cost of discipleship and the joy of discipleship, but the dominant motif of discipleship is not sacrifice and duty, it is love and joy. Jesus' command is to love, not to sacrifice. Sacrifice is derivative in the life of Christ and the Christian, not normative. Sacrifice is the cost the world imposes, not Jesus. Jesus emphasized the joy of the Kingdom—wedding feast, banquet, fellowship—not the duties. Someone has counted forty passages in the New Testament that say "rejoice," five that say "rejoicing," and sixty-three that say "joy." Joy is part of the character of the Christian, not the circumstances of the Christian. The kind of joy that Jesus prayed would be in us is grounded so firmly in relationship with God that no change of circumstance can ever shake it (see John 15:1-17). It was from prison that Paul wrote Philippians, which has been rightly called the "book of joy." Joy is a fruit of the Spirit of God—a product of God's love in us. Joy is an expression of Easter morning hope.

To be in Christ is to know God as Father, whom to know is to trust, to trust is to love, and to love is to obey with gladness from a full heart. The Christian life is not some*thing* one knows, or one has, or one does. It is not even some*one* one *knows*. The Christian life is someone one *is*. Thus our ethic is not ultimately an ethic of sentimental love but an ethic of conformity to Jesus Christ in obedience to the Father. As Stanley Hauerwas has said, "[The] very heart of following the way of God's kingdom involves nothing less than learning to be like God. We learn to be like God by following the teachings of Jesus and thus learning to be his disciples."[20]

Like Father, like Son—like us. It is ironic, to say the least, that what got humankind (and each of us individually) off to such a bad start in the beginning was the desire to "be like God" (Gen. 3:5). And that is exactly what Jesus came to show us how to do—through his life, his cross, his resurrection—to be like God. What Jesus was by nature (Son of God), we

---

[18] Coffin, *Credo*, p. 24.

[19] Marney, *ibid*, p. 81, emphasis added.

[20] Hauerwas, "Jesus and the Social Embodiment of the Peaceable Kingdom," *The Hauerwas Reader*, Berkman and Cartwright, eds., p. 120.

become by adoption. *Like Father, like Son—like us!*

*****

Easter Hope in a Good Friday World

Easter says that love is more powerful than death; bigger than the
dark....
Anne Lamott [21]

During my lifetime, which is almost overnight when seen in historical
perspective, humankind has found itself confronted by a multitude of
unprecedented crises. Back in 1975 economist-futurist Robert L.
Heilbroner was just one of many contemporary thinkers who were asking,
"Is there hope for man?"[22] It may not be surprising that Heilbroner and
many others then and now answer that question pessimistically, given the
rate of change in the world and the increasing connectedness that makes it
impossible to address serious issues in isolation from other serious issues.
Globalization is breaking down borders that have defined us for
generations, and not everyone is happy at the results or the prospects.
Nanotechnology, genetic engineering, and robotics offer wonderful
potential for increased health and longevity, while at the same time blurring
the borders of what it means to be "human." Increased consumption of
resources by growing and more affluent populations may well lead to the
possibility of an unprecedented biodiversity collapse that could result in
extinction of species in an order of magnitude of 100 to 1000 times greater
than at any time since God created human beings. Micro-terrorists and
macro-world powers vying for security and success threaten the prospects
of meaningful peace for many, perhaps most, of the world's peoples.

The glut of information in the age of Internet access to news 24/7 may
make us more informed, while at the same time make us feel more
overwhelmed and out of control. Some observers even wonder if the
Internet is reducing our capabilities of giving sustained attention to
anything, with the result that all of these increasingly complex issues tend
to be presented as sound bites. Our attention span has been reduced from
reading books to reading bumper stickers. Discourse has become sound
bites. Reasoned debate has given way to opposing talking points. The desire
for self-determination has multiplied the number of nation states and
reduced the span of our interests to ever smaller circles of narrowly defined

---

[21] Lamott, *Plan B: Further Thoughts on Faith*, p. 268.
[22] Heilbroner, *An Inquiry into the Human Prospect*, p. 13.

self interests and individual rights. In the midst of all of this, religion more often divides than unites.

If hope has not become a fatality of modern anxiety, it has certainly been seriously wounded; and it is a wound felt deep within the human condition. We might well echo the words of King David to Israel: "Our days on the earth are like a shadow, there is no hope" (1 Chron. 29: 15 NRSV). But David did not end there, and neither do we. In his study of human existence Carl Braaten concluded that hope "is at the heart of existence. It seeks outlet at every level of human life. Where there is life there is hope."[23] Indeed, hope keeps springing up like spring flowers. Eric Fromm, the renowned psychoanalyst, stated that without hope, "life has ended, actually or potentially. Hope is an intrinsic element of the structures of life."[24] Lutheran theologian Hans Schwarz has gone even further, asserting, "Hope is as necessary for human life as oxygen."[25] It seems that, rather than "Where there is life there is hope," it is more likely that "only where there is hope is there life."

There is an element of contradiction in hope, for the message of hope is that humankind is in distress. There is no need for hope when nothing is wrong or lacking. As the apostle Paul noted, it takes faith to hope "when hope seems hopeless" (Rom. 4:18). Hope lives in the tension from the negative toward the positive, from the sufferings of the present time toward a redemption that is longed for. Christian hope is not a kind of sunny optimism that sees new possibilities in the moment. It is precisely in the impossible situation which confronts us that we see God's new creative act: "God's new reality is always like a *novum ex nihilo*."[26] The Christian hope is that something new can come out of that which is nothing, that something good can come out of that which is chaos. It is not through the possibilities in the moment but through God that "the old order has gone, and a new order has already begun" (1 Cor. 5:18). This is a hope born of the cross, a "hope against hope." It is not that the Christian denies the *reality* of death: "it is the lot of men to die once" (Heb. 9:27); but, the Christian denies the *victory* of death: "'Death is swallowed up, victory is won!' 'O Death, where is your victory? O Death, where is your sting?'... Whether...we live or die, we belong to the Lord" (1 Cor. 15:55; Rom. 14: 8). As Colin Morris has noted, that is the basis for Christian hope: "Just

---

[23] Braaten, *The Future of God*, p.38.

[24] Fromm, *The Revolution of Hope*, p. 13.

[25] Schwarz, *On the Way to the Future*, p.22.

[26] Jurgen Moltmann, *Religion, Revolution, and the Future*, p. 9.

that. God on both sides of the void…."[27]

Christian hope lives in a Good Friday world where death is a reality driven home in the crucifixion of Jesus, the deepest abyss of God-forsakenness and hopelessness on earth. But Christian hope does not stop at the cross and the tomb; it goes further: it also believes in Easter.

> Out of chaos, darkness, and flood God created the world. In the context of nothingness he revealed his creative power. Out of the humiliated, poor, and abandoned Jesus who was crucified in disgrace, God makes his Messiah of the future, of freedom, and of life. [28]

Thus, contradiction (even paradox) lies at the very heart of Christian hope.

There is also a risk in Christian hope's grounding in the future in that it may foster mere acquiescence in the present. We live suspended, as it were, between a memory that binds us to a past that no longer is and a hope that rests upon a future that is not yet. But, as Moltmann has noted, the resurrection of Jesus is not only the promise of future resurrection; the Easter appearances are commissioning appearances for Jesus' followers. The realm of the present is the realm for seeking the possibilities that lie on the eschatological horizon.[29] The universal horizon of eschatology reveals the reality of the world as history, qualifying both the past and the present as the history of the future God. While the *ultimate* future exercises the final pressure on the present; the *penultimate* nature of the "not yet" is also part of the Christian present in which the future is being lived: "The present becomes the frontier where the future is gained or lost."[30]

Not many years before her death, my aunt Juanita, who had served as a missionary in China in the early 1900s, wrote hauntingly of the nature of horizons in these words: "As we travel, the hither horizon follows us even as the yonder horizon recedes and we feel surrounded by the mystery beyond every horizon." From over the horizon of the unknown future flow possibilities for both good and evil, and the future will be our heaven or hell, with the present being, in Moltmann's terms, "something like a purgatory."[31] Living in Moltmann's purgatory, surrounded by Juanita's mystery, it is in the gap between what is and what can be that the Christian

---

[27] Morris, *The Hammer of the Lord*, p. 149.

[28] Moltmann, *Religion, Revolution, and the Future*, p. 17.

[29] Moltmann, *Theology of Hope*, p. 26.

[30] Moltmann, *Religion, Revolution, and the Future* p. 202.

[31] Moltmann, *ibid*, p. xvi.

is called into action. It is in the church that Christian hope mobilizes for the future. The church is to be an eschatological community of hope that exists in the world and for the world.

Wes Seeliger wrote a delightful book that I first read back in 1975 called *Western Theology*, which he described as "a cartoon sketch of two spirits: the settler spirit and the pioneer spirit," both of which were contrasting pictures of the church. He described the settler spirit as the picture of unfaith, "the unadventuresome soul who dies by inches in his cast iron world" and the pioneer spirit as the picture of faith, the totally alive person whose life is staked on promises.[32] In contrast to the fearful souls of Settler City, the pioneers were drawn to the wide open spaces, where they heard the voice of the Trail Boss (God):

> The voice that makes no sound. The voice that is loudest in the still of night. The voice that says 'life' where only death can be seen. The voice that says 'hope' where there is no hope. The voice that says 'courage' when fear chills to the bone. [33]

At the end of the book, Seeliger lays down the challenge: "Well, pardner, there it is. Make up your mind, put it on the line. The wagon is moving out."[34] The future horizon beckons. That's the challenge; that's the call. Do we dare hope when there is no hope? Which truth do we choose to live by, Good Friday or Easter Sunday?[35]

*****

---

[32] Seeliger, *Western Theology*, p. 12.

[33] Seeliger, *ibid*, pp. 96-97.

[34] Seeliger, *ibid*, p. 103.

[35] Seeliger's little book was one among several books that impacted me in such a way that in 1976, a year after reading this book, I closed my practice of architecture and left Settler City to go to seminary. Talk about crossing the horizon!

The first task of Christian social ethics…is not to make the 'world' better or more just, but to help Christian people form their community consistent with their conviction that the story of Christ is a truthful account of our existence.
Stanley Hauerwas [36]

People who write (and read) books like this one usually have it pretty well made; we are not only reasonably sure where our next meal is coming from, we are even familiar with the terms of our retirement benefits. But we are a minority.
Robert McAfee Brown [37]

Perhaps the greatest single weakness of the contemporary Christian Church is that millions of supposed members are not really involved at all and, what is worse, do not think it is strange that they are not.
Elton Trueblood [38]

Why aren't Christians known as the world's greatest lovers?
Leonard Sweet[39]

One of the most expressive descriptions of the church in the New Testament is "the body of Christ." One of the most powerful declarations of this can be found in Paul's letter to the church in Ephesus, in which he wrote that the church "is his body and as such holds within it the fullness of him who himself receives the entire fullness of God" (Eph. 1:23). That's a pretty powerful statement: the church, in effect, now holds the fullness of God! This is not to suggest, however, that the church is on the same level as Christ, who is the church's head; for, as Paul noted and as we can well attest, the church has not yet attained "the unity inherent in our faith and our knowledge of the Son of God—to mature manhood, measured by nothing less than the full stature of Christ" (Eph. 4:13). Nevertheless, within the church, where humanity is being conformed to Christ, there is a "new creation" (2 Cor. 5:17) of which Christ himself is the "first fruits" (1 Cor. 15:23).

---

[36] Hauerwas, "Reforming Christian Social Ethics: Ten Theses," *The Hauerwas Reader*, Berkman and Cartwright, eds., p. 112.
[37] Brown, *Theology in a New Key*, p. 13.
[38] Trueblood, *The Company of the Committed*, p. 38.
[39] Sweet, *The Three Hardest Words*, p. 99.

An obvious corollary of this understanding of the church is that the church must conform to the image of God in the incarnation, and the church's ministry becomes thereby a participation in the ministry of Jesus Christ, which was "the ministry of reconciliation" (2 Cor. 5:18). This understanding is not merely an abstract theological construct, because the New Testament clearly represents Jesus as having entrusted his ministry to his disciples. The "classic" example of this is in the so-called "Great Commission" (Matt. 28:19-20), but it is also evident in other gospels, the book of Acts, and in Paul's writings.[40] The shape of Jesus' ministry was informed largely by his self-understanding as the "servant of God" derived from Isaiah, the text of his first teaching:

> The spirit of the Lord is upon me
> because the Lord has anointed me;
> he has sent me to bring good news to the humble,
> to bind up the broken-hearted,
> to proclaim liberty to the captives
> and release them from prison;
> to proclaim a year of the Lord's favour
> and a day of the vengeance of our God;
> to comfort all who mourn,
> to give them garlands instead of ashes,
> oil of gladness instead of mourners' tears,
> a garment of splendour for the heavy heart. [41]

Since being a Christian is nothing other than being conformed to Christ, the church is called to participate in this servant ministry.

Jesus also knew himself to be one "sent" of God on mission, and the idea of mission is carried over into the concept of the church as part of the movement from creation to re-creation. This mission is universal in its breadth; consequently, the church is to be an expanding community encompassing all humankind in the reconciliation of the lost creation in oneness in Christ (Eph. 1:9-10). Salvation is not the special privilege of an elect few but is the gracious gift of God to all who are estranged from God and who respond to the urging of God's spirit. Jesus' own standard for this is based more on the evidence of a person's life than on a person's formal commitment to "essential" doctrines. The evidence for this is plentiful, but to consider just two, look at the Parable of the Good Samaritan (Luke 10:29-37), where the one fulfilling the law of loving God and loving

---

[40] See, for example, Luke 24:7; John 17:18; Acts 1:8; 2 Corinthians 5:18-20.
[41] Isaiah 61:1-2; see Luke 4:18; Matthew 11:4-5.

171

neighbor was the one who acted as a neighbor to one in need. Look at the conversation with (and conversion of) a Samaritan woman who needed both salvation and community (John 4:7-30). According to the word of Jesus (who *is* the Word), citizenship in the kingdom of God is decided by the pragmatic evidence of a person's and a nation's life in such actions as feeding the hungry, giving water to the thirsty, taking the stranger into one's home, clothing those without clothes, visiting and aiding the sick, and visiting those in prison (Matt. 25:31-46).

It is obvious in this passage that one's identity as a reconciling agent of God applies both to those who name Christ and to those who do not. In the account just cited from Matthew, both groups—those who performed the acts of compassion and those who did not—were surprised to find themselves in the group they were in. Jesus knew only too well how easily someone can claim to follow him and then live a life that gives no evidence of it. He stated clearly that "Not everyone who calls me 'Lord, Lord' will enter the kingdom of Heaven, but only those who *do* the will of my heavenly Father" (Matt. 7:21, emphasis added). Salvation comes not through Christianity but through Christ, not through calling the name but in following the person. As Matthew 25 makes plain, Christ judges all people of all religions, including Christians. It is not as if the church is set in a special place of guaranteed salvation over against the rest of God's creation who are automatically lost. Rather, the church stands with all humanity before the Lord, who is not only Lord of the church but of all creation. Just because the church calls Jesus "Lord, Lord" does not make Jesus the church's private possession.

We find ourselves in the same position of those who heard Jesus' inaugural sermon and were surprised and angered to learn that being a Jew was not an automatic free ticket to salvation; neither is being in the church. This awareness helps avoid the arrogance, condescension, and condemnation that so often have characterized the church. Some would argue that this approach would also undercut the missionary motive of the church, which has largely been based on the "we are saved; they are lost" assumption. On the contrary, I believe that standing with all humanity as neighbors and brothers and sisters created in the image of God increases our motivation to act toward everyone in the love of Christ. We are to love God's world with God's love and give ourselves for it. We are not just to give witness to the Good News; we are to *be* the Good News.

The church must be open to God's truth wherever it is found, confident in the conviction that all truth is of God. This statement does not propose some kind of syncretistic universalism, because all truth must be judged against the ultimate revelation of the truth in Jesus Christ. Augustine recognized as early as the fifth century that the truth of Christianity is

172

linked with a Truth that is timeless in its essence:

> That which is called the Christian Religion existed among the
> Ancients, and never did not exist, from the beginning of the
> Human Race until Christ came in the flesh, at which time the true
> religion, which already existed, began to be called Christianity. [42]

I would add to Augustine's concept that the eternal *Logos* is also the universal *Logos*, and the truth that may be found in each of the world's religions is in some sense the presence of Christ hidden therein. Therefore, the role of the church is not so much that of bringing Christ to the religious non-Christians for the first time (for this would deny Christ's universal Lordship) as it is awakening the non-Christians to a more explicit consciousness of the Christ who is already hidden in their faith. C. F. Andrews, a Christian missionary to India in the early 1900s, is quoted as replying to a question concerning his approach to the Indian people, "I always assume that they are Christian; and after I have talked with them for awhile I sometimes see the light of Christ in their eyes."[43]

The world's religions may be understood as the work of the cosmic *Logos* which is proclaimed explicitly in the Christian gospel of the incarnate *Logos*. This means that all Christian communication of Christ with persons of other faiths should be dialogical and reciprocal. Even though I personally affirm without reservation that it is through the Word of God in Jesus that I know and understand God's truth, I cannot assume at any time that I, other Christians, or the church universal fully possess that truth. Joan Chittister gives us a proper caution against confusing our words about God with the Word of God:

> There is no one truth that is the total truth of God. We each
> embody a bit of it; we all lack the rest of it. Even together we are
> not the voice of God because we simply do not speak the
> language or understand the language or know the whole of the
> language that is the Word of God. [44]

In fact, following Christ has less to do with possessing the truth than being possessed *by* the truth. By being open to God's presence everywhere, we will find God in some unexpected places, including other religions

---

[42] Quoted by Harry Emerson Fosdick, *What Is Vital in Religion*, p. 32.

[43] Fosdick, *What Is Vital in Religion*, p. 28.

[44] Chittister, *Welcome to the Wisdom of the World*, p. 121.

which may well be examples of what Robert McAfee Brown refers to as "'the pseudonyms of God,' the strange names he uses in the world to accomplish his purposes."[45] Hence, the presence in other religions of God's characteristics—such as the reverence for life, adherence to non-violence, overcoming racial differences, respect and care for God's creation—can cause us Christians to recognize what sometimes may be neglected elements in our own religion. I am not proposing an uncritical universalism in which dialog itself becomes the absolute and truth is sacrificed on the altar of naive openness. I do not suggest that the church must relinquish its claim to know the truth, only to have the humility never to claim to know the truth fully, much less to *own* the truth.

The servant image present in Isaiah and claimed by Jesus makes it clear that the church is called to be an extension of the self-giving ministry of reconciliation of the incarnation. The church is to be "Christ" in the world and *for* the world, reaching out to bring wholeness where there is division, fullness where there is incompleteness, hope where there is despair, healing where there is hurt, peace where there is turmoil, joy where there is sorrow, love where there is fear, faith where there is doubt, freedom where there is bondage, life where there is death. This work of reconciliation must be expressed at both personal (individual) and institutional (societal) levels, reflecting the comprehensiveness of God's reconciling love which embraces the whole person and the whole world. That is certainly a big enough challenge to motivate the Christian to missionary action.

Given the biblical understanding of humankind as a unity made up of people created in God's image, the church's ministry must include more than merely mouthing pious platitudes of peace to the poor without ever moving to meet their needs:

> My brothers, what use is it for a man to say he has faith when he does nothing to show it? Can that faith save him? Suppose a brother or a sister is in rags with not enough food for the day, and one of you says, 'Good luck to you, keep yourselves warm and have plenty to eat', but does nothing to supply their bodily needs, what is the good of that? So with faith; if it does not lead to action, it is in itself a lifeless thing. [46]

This is not a misreading of the gospel on the part of James. When Jesus sent out his disciples, he commanded them to continue his ministry of healing the peoples' hurts: to proclaim "the message, 'The kingdom of

---

[45] Brown, *The Pseudonyms of God*, p. 35.
[46] James 2:14-17.

Heaven is upon you.' Heal the sick, raise the dead, cleanse lepers, cast out devils" (Matt. 10: 7-8). This ministry does involve proclamation, but it also requires actions. That God is love is not a premise to be argued logically but a presence to be demonstrated relationally. Hugh Prather (not a Christian as far as I know) has written honestly of the difficulty of loving:

> I can't force myself to love someone I have no feeling for, but that situation is so rare—what about the 99% of the time that I *could* feel love if I would only let go?... Love is not an act of the will, but sometimes I need the force of my volition to break with my habitual responses and pass along the love already here. [47]

Love, as affection based on attraction to the other, cannot be commanded. But, as Anne Lamott has reminded us, "[If] you want to change the way you feel about people, you have to change the way you treat them."[48] When we have come to see others as family, it is more likely that we will realize, and act out of, the love of Christ that is already in us. And in the meantime (maybe not 99% of the time at the beginning, but a lot of the time) we can pass along the love that is already there. The rest of the time, we will have to work at treating them better and act out of love expressed as justice, which is not dependent on our feelings of love, but which is nonetheless a proper compassion and gracious response to the other's need. "Compassion" means "to suffer with," which puts us alongside the other who is suffering, sharing in the suffering on the other's behalf. Jesus gave a good summary of his ethics in Luke 6:36: "Be compassionate as your Father is compassionate."

Love cannot be complete, and certainly cannot be Christ-like (which is like the Father), without genuine emotional empathy; but love is not essentially emotional in a "warm and fuzzy get-all-mushy-inside" kind of way. It is, rather, a resolute purpose on the part of Christians to seek in all circumstances the other's good with the same zeal as we seek our own. Glen Stassen points out that Jesus does not say, "Feel about others as you would have them feel about you." Rather he says, "*Do* unto others."[49] Robert McAfee Brown adds further insight into the relationship between love and justice: "[The] line between love and justice is exceedingly thin and finally nonexistent. There is no love without justice, no justice without love."[50] Justice is a poor substitute for love, but it is a necessary substitute

---

[47] Prather, *I Touch the Earth, the Earth Touches Me*, n. p., emphasis in the original.

[48] Lamott, *Plan B: Further Thoughts on Faith*, p. 143.

[49] See Stassen, *Living the Sermon on the Mount*, p. 175.

[50] Brown, *Unexpected News*, p. 70.

in the absence of love or for an inadequate love. The delivering and restorative justice of Isaiah is the threshold of compassion, and such justice moves us well along the way to community and peace. God requires this kind of justice, but God desires love.

The ministry of reconciliation is the unchanging and universal mandate for action by the church, because it is rooted in the eternal and unchanging character and purpose of God. In the challenging words of Reynolds Price, "Any religion which fails to demand that its powerful adherents pay steady attention to mitigating the lives of those in such [awful] plights can hardly call its God a loving God." [51] So, ministry as God's love at work in the world is both universal and timeless for Christians, but as incarnational love the specific forms of this ministry must always be local, adjusted to the changing contours of specific human need. With the sensitivity of God's Spirit, the church must seek out human need and speak a prophetic word, while at the same time moving to meet the need. The breadth of human need is so great that it is easy to be overwhelmed and to succumb to a form of spiritual helplessness. Such a response may particularly be the case when a lack of priorities obscures the underlying reality that human problems cannot be addressed piecemeal and in isolation from one another. Avoiding a piecemeal response becomes even more critical at a time like ours, when society is becoming increasingly institutional in nature, with corresponding losses of individual freedom and self-determination.

*****

God and Country

[There] is no salvation in love of country. There is salvation only in love of Jesus Christ; and if you confuse the two, the greatest defeat will have been achieved.
Peter Gomes [52]

The church's highest priorities today must be assigned to effecting change in the social structures that contribute to alienation, deprivation, and dehumanization wherever that may be. Such action will almost certainly place the church in a more confrontational stance with government than has been especially true in recent years. During the span of my life, we Americans have been living in a mood of intense nationalism. The implication of our rhetoric has been consistently that we

---

[51] Price, *A Serious Way of Wondering*, p. 110.
[52] Gomes, *Strength for the Journey*, p. 142.

176

are pure, our enemies are evil. Robert McAfee Brown has expressed his concern with those who would say, "America is right. America is God's nation. To criticize America is unpatriotic and un-Christian." He then went on to say,

> It is a curious fact about the present American scene [words written in 1972, but no less true today] that those who must blatantly shout about their 'Americanism' are precisely those most determined to deny the right of dissent to those who disagree with them.... In the name of 'patriotism,' another word they abuse, they insist that all Americans must think alike, namely the way *they* do, for their point of view is (a) American, (b) right, and (c) Christian. [53]

We Americans today are certainly no exception to Brown's assessment that the "nation is the most pervasive of all the gods, in any time, in any culture."[54] We are guilty of the sin of pride of nation—the deification of national interests, so that God is on our side no matter what we do. We are not alone in this, of course. No nation has ever operated on the principle that God has no favorites and that power is to be equated with duty and responsibility, not privilege. Every nation, in its pride and lust for power, is apt to deify its own interests and define good and evil in ways that have more to do with national interests than with God's universal laws. Stephen Decatur's toast, "Our country, may she always be in the right; but our country, right or wrong!" sounds plausible and patriotic, even noble, but in its essence it is idolatrous—placing nation over God.

In America, with our long history of Exceptionalism, the problem is further compounded by the widely held belief that God founded this nation to carry out the divine purpose and guides our destiny in ways that make it difficult to conceive that God and country are not just two ways of saying the same thing. We have done a perverse twist on the old saying, "What's good for General Motors is good for America" and tend to act as if "What's good for America is good for God." Glen Stassen warns us against those who would raise

> a national flag...or an image of our nation that stands for goodness against another nation that stands for evil and inflames us to make war and arouses our passions to serve the image rather than serve God who is revealed in Jesus

---

[53] Robert McAfee Brown, *The Pseudonyms of God*, pp. 132, 136, emphasis in the original.
[54] Brown, *Unexpected News*, p. 159.

Christ and the Holy Spirit.[55]

In 1978 in Louisville, KY (where I lived at that time) an article in the *Courier-Journal* newspaper quoted a lay evangelist, who was first vice-president of the Louisville chapter of the Full Gospel Business Men's Fellowship, as saying,

> Full Gospel is involved in the American spirit. We sing Americanism songs. The better American you are, the better country this will be. We can't separate God and this country.[56]

Now, lest you misunderstand me, I am not anti-American. I love this country and live here because there is no other place I would rather live. I thank God that I am blessed enough to live in the United States. But when we reach the point where we are unable to separate God and country, we are in trouble.

This was ancient Israel's problem long before it was ours. From the exodus on, Israel increasingly deified the nation; and the prophets were lonely voices crying in the wilderness as they sought to awaken the people to the reality of their relationship with God. They smugly thumbed their noses at other nations, saying we have nothing to fear for "God is with us," and they longed for the day of the Lord—because that would be the day that all of those other nations would get their comeuppance. But Amos warned them: "Fools who long for the day of the Lord, what will that day mean to you? It will be darkness, not light" (Amos 5:18). And Isaiah thundered the Word of God: "It is the Lord of Hosts whom you must count 'hard'; he it is whom you must fear and dread. He will become your hardship…" (Isa. 8:13-14a). This was shortly before the nation fell to the onslaughts of Assyria and was carted off into exile. The nation of Israel continues to suffer from a self-serving concept of what it means to be God's people today. But so do we, and as Americans, we must first repent of our own sin of pride before we call upon others to repent or join with them in their own national deification.

We would do well to re-read the Old Testament prophets and profit thereby. However, rather than having a prophetic stance that distinguishes the church from government, the most active and vocal representatives of the church in America in the past three decades have increasingly acted as if church and nation are one and the same. We need urgently to heed the caution voiced by Stanley Hauerwas:

---

[55] Stassen, *Living the Sermon on the Mount*, p. 190.
[56] *Courier-Journal*, September 9, 1978, n. p.

> The church does not exist to provide an ethos for democracy or any other form of social organization, but stands as a political alternative to every nation, witnessing to the kind of social life possible for those that have been formed by the story of Christ. [57]

To quote Brown again: "It is not 'this nation, which is God,' or 'this nation, alongside God,' but 'this nation, *under* God,' that expresses the true context for patriotism."[58] No form of government, no matter how benevolent, can ever be the body of Christ in the world. That role is assigned to the church by Christ himself, and the church fails in its responsibility when it mistakes any government as the fulfillment of the prayer that Jesus taught us to pray, saying "thy kingdom come on earth." God's kingdom, not any national kingdom, is what Jesus taught us to pray for and to work for in his name.

*****

Koinonia **and the Cross**

The church must not only live its witness, it must also speak its witness, for it is only through our words that our deeds become intelligible as pointing to Christ, who is the Word. "The spoken word is never really effective unless it is backed up by a life, but it is also true that the living deed is never adequate without the support which the spoken word can provide. This is because no life is ever good enough."[59] The ministry of reconciliation requires that each person be reconciled to Christ in such ways that each one can make a confessional response to the question of Jesus: "Who do you say that I am?"

The early church was incurably evangelistic, but we are sometimes prone to forget that the first disciples were not theologians. Their evangelistic fervor was not so much the result of systematic thought as of a contagious spirit. C. S. Lewis has used the term "good infection" to describe the way Jesus spread his kind of life to those around him. As the disciples followed him they came to know and love him and grew more and more to possess his nature, his disposition, his way of looking at things. Living with Jesus, they became infected with his life; and they in turn

---

[57] Hauerwas, "Reforming Christian Social Ethics: Ten Theses," *The Hauerwas Reader*, Berkman and Cartwright, eds., pp. 114-115.

[58] Brown, *The Pseudonyms of God*, p. 136, emphasis in the original.

[59] Elton Trueblood, *The Company of the Committed*, p. 53.

179

infected others with the contagion of their spirit. They had experienced Christ and had to share the experience. The method of reconciliation is first and foremost the spontaneous overflowing of a sense of gratitude from one who has experienced God's love in Christ. The abiding motive is love—love which is self-giving on the part of the one loving and other-affirming toward the one loved. Love is the inevitable response of one who has known the fullness of God's love, for love begets love: "The love of Christ leaves us no choice" (2 Cor. 5:14).

A "word study" of the Greek word *koinonia* will help further our understanding of the nature of the church. The basic meaning of *koinonia* is "to share with someone in something." There are at least four ways in which *koinonia* is used in the New Testament in relation to the church: social *koinonia*, spiritual *koinonia*, practical *koinonia*, and sacrificial *koinonia*.

"Social" *koinonia* is usually translated as "fellowship," and in this usage is often nothing more than part of the familiar church trinity of "fun, food, and fellowship." Rather than growing out of what it means to be church, this kind of *koinonia* can easily become the means of being church. The often heard statement, "I go there (to that particular church) because I like the fellowship," can indicate nothing more than church conceived as a social gathering of like-minded, congenial people who enjoy one another's company. I do not mean to disparage friendliness and congeniality in the church, but these are not the basis for true church. That the New Testament concept includes a strong social emphasis is undeniable: "They met constantly to hear the apostles teach, and to share in the common [*koinonia*] life" (Acts 2:42). But this life was the fruit of true koinonia, not its root. Social *koinonia* is a kind of "cheap *koinonia*" along the lines of Bonhoeffer's assessment of "cheap grace." It costs little to nothing. I am reminded of words from "St. Hereticus":

> He leadeth me: O blessed thought!
> To air-conditioned chapels fraught
> With cushioned pews—where I may see
> The minister on closed TV. [60]

"Spiritual" *koinonia* is based in the unity of the Holy Spirit in the two-fold dimensions of loving God, through the mediation of Jesus Christ in the power of the Holy Spirit, and participating in this divine love with each other. This *koinonia* is the presence and life of God in our midst. Various New Testament references support this kind of understanding of *koinonia*:

---

[60] Robert McAfee Brown, *The Collected Writings of St. Hereticus*, p. 39.

I thank my God whenever I think of you; and when I pray for you all, my prayers are always joyful, because of the part [*koinonia*] you have taken in the work of the gospel from the first day until now. [61]

It is God himself who called you to share [*koinonia*] in the life of his Son Jesus Christ our Lord. [62]

The grace of the Lord Jesus Christ, and the love of God, and fellowship [*koinonia*] in the Holy Spirit, be with you all. [63]

This conception of *koinonia* is the sharing in the fellowship of the community of the gospel of Jesus Christ in the Holy Spirit. But this understanding seems too lofty, too abstract. We may find it inspiring, but it doesn't give us much content in the concept.

"Practical" *koinonia* brings us down off the spiritual high to where *koinonia* begins to take shape, and the shape it takes may leave us uncomfortable. As quoted above in Acts 2:42, "They met constantly to hear the apostles teach, and to share the common [*koinonia*] life," and we can say "Yes! Amen! Let's have that kind of *koinonia* here." The passage continues: "to break bread, and to pray." And we say again, "Amen! Bread and prayer." The passage goes on: "A sense of awe was everywhere," and we say "Yes! Praise the Lord! Let's hear an 'amen' for the sense of awe!" It continues: "many marvels and signs were brought about through the apostles." And our refrain once again: "Yes, Lord. We want marvels and signs." But there's more: "All whose faith had drawn them together held everything in common [*koinonia*]." And we pause a moment: "Hummmm. This may be taking a bad turn." And then comes the punch line: "They would sell their property and possessions and make a general distribution as the need required."

Now, we're beginning to see real *koinonia*. Funny, isn't it? We read in 1 Corinthians that the cross was a stumbling block. But we don't stumble much over the cross. We have sanitized the cross, made jewelry out of it, put it up on top of our steeples, and kept it safely out of the way. Or, we have made gory movies about it, with images which disturb us and convict us about Jesus' suffering for us. (Eugene Peterson refers to such images as "spiritual pornography," citing the Mel Gibson movie, "The Passion of the Christ" as a conspicuous example.[64]) We may appreciate Jesus' sacrifice on

---

[61] Philippians 1:3-5.
[62] 1 Corinthians 1:9.
[63] 2 Corinthians 13:14.
[64] Peterson, *Tell It Slant*, p. 257.

the cross, but we don't really stumble over Jesus' cross. However, let someone start talking about *koinonia* of property and possessions, and we stumble all over the place. We have a ready defense against this kind of *koinonia*; we simply call it socialism and dismiss it out of hand.

Paul viewed *koinonia* in a very practical way in connection with the collection for the church in Jerusalem. In 2 Corinthians 9:13 he appealed to the Corinthian church to be generous in their "contribution" (*koinonia*). Earlier in the letter he had commended the generosity of the congregations in Macedonia:

> We must tell you, friends, about the grace of generosity which God has imparted to our congregations in Macedonia. The troubles they have been through have tried them hard, yet in all this they have been so *exuberantly happy* that *from the depths of their poverty* they have shown themselves lavishly open-handed. Going to the limit of their resources, as I can testify, and even beyond that limit, *they begged us* most insistently, and on their own initiative, *to be allowed to share* [*koinonia*] *in this generous service to their fellow-Christians*."[65]

Note that Paul didn't say that their money represented *koinonia*; rather, it *was* the *koinonia*. The collection wasn't just money; it was an expression of their motivation arising out of their exuberant happiness. In this understanding of koinonia the gift and the giver are one. The gift and the recipient become one. Hence, *koinonia* is the sharing of personhood in the form of caring for one another's needs. This leads us now to the deepest meaning of *koinonia*.

"Sacrificial" *koinonia* brings us to the essence of *koinonia*, which at its core is cross-shaped. We Christians often refer to the Lord's Supper as "communion," which is itself a form of the word *koinonia*. In 1 Corinthians Paul told us that the cup which we bless in the Lord's Supper is a sharing (*koinonia*) in the blood of Christ; and the bread we break is also a sharing (*koinonia*) in the body of Christ. There is no cheap *koinonia* here. This is cross-shaped *koinonia*. The fellowship, the sharing, the communion that makes church true *koinonia* is union with Christ in his death. The cross is where cheap *koinonia* pays the price. This *koinonia* is not just sharing property; nor is it in collections for the poor (both of which are challenge enough). It is the *koinonia* of the cross.

In his letter to the church in Philippi, Paul wrote of this kind of *koinonia* in his life: "All I care for is to know Christ, to experience the power of his

---

[65] 2 Corinthians 8:1-4, emphasis added; see also Romans 15:26.

resurrection, and to share [*koinonia*] his sufferings" (Phil. 3:10a). This is not just an Easter Sunday kind of remembering and giving thanks for Christ's sufferings. This is *our* acceptance of personal suffering because of our *koinonia* with Christ, because we *are* Christ's body as the church: "Now *you* are Christ's body" (1 Cor. 12: 27a, emphasis added). Christ's sufferings were on behalf of the world. In like manner the church is called to the *koinonia* of suffering for the world who are lost, hurting, and dying. William Sloane Coffin is right on the point: "Our calling today is like God's call to Moses: arising from the world's pain, it is a call to alleviate that pain by sharing it."[66] In Robert McAfee Brown's words, the church must be "a place where the only credential necessary to gain a hearing is a cry of pain."[67]

*****

Turning the World Upside Down

> One of the functions of history writing and telling is to define who are the good and who are the bad guys....This is why the winners never allow the losers to become historians....The Bible has the peculiarity of having been written by those who experienced weakness and defeat, i. e., a community which *of necessity* had to be opposed to the triumphant definitions of power....The result is disturbing. The Bible turns the normal plot upside down. Villains become heroes and heroes become villains.
> Rubem Alves[68]

Over the past five centuries, Christianity has been largely defined by Europe and the nations spawned by European culture. Within the past century, Christianity has been increasingly defined by North American theology and ideology. Also during the past two centuries, the Western and Northern world have experienced unparalleled economic growth; but the benefits of this growth have not been equally shared, due in large measure to a style of capitalism which has increasingly rewarded the rich and deprived the poor. Not surprisingly, Western/Northern religion has become in large measure the religion of the haves, with very little awareness of or concern for the rest of the world, except in seeing it as a "mission field" for evangelism, which has sometimes been mixed with nationalistic

---

[66] Coffin, *A Passion for the Possible*, p. 83.
[67] Brown, *Theology in a New Key*, p. 172.
[68] Alves, *Tomorrow's Child*, pp. 129, 130, emphasis in the original.

imperialism. But in the last 100 years the world of Christianity has been undergoing a shift of theological "tectonic plates," with the center of gravity moving southward, especially to Africa and South America.

During my lifetime, the challenge for North American Christianity has increasingly been the need to find ways to theologize with those who are south of the equator about their concerns, or to become increasingly irrelevant to much of the world. For me, this theological challenge has taken shape under the influence of theologies of liberation and hope. As Dom Helder Camara noted in the 1970s, it is among the oppressed people south of the equator that the voice of God is being heard:

> If we are not deaf we hear the cries of the oppressed. Their cries
> are the voice of God.... The pleas of those who have no voice
> and no hope are the voice of God.... And the voice of the
> countries suffering these injustices is the voice of God. [69]

The crying need in being Christian today is to respond to the need of the crying.

When is the last time that your church, my church—any church we know that we would be comfortable in (and there's the problem; we expect to be comfortable in church)—when is the last time our church suffered because of its incarnation of the presence of Christ in the community? In 1980 I clipped a page from a state denominational paper that had two items near each other (with no apparent irony intended). The first item, sounding a lot like Paul's comments about the church in Macedonia, quoted from a letter received by the coordinator for relief and development of the Baptist World Alliance from the general secretary of the Garo Baptist Union in Bangladesh:

> The Garo Baptist Union of Bangladesh is sending you $100 for
> Cambodian relief.... It is a small gift, but it comes from the
> hearts of the drought and flood stricken Baptists who are in deep
> sympathy with the starving brothers and sisters of Cambodia.

The second item was an advertisement: "Church Pew Cushions: Padded seats or reversible cushions."[70] Which item do you think more accurately expresses the meaning of *koinonia*?

In our prayers we often list our blessings (for which we give thanks) and our woes (from which we ask deliverance). Our lists may look

---

[69] Camara, *The Desert Is Fertile*, p. 16.
[70] *Baptist Courier*, March 6, 1980, p. 12.

something like this:

Blessings:	material goods and money
	plenty to eat
	enjoyment of life
	praise and recognition from others
Woes:	living in need
	not having enough to eat
	a life full of tears
	being hated and insulted by others

These are pretty good lists. In fact, Jesus made the same two lists (see Luke 6:20-26); only he turned them upside down. Jesus listed our blessing as our woes and our woes as our blessings. Read the text. Jesus turns our world upside down. Can we read Jesus' lists and truly say, "The Word of the Lord. Thanks be to God."?

As I noted earlier, at least some of the early Christians lived in such ways that they were accused of "turning the world upside down" (Acts 17:6, NRSV). Is our faith strong enough that we dare to live upside down? Even a casual reading of the book of Acts and the New Testament epistles is sufficient to demonstrate that the early church suffered much persecution. What we may overlook is that it suffered this persecution because it was counted worthy of persecution. When we seek to explain why we are not similarly persecuted, we must be honest enough to admit that it is not because of some miraculous improvement in human nature. Our churches (I'm confessing from within the church as it is in the United States) are not persecuted, primarily because we no longer disturb or upset. The incarnation has been reduced either to a personal and institutional sense of vague good will or to a list of moral requirements based more on protecting God and the church than on expressing God's love through the church. Michael Harper, writing in *A New Way of Living*, nails it: "The church is neither loved nor hated. It is ignored by most, and pitied by some."[71]

Our *koinonia* has gotten too far away from Christ—from the cross. It's not that we are unfamiliar with the idea of Christian sacrifice. Our hymns urge us on the upward way; we are exhorted to bear the cross; the act of baptism is a sign of death and resurrection; and the repetition of the Lord's Supper provides us with fresh reminders of the sacrifice that lies at the heart of our faith. We know well the language of sacrifice; it is the

---

[71] Harper, *A New Way of Living*, p. 47.

experience we lack. We want life to be safe and secure from all alarms. We want all of life's stories—especially our *own* stories—to end, "and they lived happily ever after." We want to hear God's commendation of "Well done, good and faithful servant" without actually having to *be* a servant.

The church in our day has hidden the cost of discipleship under the warm glow of an emotional gospel that doesn't speak often of the cross, except in terms of Christ's cross and what *that* has accomplished *for us*. All too often the church soft sells Christianity for fear of scaring someone away. The church in America has adopted an American model of consumerism, and has addressed its product line to the "felt needs" of the customer. But the call to follow Jesus in the narrow and demanding way of discipleship has been strangely lost. The tragedy of the church throughout much of its history has been the persistent, ingenious endeavors to make Christianity costless. The message has often been, "Jesus paid it all," so there's no cost to us to be a disciple.

We are living in a "therapeutic culture" characterized by a "prosperity gospel," where there is not only no cost in our gospel, but there is profit to be made. As described by Stephen Long, discipleship in this gospel "concentrates on the benefits package." Long goes on to observe that he is increasingly hesitant to describe Jesus as his "personal" Lord and Savior, citing Ken Woodward who finds that expression to be elitist, "like having a personal tailor."[72] Or, we might also say, like having a personal banker. The January 2009 issue of *Atlanta* (Georgia) magazine contained this quote from the founder of a local area "faith-based" bank: "We felt if we prayed and obeyed God's word and did what He said, that He would help us be successful."[73] Apparently, unlike the FDIC, God does not insure our deposits. According to the magazine, the bank failed in August 2008 and at the beginning of 2009 was under investigation for possible financial crimes. We have developed the most sophisticated, market driven means of avoiding the costliness of the Christian life and the pain of discipleship in our drive to get the most out of our religion with the least investment of ourselves. When we turn God into a commodity, our tithes and offerings are not gifts from hearts filled with gratitude; they are investments made with an expectation of return on investment.

And then, breaking in rudely on our lives, comes Jesus' call to self-denial and cross-bearing, and it strikes a chill in our heart and blocks out the sunshine of our happiness like a dark storm cloud falling over the land—maybe even like the prelude to an earthquake that splits the rocks of

---

[72] Long, "God Is Not Nice," in *God Is Not...*, ed. D. Brent Laytham, p. 49.
[73] *Atlanta*, January 2009, p. 66.

our security.[74] We want to avoid a God like that, a God that calls people to die, a God whose own life on earth ended up on a cross. This isn't a very customer friendly God at all. It certainly doesn't have the appeal of the "feel good" spirituality of Neale Donald Walsch: "If we can't depend on God to feel good, then why are we in this universe?"[75] To paraphrase Robert McAfee Brown's comments earlier about Jesus' inaugural sermon, "A church like that—who needs it?"

But Jesus warned that the life of *his* disciples would be lived in the shadow of the cross. The Christian life of discipleship is "a dying kind of living," as Clarence Jordan has expressed it.[76] C. S. Lewis has reminded us that Christ says, "Give me all. I don't want so much of your time and so much of your money and so much of your work. I want you. I have not come to torment your natural self but to kill it."[77] God has neither forgotten nor forsaken the cross. There never has been—for anyone, anywhere, at any time—any other way. If we are attracted to Christianity without our own cross, we aren't attracted to Christianity, for "the way of the cross leads home."[78]

We may wish it were otherwise, but the cross today means exactly what it has always meant: death, denial of self, a self-abandoning lifestyle that risks the shame of failure, that risks being taken advantage of, that risks the humiliation of being a public spectacle. We may not risk a literal cross today, but the test is the same: our total self-abandonment that risks all for the sake of others. And if there is no imaginable way that the test will actually be given to us, it is our responsibility to ask whether we are living the life of discipleship at all. If we wake up in the morning and are not ready to take up our cross, then maybe—no, almost certainly—we are not planning to follow Jesus that day. Someone (perhaps Dietrich Bonhoeffer) has said, with possibly no exaggeration at all, "Every Christian alive today is called upon to explain why." Are we alive today because the world no longer kills zealots, or because the world has become so Christ-like that even Jesus wouldn't be crucified today? Or is it because we have such a weak and insipid brand of Christianity that it would never occur to anyone that we are a threat worth killing?

The story has been told that a pastor was showing Clarence Jordan (founder of Koinonia Farm near Americus, Georgia) around his church,

---

[74] See Matthew 27:45ff.
[75] Quoted by Don Lattin, "Chatting up the man who talks with God."
[76] Jordan, *Cotton Patch Parables*, p. 129.
[77] Lewis, *Mere Christianity*, p. 153.
[78] Title of a hymn by Jessie B. Pounds, *The Hymnal for Worship and Celebration*, ed. Tom Fettke.

pointing with pride to features like imported pews. The sun was setting as they stepped outside, and a spotlight came on automatically and highlighted a huge cross on top of the steeple. The pastor bragged that the cross alone cost $10,000 (remember, this was about sixty years ago). Clarence looked at him and said, "You got cheated. Times were when Christians could get them for free." The challenge for the church today is to take the cross off the steeple and put it in our hearts. There is no New Testament identification of the church with a building. That came later, after Constantine made it safe to be a Christian and we began to take the church out of the world and the cross out of our lives. And nowadays when we leave the church building, we leave the cross behind. There is much truth in Robert McAfee Brown's observation: "The trouble with the church is that it is not in trouble."[79] Or, as John Biersdorf has expressed it: "There is something unseemly and basically wrong about a church that is happy and thriving while the culture is in agony."[80] As my father used to say, it is true that God's Word comforts the afflicted and afflicts the comfortable. But when we use it to comfort the comfortable, we add to the afflictions of the afflicted.

*****

Love in Action

The crucial question is not whether the church will be a fellowship. The question is whether it will be a fellowship only in the social sense of a "fellowship hall," or in the sense of the self-giving *koinonia* of Christ. God chose to incarnate the divine nature in Jesus Christ, because a human being *in relationship*, in the *world*, was and still is the most effective medium for communicating love. If the church is to fulfill its *koinonia*, it must actually *be* the body in which the living Word of God's love is lived. Love cannot be adequately described; it can only be demonstrated. *Koinonia* is in need of demonstration, not explanation. "Incarnation" means "in the flesh," not "in the words." "God is love" has to be lived, not merely talked. Jesus seemed to think it was more important to give a cup of cold water than to talk about truth.

The summary statement of Jesus' life given in Acts was that he went about doing good, not that he talked well (Acts 10:38). In the words of John, "love is not a matter of words or talk; it must be genuine, and show itself in action" (1 John 3:18). Both 2000 years ago and today, one deed of

---

[79] I have lost track of the source for this quote.
[80] Biersdorf, *Hunger for Experience*, p. 138.

love is worth a thousand words about deeds of love. Perhaps after our deeds have been noted and tested, we will have earned a hearing for our words. As is often said, the world won't care what we know until they know that we care. You remember Eliza Doolittle in *My Fair Lady*:

> Never do I want
> to hear another word.
> There isn't one
> I haven't heard...
> Say one more word and
> I'll scream!
> Sing me no song!
> Read me no rhyme!
> Don't waste my time!
> Show me![81]

Michael Harper has suggested that her words might well be addressed by the world to the church:

> We are sick of sermons, books, discussions, theologies, Bible lectures. We are not interested in hymns, anthems and choruses. Don't spout poetry at us. *Show us*. Give us demonstrations. We want to see action. Words are not enough. Your words make us sick. And we won't listen any more. [82]

How penetratingly true. God has always known that words are not enough. Even words about God are not enough. Even God's words are not enough. What the world needs is not more words about God, but more of the Word of God; and the Word always needs to be "made flesh" and "dwell among us." There is no neutrality about incarnation. Whether we like it or not, whether by intention or by default, we inevitably incarnate whatever faith we have. And while I must acknowledge this is true in my own life as an individual, I say "we" advisedly, because Christ did not just leave changed individuals, he left a community, a church, a *koinonia*. No single individual other than Jesus can ever fully express the meaning of incarnation; it takes the whole church. Hear Paul again: "A body is not one single organ, but many.... If the whole were one single organ, there would be no body at all" (1 Cor. 12: 14, 19).

---

[81] Lyrics by Michael Ball, http://www.lyricsdownload.com/michael-ball-show-me-my-fair-lady-lyrics.html, accessed March 6, 2009.
[82] Harper, *A New Way of Living*, p. 12, emphasis in the original.

This understanding of the church as the body of Christ is expressed in a unique way in John's writings. John 1:18 begins with the words, "No one has ever seen God," and 1 John 4:12 begins, "God has never been seen by any man." Both verses then go on to say how God is revealed to us. In Jesus' day, it was in Jesus himself: "God's only Son, he who is nearest to the Father's heart, he has made him known" (John 1:18b). But what about after Jesus is gone? What then? It is up to us: "God himself dwells in us if we love one another; his love is brought to perfection within us" (1 John 4:12b). Now that the world can't see Jesus in the flesh, only the church can make God's presence known in the love of Christians for one another and for the world. The nature of *koinonia* is not that we believe in God's love, but that we live God's love. Arthur Herzog throws the challenge into the face of the church in his book, *The Church Trap*:

> [Churches] will be forced to show that they bear witness to a meaningful faith, as demonstrated by their actions and lives. There is always the smallest chance that the churches—in some fashion yet undefined—are right, but the proof is up to them. [83]

William Barclay tells of an old legend about what happened when Jesus, after his death and resurrection, returned to heaven:

> One of the angels met Him and saw His wounds. The angel said, 'You must have suffered terribly down there in the world?' Jesus answered, 'I did.' 'Do all men know,' said the angel, 'how you loved and suffered for them?' 'No,' said Jesus, 'as yet only a few in a corner of Palestine know the story.' 'Well, then,' said the angel, 'what have you done about letting all men know?' Jesus said, 'I have asked Peter and James and John and the rest to tell others, and the others to tell yet others and still others until the farthest man on the widest circle has heard the story.' The angel knew men and he was very doubtful. 'Yes,' he said, 'but what if James and John and Peter forget? What if the rest fail in their task? What if years go on and on and men do not tell others about you and your sacrifice? What then? Haven't you made other plans?' Back came the answer of Jesus, 'I haven't made any other plans; *I'm counting on them.*"[84]

Elton Trueblood finished up his wonderful book, *The Company of the Committed*, with these words, which are worth quoting in full:

---

[83] Herzog, *The Church Trap*, p. 177.
[84] Barclay, *And Jesus Said*, p. 206, emphasis in the original.

Somewhere in the world there should be a society consciously and deliberately devoted to the task of seeing how love can be made real and demonstrating love in practice. Unfortunately, there is really only one candidate for this task. If God, as we believe, is truly revealed in the life of Christ, the most important thing to Him is the creation of centers of loving fellowship, which in turn infect the world. Whether the world can be redeemed in this way we do not know, but it is at least clear that there is no other way. [85]

Michael Harper is right; new songs and sermons won't do. Arthur Herzog is right; the proof is up to the church. William Barclay is right; Jesus is counting on the church. Elton Trueblood is right; there is no other way.

*****

The Revolutionary Nature of Hope

An old saying holds that religion and politics don't mix. Probably it was first said by Pharaoh when he turned down Moses' plea to 'let my people go.' Generally what it means is, 'Your religion doesn't mix with my politics.'
William Sloane Coffin [86]

Third world Christians... tell us that the basic viewpoint of the biblical writers is that of victims, those who have been cruelly used by society, the poor and oppressed. They further tell us that they are the contemporary counterparts of those biblical victims, cruelly used by contemporary society, the poor and oppressed.... If God sided with the oppressed back then, they believe God continues to side with the oppressed here and now.
Robert McAfee Brown [87]

A church without hope has nothing to offer anyone.... Despair is not merely inappropriate but downright indecent in a world shot through with the reconciling power of God.... *Hope* is possible because the one who follows the way of Christ has *faith* that there

---

[85] Trueblood, *The Company of the Committed*, p. 113.
[86] Coffin, *A Passion for the Possible*, p. 35.
[87] Brown, *Unexpected News*, p. 14.

is no situation which is impervious to *love*.
Colin Morris [88]

> This present moment invites us to discard our 'reasons' for
> hoping; to put aside our easy optimism, our all too human
> strategies, to nourish our hope at its source—the word of God....
> To hope is a duty, not a luxury. To hope is not to dream, but to
> turn dreams into reality. Happy are those who dream dreams and
> are ready to pay the price to make them come true.
> Leon Joseph Cardinal Suenens [89]

Far too often we Christians think of hope in personal terms, as if the meaning of hope is fulfilled when I have hope. But, like love, Christian hope is not private. It must always include others if it is Christian hope. I noted earlier that there is an element of contradiction in hope, for the message of hope is that humankind is in distress. What I did not really address at that time was the societal dimensions of hope and the relationship between hope and justice, hope and *koinonia*, hope and the world's truly hopeless. We let ourselves off the hook of hope way too easily when we restrict hope to the purely spiritual realm. Like love, hope is only an abstraction until it is incarnated. And like love, hope is too narrow until it includes the "least of these."

There has long been a notion abroad in the church, especially in the American church, that theology is apolitical and socially neutral. This notion may be due at least partially to a misapplication of the Jeffersonian wall of separation between church and state. Although I am not a scholar in the field of Jefferson's intentions, I do think a mistake is made when the wall is perceived as intending to place political life on one side of the wall and spiritual life on the other. What I think was intended was the separation of "organized religion," the church, from "organized community life," the state. Although many will disagree, I think the founding fathers of the nation never expected that neither would influence the other, simply that neither would control the other. Whether or not this analysis is correct, I can say with confidence that in the last 50 years or so this intention to separate church and state has changed dramatically with the rise of the evangelical Christian alliance with the right wing of the Republican Party.

William Herzog, in studying this subject in 1968, suggested that part of the church's motive in seeking to breach the wall of separation was due to the general ineffectiveness of organized religion to achieve moral change in

---

[88] Morris, *The Hammer of the Lord*, pp. 9, 105, 135, emphasis in the original.
[89] Suenens, *A New Pentecost?*, pp. xi-xii, xiii.

the life of the nation, despite the church's numeric growth of the 1950s. He charged that since the churches couldn't rely on the faithful to bring about the change, "they have been compelled to go to Caesar for help…to the point where 'In the State We Trust' might well be organized religion's motto."[90] While that might overstate the case, it does serve well to make the point. As Robert McAfee Brown noted in the early 1980s, "Those who once declared that 'religion and politics don't mix' have now decided that the issue is no longer 'politics' but only a certain kind of politics, namely, 'left-wing politics.' Right wing politics are O. K."[91] I think the right wing has gotten one thing right: theology is necessarily political in this world of competing political powers. However, I also think they have gotten just about everything else wrong—collapsing church and state into one, relying on law to bring about changed lives, focusing on secondary issues, utilizing the wrong methods, and often manifesting more anger and hate than love.

There is no such thing as ecclesiastical neutrality and apolitical theology. There are only those who are conscious of their political assumptions and consequences and those who are not. William Barclay once commented on the fact that "loyalty to Christ must take precedence over all other loyalties." He then went on to observe,

> It is a curious thing that the enemies of Christianity have seen that quite clearly. For instance, Hitler banished all professing Christians from his government because he said their loyalty to the state was endangered by their loyalty to Christianity. He knew quite well that, with a real Christian, if a clash of loyalties came then Christ would come first. [92]

Interestingly, and sadly, unlike Hitler who recognized the tension between loyalties to Christ and country, the George W. Bush administration and the right-wing evangelicals didn't want to keep Christians *out* of office; they wanted to *fill* the government with Christians on the assumption that loyalty to Christ and to the state are the same thing. I am not suggesting that Christians should be kept out of government; I am merely lamenting that so few seem to see any tension in the relationship.

As an eschatological community of hope, the church is the inheritor of the eschatological promises of biblical tradition such as liberty, peace, justice and reconciliation, which cannot be kept within the walls of the church or on the other side of a wall from the world of politics. The total

---

[90] Herzog, *The Church Trap*, pp. 111, 113.
[91] Brown, *Unexpected News*, p. 117.
[92] Barclay, *And Jesus Said*, p. 208.

thrust of an eschatological ethic is towards society. As an incarnational ethic, it must always take its stand right in the midst of history, "right on the ground of real, actual human life…breathing the air of the times."[93] An incarnational ethic inevitably means that human issues "are also fundamentally theological issues, for any issue that involves the life and death of the children of God is a theological issue, whether the proper theological formulations are pronounced or not."[94]

Our distorting glasses of a narrow and abstract Christianity must be removed and our theological perspective broadened to see everything through the eyes of Christ, who stands where persons stand, live, and die—"whether Christians or non-Christians, communists or non-communists, white or colored, civilized or poor, hungry, and ignorant."[95] And when we see through Christ's eyes, we realize that in this world of interlocking complexities, it is quite true that the one who is not "oppressed" is literally the "oppressor." There is no neutrality. We are either the Rich Man or Lazarus. Even more important, if God is present in our historical situation, God too must take sides—either with or against the status quo. Based on the biblical record, God seems consistently to be on the side of justice and righteousness, which are seldom found to be characteristics of the status quo. For those of us who benefit from the current status quo, this means that we must develop a theology of letting go; of making do with less; of cooperation rather than competition; of dependency on God rather than reliance on self, or state, or progress, or materialism, or whatever it is that keeps us from living out of a faith that God really *is* a loving parent and that God really *is* in the midst of life with us.

Given that the theological task is not merely to interpret the world but to change it, an eschatological ethic seeks the transformation of the present condition, even when this results in revolutionary dynamics. "The ingredients brewed by Christian hope are an explosive mix. They are the stuff of which 'eschatological revolutionaries' are made…."[96] As Carl Braaten has asserted, the simple fact of preaching the gospel is like setting dynamite at the foundations of the social structure.[97] When the dynamics (or dynamite) of the Christian gospel are released into the world, they set off shock waves of expectations that threaten the structures of injustice and

[93] Johannes B. Metz, "The Privatization of Religion," *The Scope of Political Theology*, ed. Alistair Kee, p. 9.
[94] Robert McAfee Brown, *The Pseudonyms of God*, p. 57.
[95] Joseph L. Hromadka, *Theology between Yesterday and Tomorrow*, p.72.
[96] Gabriel Fackre, *The Rainbow Sign*, p. 57.
[97] Braaten, *The Future of God*, p. 143.

inequality.

The God whom Jesus proclaimed and revealed is not the guarantor of the status quo—any status quo. Quite the contrary, God is the power of the ultimate future that *always* presses for radical conversion of any of our penultimate futures. Christianity calls for conversion, and it is a calling directed not only to each individual separately but also to societies as a whole. The coming of the kingdom of God (or the reign of God) is always contrary to any other kingdom or reigning power. Christ is both redemptive and revolutionary, and we as individual Christians and collectively as the church can act faithfully only when we act consistently with our prayer that God's kingdom may come on earth as in heaven.

The gospel of Jesus Christ is a liberating gospel, freeing us from all that binds us. The gospel story is "the story of deliverance, of freedom, and joy."[98] The freedom of the Christian faith is to be lived out in political freedom as well as spiritual freedom. The love of God frees us not only from our sin but also from everything that enslaves us. The exodus story of the misery-seeing, cry-hearing, heed-taking, down-coming, rescuing God is not itself a story of liberation from sin but from political oppression (Ex. 3: 7-10). Jesus' death was not the result of calling people to repent of spiritual sin apart from the realities of life. His death was at its heart a political execution. Jesus' threat to the power structure of religion and government was what got him killed. Carl Braaten rightly notes that "Christianity is a conspiracy for freedom."[99] The freedom of Christian faith is surely spiritual freedom, but it is to be lived in political freedom. The freedom of an eschatological ethic urges us toward liberating actions as we become "painfully aware of suffering in situations of exploitation, oppression, alienation, and captivity."[100] When we have come to know the freedom of the gospel, we no longer accept slavery as our destiny. Through the eyes of Christ, we see that evil, suffering and pain are the negative image of the positive hope for God's future.

> When freedom has come near, the chains begin to hurt. When life is close, death becomes deadly.... We begin to suffer from the conditions of our world if we begin to love the world. And we begin to love the world if we are able to discover hope for it. And we begin to discover hope for this world if we hear the promise of a future which stands against frustration, transiency,

---

[98] Joseph L. Hromadka, *Theology between Yesterday and Tomorrow*, p. 88.

[99] Braaten, *Christ and Counter-Christ*, p. 117.

[100] Jurgen Moltmann, *The Crucified God*, p. 317.

and death. [101]

The church has been sent through Easter into history with just such a hope, which must make us no longer content with anxious affirmations of the status quo. We can express our hope, mediate our love of God, and become a likeness of Christ "only by holding the future open for the hopeless of the earth and representing to them in word and deed the new hope of mankind which was born from the grave."[102] As Moltmann asserts, this kind of liberating action must embrace five dimensions of human relationships:

> [In] the vicious circle of poverty, liberation must be called social justice; in the vicious circle of force, it must be called democratic human rights; in the vicious circle of alienation, it must be called identity in recognition; in the vicious circle of ecology, it must be called peace with nature; and in the vicious circle of meaninglessness, it must be called courage to be, and faith. [103]

*****

The Question of Violence

Internationally and historically, killing is the predominant method of choice to make the world a better place.
Eugene Paterson [104]

What we now need to discover in the social realm is the moral equivalent of war: something heroic that will speak to men as universally as war does, and yet will be as compatible with their spiritual selves as war has proven itself to be incompatible.
William James [105]

Those who make peaceful evolution impossible make violent revolution inevitable.
John F. Kennedy [106]

---

[101] Moltmann, *Religion, Revolution, and the Future*, pp. 61-62.
[102] Carl Braaten, *The Future of God*, p. 102.
[103] Moltmann, *The Crucified God*, pp. 336-337.
[104] Peterson, *Tell It Slant*, p. 69.
[105] James, *The Varieties of Religious Experience*, p. 290.
[106] Quoted in William Sloane Coffin, *A Passion for the Possible*, p. 45.

The revolutionary nature of an eschatological ethic of hope inevitably raises the question of the necessity for violence. This question is directly related to the fact that up to the present moment, practically all true political revolutions have been accomplished by means of violence. But the issue of violence is somewhat illusory, for there is a great deal of violence present in all social and political systems where it is used by those in power at the present to maintain their political positions. Violence can and often does reside in the status quo as well as in the efforts of those who seek change.

It has been pointed out, quite correctly I think, that those who are in power determine the level of violence of any struggle, for it is up to them to decide whether the status quo can make way for change without the necessity of violence. I do not argue that this assertion justifies the use of violence at any time, but it does put the primary responsibility for dealing with the question of violence where it belongs. When bloody violence occurs in the confrontation of the new with the old, it is usually because the partisans of the old order have neglected "to build bridges to the future."[107] Therefore, participating in violent reactionary efforts to preserve the present is just as future-denying as participating in the violence that usually erupts when the pull of the future hope of freedom becomes too strong to suppress. However, the issue of violence as a means of social change cannot be left here, since to do so is tantamount to a deterministic acceptance of the necessity of violence.

Biblical ethics, in both the Old and New Testaments, are rooted in the understanding of the nature of God. As I have asserted, basic to my understanding is the nature of God as love—an electing, covenanting, delivering, sacrificing love. In the Old Testament, this love received its most revealing expression in the exodus experience and Israel's subsequent covenant relationship in which they learned that God is reliable, trustworthy, faithful, and active to deliver the oppressed from bondage. The appropriate human response to God's elective love is moral responsibility and service to God, which received its foundational statement in the Decalogue. Both Torah and the prophets elaborated on the covenant requirements to show that covenant love is to be expressed in "impartiality towards all and compassion for the oppressed and weak," in the words of ethicist Glen Stassen. Whether in political, social, economic, or religious activities, God's people are called to a righteousness that maintains the covenant relationship and reflects God's character as expressed in the writings of the 8th and 6th century BCE prophets as the

---

[107] Carl Braaten, *The Future of God*, p. 144.

"whole duty of man." A key expression of this concept is found in Micah 6:8:

> God has told you what is good;
> and what is it that the Lord asks of you?
> Only to act justly, to love loyalty,
> to walk wisely before your God. [108]

The New Testament similarly roots its ethical understanding in the nature of God, reflecting further the understanding of delivering love as revealed supremely in Jesus Christ. The prima facie case against violence in the name and cause of Christ is a strong one. It is difficult if not impossible to reconcile killing in the name of the God who is love. The Messiah of God's freedom came not as humankind's master but in the form of a servant. "It follows that the freedom of God comes to earth not through crowns, that is to say, the struggle for power, but through love and solidarity with the powerless."[109] God's nature is a willingness to suffer for the creation of the new. An eschatological hope derived from God's self identification with human suffering through Jesus' death and resurrection is obviously called to endure violence rather than inflict it. There is a basic incoherence of means and end when we seek to achieve the *shalom* of God's kingdom of non-violence by means of violent actions. Moltmann quotes a student in Tubingen who transformed the saying of Che Guevara, "The vocation of every lover is to bring about revolution," into "The duty of every revolution is to bring about love."[110]

Anyone following world news in recent years must be aware that the primary differences in international conflict resolution today and personal conflict resolution in pre-historical times are the result of technological sophistication and magnification rather than advancement in the moral stature or intelligence of the human species itself. While this assertion may be an oversimplification, it does serve to suggest that systems of conflict resolution among the nations of the world depend more on military firepower than on moral fiber. The problem of human conflict is certainly not new. What is new is the magnitude of potential catastrophe that waits to be released because of our narrow focus on military solutions to human problems. The development and proliferation of nuclear weapons and

---

[108] See also Deuteronomy 10:12; Amos 5:24; Isaiah 1:16-17; 58:5ff.; Psalm 24:3-6; 40:6-8; 50:7-15; 51:16-17; Jeremiah 7: 22-23; et al.

[109] Jurgen Moltmann, *Religion, Revolution, and the Future*, p. 68.

[110] Moltmann, *ibid*, p. 68.

other "weapons of mass destruction" within my lifetime, along with increasingly sophisticated technological means of delivering and employing these weapons, have placed a new urgency on the issue of war. We mistakenly persist in the belief that violence can end a conflict among people, that war can bring peace, and that weapons of war can be called peacekeepers.

Yet there is some evidence that a growing number of people—both those with the intellectual sophistication of scholars and those with the common sense of the masses—are realizing that war becomes less and less well suited to the ends of peace and justice as it grows increasingly destructive. This truth is conceded by many thoughtful observers, whatever their ultimate stance may be regarding the moral legitimacy of war. Positions held by those professing to follow Christ range from "holy war" to "just war" to a kind of "ethical realism" to "pacifism." I simply find "holy war" to be an oxymoron when employed in the name of Jesus Christ. To harmonize the spirit of war with the spirit of the self-sacrificing love lived and taught by Jesus is way too difficult. For the same reason, I also cannot accept the concept of "just war," although I can respect those Christians who take this position after rigorous thought and sincere prayer.

"Ethical realism" seems to me to be simply a moral copout for a Christian. It may well be a correct assessment of human nature, society and politics; and it is undeniably true that many people, even Christians, violate the spirit and standard of Jesus' command to love one another, much less the command to love and pray for our enemies and those who wrong us. The religiously prophetic opponents of war can easily be dismissed by the "ethical realists" as naive and even dangerous in their call for others to live like Christ in this fallen world. However in a day when strife is measured in mega-tonnage of weapons of mass destruction, and when the prospects of survival, much less security and peace, are obscured by the images of falling towers in New York City and the prospects of having the sun blacked out by mushroom-shaped clouds over our own cities, Jesus' belief in the redemptive power of love should not be abandoned too soon. If nothing else can be claimed for Jesus' method, at least it is based on the best in us and not the beast in us.

There is certainly prima facie evidence that would seem to support those who doubt that human beings are really capable of peace on earth and loving one another. Yet, closer examination of human history shows that what has been repudiated is not Jesus' method but a naive expectation that it can be followed without the risk of suffering and sacrifice. To act like Christ makes us vulnerable. And to that I say, exactly! That's what it means to be Christian. This approach is not irresponsible escapism, or naive optimism, but the Christian hope of the cross. To be vulnerable to nuclear armed power or the explosive creativity of terrorists is to cast oneself upon the hope and faith of the gospel rather than on a "realistic" counter-deterrence of even greater armed might. If God is love and if living the love of God looks like the life of Jesus, then it is clear to me that we can't fight our way to love in the name of the Jesus. It is impossible to understand Jesus apart from the image of the Suffering Servant of God spoken of by Isaiah.[111] This Servant is committed to nonviolence:

> He was afflicted, he submitted to be struck down
> and did not open his mouth;
> he was led like a lamb to the slaughter...
> without protection, without justice, he was taken away...
> He was assigned a grave with the wicked,
> a burial-place among the refuse of mankind,
> though he had done no violence
> and spoken no word of treachery.[112]

There is, for me, simply no basis in Jesus for violence and no hope for surviving violence apart from suffering love.

I have taken my stand as a pacifist, in the personal conviction that Jesus gives us no foundation for building a case for military defense and the exercise of warfare. From my own reading of the Bible, I can find no support in Christ's name for expediency, reasonableness, pragmatism, and the like as being appropriate standards for the Christian life. Surely, by these standards one could argue plausibly that Jesus blew the whole game when he let himself be killed at only 33 years of age. But, apparently, he lived by a different criterion, one embodying the self-giving, liberating, faithful character of God's love.

Bumper stickers are a poor source for theology, but I saw one that at least causes a proper pause for thought: "Who would Jesus kill?" Before we would kill in Jesus' name, we have to be very comfortable that Jesus himself would pull the trigger or push the red button. Jesus never cautioned his disciples against the terrorists of this world, "those who can kill the body, but cannot kill the soul." Instead, he counseled, "Fear him rather who is able to destroy both body and soul in hell" (Matt. 10:28). Killing, especially in the name of Christ, stains our soul with the blood splatters of other people—the soul that Jesus shed his own blood to cleanse and people whom Jesus died to save.

Sure, Jesus rebuked the hateful mobs, but he called them to an ethic of love. He chased religious charlatans from the temple with a whip, but that

---

[111] See Isaiah 42:1-4, 49:1-7, 50: 4-9, 52:13-53:12.
[112] Isaiah 53: 7-9.

200

is a precedent for us to cleanse our own places of worship, not to wage war. War, especially nuclear war, used by nations to achieve their own self-serving national ends is not the moral equivalent of a whip used by Jesus to cleanse the temple. Among the last words that Jesus spoke directly to his closest disciples were those he addressed to Peter after Peter had cut off the ear of the High Priest's servant who had come to take Jesus away. To Peter, who was full of fight, Jesus said, "Put up your sword."[113] There is no place for swords in the gospel story.

Jesus did not bring a sword, but a cross, as his instrument of peace. It is the peacemakers whom Jesus called children of God, and he was not referring to soldiers when he said peacemakers. No open-minded reading of the Bible leads to the conclusion that Jesus is a role model for anything other than love, forgiveness, and self-denial. The issue is not to have Jesus on our side, but to be on his. Surely the burden of proof is always on the Christian who would wage war rather than on the one who refuses to do so. It is sad that American Christians have mostly supported our wars and the soldiers that fight in our wars, while condemning the conscientious objectors who oppose war in the name of Jesus.

The apostle Paul got it right: "Never pay back evil for evil...do not seek revenge... Do not let evil conquer you, but use good to defeat evil" (Rom. 12:17-20). And then he challenged us:

> [Find] your strength in the Lord, in his mighty power. Put on all the armour which God provides.... Fasten on the belt of truth; for coat of mail put on integrity; let the shoes on your feet be the gospel of peace, to give you firm footing; and, with all these, take up the great shield of faith.... Take salvation for helmet; for sword, take that which the Spirit gives you—*the words that come from God.* [114]

These are the "body armor" and "weapons" of faith. It has never before been more critical than now that we find out how they work. We have centuries of proof that violence is not the antidote to violence. Clearly, a little violence does not inoculate us from the disease of more violence. Violence is not the cure; violence is the disease. As a Christian I find it logically inconsistent to accept any other norm for my life and ethics than knowing God as love as lived in Jesus. With that as my starting point, I am called to a life of love that must be liberating, life-affirming, and community-creating. Taking human life is too decisive a contradiction of my belief and too decisive an action for me to ever justify usurping God's

---

[113] Matthew 26: 52.
[114] Ephesians 6:10-17, emphasis added.

authority over life and death.

I do believe, however, that it is incumbent upon those of us who wish to get rid of war either to find alternative means of fulfilling its functions or to bring about changes which render those functions unnecessary. Simple abhorrence of war and avoidance of violence are insufficient to assure either peace or justice. One of the more frightening truisms of modern life is that we cannot unlearn our technical know-how. Complete disarmament alone, even if it were possible, would leave human problems unresolved; and renewed conflict in international relations could all too easily lead to rearmament. What is required is not just a mistrust of the ways of violence, but a new and deeper trust in the ways of nonviolence. Glen Stassen has pointed a clear way toward "just peacemaking" in his books of that title.[115]

In his book, *Revolutionary Nonviolence*, Dave Dellinger offers a helpful and potentially fruitful insight in drawing a distinction between human rights and national rights:

> Nonviolence is a person-to-person and people-to-people method, and once people begin to think of themselves and others as citizens of rival governments, they can hardly practice it. Nonviolence must be used to defend *human rights*, not *national rights*. [116]

This is critical to understanding and following Jesus and addressing the issue of social conflict and violence in Jesus' name. The first step on the way to peace is to see the "other" as one who is made in the image of God, who is loved by God, and for whom Jesus died. Jesus made clear that the greatest commandment is to love God and that the second is to love one another the way we love ourselves. Recent discoveries of the Genome Project and DNA research by geneticists have confirmed what the Bible has always asserted: we all are related to one another (see Acts 17:26). We are one extended family, generation upon generation of brothers and sisters, parents and children.

Jesus and the "ethical realists" throughout history have looked at the world and seen different things. "Ethical realists" have seen individuals as subsumed in society, whereas Jesus saw society as made up of individuals. I suggest that Jesus' view offers the understanding that is most needed as a corrective for too many centuries of "ethical realism." Peace, certainly not

---

[115] See *Just Peacemaking: Ten Practices for Abolishing War* and *Just Peacemaking: Transforming Initiatives for Justice and Peace*.
[116] Dellinger, *Revolutionary Nonviolence*, p. 203, emphasis in the original.

the kind of peace that surpasses all understanding, will never be achieved between governments. It can only be achieved, if at all, between people. Peacemaking is a person-to-person and people-to-people activity. Our best hopes for peace today, as always, lie not with governments but with individuals who reach out to claim and live out the oneness of humanity. War, the preparation for war, and even the so-called peace that is preserved by war dehumanize of necessity. For, as H. J. N. Horsburgh cogently observes,

> In time of war it can be vitally important not to see the enemy as a mixed assortment of ordinary human beings. It is for this reason that, even in peacetime, scenes from everyday life in potentially hostile countries are seldom televised. In a few moments they can undo the work of years, seriously undermining the monstrous misconceptions that politicians and publicists have been labouring to impress upon the popular mind. [117]

Eventual success of nonviolent methods cannot be guaranteed, of course, but still less can the success of more orthodox, violent systems. If the proof of the pudding is in the eating, we have too long eaten the bitter pudding of war and violence. Jesus put the issue this way: "All who take the sword die by the sword" (Matt. 26:52). The modern version in international relations can be put in these words: the nation that prepares for war dies by war. As I write these words on Christmas Day, the day of celebrating the birth of the Prince of Peace, I hear echoes of the voice of the prophet from long ago: "In the wilderness, prepare a way for the Lord." In the widely quoted words that probably originated with a French underground fighter in World War II, "There is no way to peace; peace is the way." In the words of the Prince of Peace, "I am the way. Follow me."

Idealism? So it may be. May it also prove to be realism.

Now, however, I must confess an "existential inconsistency" in my stance. While I can defend my position as logically consistent with my faith and my hope in Christ, I am unable to resolve the emotional tensions quite so neatly. I believe if circumstances called upon me to defend my life by taking another's, that I could live up to the claims of my pacifism. Even if the cause were "noble and good," I hope I would have the moral courage to be more willing to die for it than to kill. But the point of greatest existential conflict for me occurs in the matter of protecting not my life but the lives of others, particularly of loved ones. I have little doubt that, if "backed into a corner," I would take someone's life rather than stand idly by and let my wife or children or grandchildren be killed. I would not,

---

[117] Horsburgh, *Non-Violence and Aggression*, p. 17.

however, try to defend my failure to live by my convictions as being proper action in the name of Christ. Such action might be "ethically realistic," but I could never claim it was Christian.

Ultimately, I am driven to confess my spiritual inadequacy and to give thanks to God that God's demands are always preceded by God's grace and love, and that "Christ died for us while we were yet sinners, and that is God's own proof of his love towards us" (Rom. 5:8). I can only hope, we can only hope, that God's grace and love are large enough to forgive even our collective and institutionalized forms of human failure. But this hope is scarcely an excuse for us to "persist in sin, so that there may be all the more grace" (Rom. 6:1). Instead, we must work to eliminate the inhuman (in the best sense of "human" meaning to have been created in God's image) reliance on war and death as expressions of our perverted nature, lest God indeed give us up to our "own depraved reason" (Rom. 1:28; See the remainder of this passage through v. 32).

*****

A Cross, Some Clowns, and Dancing

In dark times, give off light.
Anne Lamott [118]

For God's foolishness is wiser than human wisdom, and God's weakness is stronger than human strength.
The Apostle Paul [119]

[Where] it is real, laughter is the voice of faith.... Laughter is hope's last weapon. Crowded on all sides with idiocy and ugliness, pushed to concede that the final apocalypse seems to be upon us, we seem nonetheless to nourish laughter as our only remaining defense.... It shows that despite the disappearance for any empirical basis for hope, we have not stopped hoping.
Harvey Cox [120]

There was some one thing that was too great for God to show us when he walked upon the earth; and I have sometimes fancied that it was his mirth.
G. K. Chesterton [121]

---

[118] Lamott, *Plan B: Further Thoughts on faith*, p. 181.
[119] 1 Corinthians 1:25, NRSV.
[120] Cox, *The Feast of Fools*, pp. 155, 157.
[121] Chesterton, *Orthodoxy*, p. 155.

In [the Christian God] is found that eternal joy which causes the
whole creation to sing and dance.
Jurgen Moltmann [122]

God's time is dance time. Even in the midst of a cultural free-for-
all and free-fall, disciples dance.
Leonard Sweet [123]

Life isn't about how to survive the storm, but how to dance in
the rain.
Source Unknown

Worried Christian legalist: 'Can a Christian dance?'
Dr. Maltby (after reflecting): 'Well, some can, and some can't.'
Robert McAfee Brown [124]

Is there hope for us? I say, "Yes!" It is not a "cheap hope," however, because it is not derived from "cheap love." Christian hope comes with the price of being a child of God who creates life from death by suffering. But that hope lies in the recognition that suffering is not the end of the story. Suffering is not the plot of the story. The one in whom I hope came to give life and to give it abundantly (John 10:10). And this abundant life is nothing less than the "death of death."[125]

Eugene O'Neill has a wonderful little play entitled "Lazarus Laughed," in which he portrays Lazarus after Jesus has brought him out of the tomb. The play is about the tension between how Lazarus then understood life and death and the understanding of the common folk and the religious leaders. For Lazarus, there was no more death, and fear was no more. There was only laughter. When Lazarus came forth from the tomb, he laughed. One of the bystanders described the scene as Jesus later departed: "Lazarus, looking after Him, began to laugh softly like a man in love with God! Such a laugh I never heard! It made my ears drunk!" And Lazarus exulted: "There is only life! I heard the heart of Jesus laughing in my heart.... And my heart reborn to love of life cried 'Yes!' and I laughed in the laughter of God!" In contrast, at the end of the play the chorus of old men and the crowd assert that "Life is a fearing.... Life is death."[126] They forgot life and laughter and remembered only death and fear.

---

[122] Moltmann, *Religion, Revolution, and the Future*, p. 147.

[123] Sweet, *Soul Salsa*, p. 185.

[124] Brown, *The Significance of the Church*, p. 81.

[125] Moltmann, *ibid*, p. 34.

[126] O'Neill, *The Plays of Eugene O'Neill*, pp. 277, 279, 297.

But the end of our story, with Jesus, like Lazarus, is that death, not life, is transient: "There shall be an end to death...for the old order has passed away!" (Rev. 21:4). Do we dare believe it? It does appear foolish, but that is part of the paradox. In seeking wisdom, we have become fools (Rom. 1:22). In becoming fools for Christ's sake (and for the sake of those for whom he died), we become wise (1 Cor. 4:10). As someone has observed, there are two kinds of fools in the world: damned fools and fools for Christ's sake.

In circuses and rodeos, when things go wrong, it's time to send in the clowns. Clowns are interesting, because they look so foolish, yet they have such a serious role to play. Clowns are figures of laughter, but they are also figures of rescue and hope. Colin Morris is right when he sees the clown as the symbol of hope in the midst of the threatening seriousness of life:

> The clown dares to live out his dreams, whatever the personal
> cost. And such men are dangerous. They introduce a wild,
> unpredictable element into an otherwise tidy, soulless, prudential
> existence.... The strategy of laughter is man's last protection
> against the idolatry of all forms of earthly power. Laughter is
> hope's final weapon. [127]

It's time to send in the clowns:

> Enter Christ the harlequin: the personification of festivity and
> fantasy in an age that had almost lost both.... Only by learning to
> laugh at the hopelessness around us can we touch the hem of
> hope.... In tragedy we weep and are purged. In comedy we laugh
> and hope.... The comic, more than the tragic, because it ignites
> hope, leads to more, not less, participation in the struggle for a
> just world. [128]

This is not a time for funerals, but for celebration, for what religious philosopher Geddes MacGregor has called a "theology of mirth." In his little book, *The Humor of Christ*, Elton Trueblood said that Christians have a great deal to laugh about, because they understand that "though there is an ocean of darkness and death, there is also an ocean of light and love which flows over the ocean of darkness."[129] More profoundly, Jesus calls us to a kind of life that can rejoice and dance for joy even in the face of persecution because of our faith (Luke 6:22-23).

As Christians, we are to let the heart of Jesus laugh in our hearts.

---

[127] Morris, *The Hammer of the Lord*, pp. 93-94, 95-96.
[128] Harvey Cox, *The Feast of Fools*, pp. 139, 142, 150, 153.
[129] Trueblood, *The Humor of Christ*, p. 25.

Christians are called to be God's happy people: "They sing and dance and laugh a lot," because the future is a source of festivity.[130] Medieval theologians often conceived of the orderly movements of the heavenly bodies as the cosmic choreography of a joyful dance. Picking up on this notion, C. S. Lewis often referred to the life of Christian faith and worship as the "great dance" in which the universe sways to the rhythm of God's created intention. I probably would never turn to Michael Jackson's words for theological insight, but there are few equals and perhaps none better to turn to for words about dance. In these words I recently came across, Michael speaks eloquently about dance in words that echo medieval spirituality:

> This world we live in is the dance of the creator. Dancers come and go in the twinkling of an eye but the dance lives on. On many an occasion, when I am dancing, I have felt something sacred....I keep on dancing and then, it is the eternal dance of creation. The creator and the creation merge into one wholeness of joy. I keep on dancing—until there is only...the dance.[131]

Leonard Sweet has suggested that "Jesus came to make all of life a dance," pointing to Jesus' metaphor of piping and dancing in Matthew 11:17. He then comments further,

> [The] Aramaic word for 'rejoice' is the same as the word for 'dance,' leading one to wonder whether Jesus was actually telling the people to experience the joy of living or to get into the dance of life. The gospel of Jesus can be expressed in one sentence: There is some music you face; there is other music you dance to. In the energy and movement and teachings of Jesus, I have found the music to dance my way through life.... God's people deserve to dance. And God deserves dancing people. You are a gift to life, and life is a gift to you. Rejoice and be glad in it. [132]

Sam Keen quotes Arthur Darby Nock, who said "Primitive religion is not believed. It is danced." Keen then goes on to say,

> Words, concepts, doctrines, ideas are all necessary for clarity and for consistent action. There is a time for words. It lasted from the

---

[130] David O. Woodyard, *Beyond Cynicism: The Practice of Hope*, p. 107.

[131] www.tobyjohnson.com/perelandra.html, accessed September 22, 2009 .

[132] Sweet, *Soul Salsa*, pp. 14, 152.

Reformation to the present. Now we are sick of being inundated in an ocean of verbiage. The word must be rediscovered in the flesh. Religions must return to dance. [133]

Sydney Carter has written a wonderful song entitled "I Danced in the Morning" expressing the mood of God's creative and redemptive activities as a dance in which we are invited to join.

> I danced in the morning when the world was begun,
> And I danced in the moon and the stars and the sun,
> And I came down from heaven and I danced on earth;
> At Bethlehem I had my birth.
>
> Dance, then, wherever you may be;
> I am the Lord of the Dance, said He,
> And I'll lead you all, wherever you may be,
> And I'll lead you all in the dance, said he.[134]

These words below from Sydney Carter speaking about his song remind me of Jesus' metaphor of piping and dancing mentioned earlier:

> I see Christ as the incarnation of the piper who is calling us. He dances that shape and pattern which is at the heart of our reality. By Christ I mean not only Jesus; in other times and places, other planets, there may be other Lords of the dance. But Jesus is the one I know of first and best. I sing of the dancing pattern in the life and words of Jesus.[135]

I, too, sing of Jesus, and it is to the piping of the music of Jesus that I aspire to dance.

In his delightful little book from the 1960s, *The Gospel According to Peanuts*, Robert Short saw in Snoopy an example of the Christian life that knows the joy of Christ while bearing the humiliations that often come with that life. Snoopy is often leaping for joy, giving full body expression to his belief that "To live is to dance. To dance is to live."[136] My wife finds it amusing that I am drawn to the metaphor of the Christian life as a dance. I cannot dance. Remember, I grew up as the son of a Baptist pastor in a small southern town. Growing up, I was not allowed to dance. Somewhere

---

[133] Keen, *To a Dancing God*, p. 160.
[134] Carter, "I Danced in the Morning,"
[135] Carter, *ibid*.
[136] Short, *The Gospel According to Peanuts*, p. 112.

along the way, my "dance" gene apparently became recessive. Now that I am older and have an understanding of the Christian life that would allow me to dance, I still can't dance, as anyone who has ever watched me try will attest to. I can keep time with the music, but I always seem to be on the off-beat. That's why I like Snoopy. I can't dance, but, with Snoopy, I can jump for joy—not in time with this world's music but with the music of God's future.

It is not just memories of the past acts of God, but an eschatological hope in God's future which we experience in the here-and-now that keeps us dancing on the off-beat, "always dancing slightly out of step with the times."[137] Rubem Alves gives us a wonderful picture of life as the dance of faith:

> Living is like dancing. As you dance you move your body according to a rhythm and a harmony which fill the space....You may dance to the tune played by the present reality.... Or you may choose to move your body under the spell of a mysterious tune and rhythm which comes from a world we do not see, the world of our hopes and aspirations. *Hope is hearing the melody of the future. Faith is to dance it.* [138]

The wisdom writer of Ecclesiastes wrote that there is a season for everything, including a time for dancing (Eccles. 3:4b). This is a time for living. Now is the season for dancing. A faith that isn't hope-full is a faith that isn't dancing. The Lord of the Dance is waiting.

Shall we dance? ...

---

[137] Carl Braaten, *Christ and Counter-Christ*, p. 87.
[138] Alves, *Tomorrow's Child*, p. 195, emphasis added.

PART SEVEN: THE INTERLOGUE...

> It was there from the beginning; we have heard it; we have
> seen it with our own eyes; we looked upon it, and felt it with our
> own hands; and it is of this we tell. *Our theme is the word of life.* [1]

> God did not finish creation. We are put here to do our part
> in completing the project. What else can possibly be worth a life?
> Joan Chittister[2]

This is not the "last word," so I can't call it the "epilogue." And, given
my use of "word/*logos*" as the framework of revelation of the biblical story,
to call it the "interlude" doesn't seem adequate. So, I am resorting to
making up a word: "interlogue," consisting of the prefix "inter" (in the
sense of "in the midst of") and "*logos*" (word). I am suggesting that we are
to live "in the midst of the Word." And, as indicated above in the heading,
the proper punctuation to follow "interlogue" is an ellipsis.

During a Sunday school class discussion a few years ago, someone
commented that there was more to say about the topic under discussion at
that moment. That observation struck me at that time, and it has lingered
with me and become another one of the stack poles around which I gather
truth. Whenever we talk about Truth, God, Love, Reality—or any of the
other "capitalized words" of life—regardless of what we say or where we
stop, *there is always more.* Talking about anything that matters *Ultimately* is
never the Last Word. Only God can utter the Last Word; we can only
speak penultimately at our best. We don't reach the End, we just run out
of breath, out of thoughts, out of understanding, out of words.
(Unfortunately, we too often run out of thoughts before we run out of
words, but that is another issue entirely.) Further, where we stop talking is

---

[1] 1 John 1:1, emphasis added.
[2] Chittister, *Welcome to the Wisdom of the World*, p. 132.

never the End; it is always a pause, no matter how dogmatically and eloquently we may have spoken. Only God can put a period or, more aptly, an exclamation mark at the end of an utterance. We can only "end" with an ellipsis...

So, I wind down...

For the moment...

But there is more...

There is always more...

*****

About the Author

Davis Byrd has lived his life in the context of his Christian faith. Growing up as the son of the pastor of the First Baptist Church in a county-seat town in South Carolina, his early life was shaped by the faith of his parents.

During his college years at Rice University, his childhood faith, largely inherited without question from his parents, began to become his personal faith as an independent person among people who did not preconceive him as the "pastor's son." After several years in the practice of architecture and city planning, he felt God's call into ministry and closed his architectural office and went to seminary. At seminary, he served on the administrative staff while receiving a Master of Divinity and doing graduate work in Christian Ethics. After completing his seminary education, he combined has architectural and ministry training and provided architectural and consulting services for churches, working personally with over 200 churches and heading an office that worked with over 2000 church projects under his leadership. He was a member of the American Institute of Architects and the American Planning Association and was a charter member of the American Institute of Certified Planners.

He was ordained to the gospel ministry during his seminary days and has been an active churchman all of his life, serving in various churches as supply preacher, Sunday school teacher, deacon, choir member, and member and chairman of various committees.

Byrd has had articles and book reviews published in newspapers, magazines and scholarly journals.

BIBLIOGRAPHY

Alves, Rubem. *Tomorrow's Child: Imagination, Creativity, and the Rebirth of Culture.* New York: Harper & Row, Publishers, 1972.

Anderson, Bernhard W. *The Unfolding Drama of the Bible.* New York, NY: Association Press, 1957.

_____. *Understanding the Old Testament.* Englewood Cliffs, New Jersey: Prentice-Hall, Inc., Third Edition, 1975.

Atkinson, Gordon. "Turtles All the Way Down," http://www.christiancentury.org/article.lasso?id=1037, accessed 9/12/08.

Baillie, John. *The Idea of Revelation in Recent Thought.* New York: Columbia University Press, 1976.

Balcomb, Raymond E. *Try Reading the Bible This Way.* Philadelphia: The Westminster Press, 1971.

Ball, Michael. *Show Me (My fair Lady)*, http://www.lyricsdownload.com/michael-ball-show-me-my-fair-lady-lyrics.html, accessed 3/6/09.

Baptist Courier, March 6, 1980.

Barclay, William. *And Jesus Said: A Handbook on the Parables of Jesus.* Philadelphia: The Westminster Press, 1970.

_____. *More New Testament Words.* New York: Harper & Brothers Publishers, 1958.

Barth, Karl. *The Doctrine of Reconciliation: Church Dogmatics, Volume IV, 3, II.* Edinburgh: T. & T. Clark Ltd., 1962.

Berkman, John and Michael Cartwright, eds. *The Hauerwas Reader.* Durham, NC: Duke University Press, 2001.

Biersdorf, John. *Hunger for Experience: Vital Religious Communities in America.* New York, NY: The Seabury Press, Inc., 1975.

Blackaby, Henry T. and Claude V. King. *Experiencing God: How to Live the Full Adventure of Knowing and Doing the Will of God.* Nashville, Tennessee: Broadman & Holman Publishers, 1994.

Blount, Brian K. "Biblical Authority," *Struggling with Scripture.* Louisville, KY: Westminster John Knox Press, 2002.

Bonhoeffer, Dietrich. *Creation and Fall – Temptation: Two Biblical Studies.* New York, New York: The Macmillan Company, 1959.

Boomershine, Thomas E. *Story Journey: An Invitation to the Gospel as Storytelling*. Nashville, Tennessee: Abingdon Press, 1988.

Borg, Marcus. *Reading the Bible Again for the First Time: Taking the Bible Seriously but Not Literally*. San Francisco: HarperCollins Publishers, 2002.

Botterweck, G. Johannes, and Helmer Ringgren, eds. *Theological Dictionary of the Old Testament*, Volume III. Grand Rapids, Michigan: William B. Eerdmans Publishing Company, 1978.

Braaten, Carl E. *Christ and Counter-Christ*. Philadelphia: Fortress Press, 1972.

_____. *The Future of God: The Revolutionary Dynamics of Hope*. New York: Harper & Row, Publishers, 1969.

_____. "Toward a Theology of Hope," *Theology Today*, XXIV, July, 1967.

Bradbury, Ray. *Dandelion Wine*. New York: Bantam Books, revised Bantam Edition, 1976.

Brown, Charles, ed. *Sing 'n' Celebrate!*. Waco, Texas: Word Incorporated, 1971.

Brown, Robert McAfee. *Theology in a New Key: Responding to Liberation Themes*. Philadelphia, Pennsylvania: The Westminster Press, 1978.

_____. *The Bible Speaks to You*. Philadelphia: The Westminster Press, 1955.

_____. *The Collected Writings of St. Hereticus*. Philadelphia: The Westminster Press, 1964.

_____. *The Pseudonyms of God*. Philadelphia, Pennsylvania: The Westminster Press, 1972.

_____. *The Significance of the Church*. Philadelphia: The Westminster Press, 1956.

_____. *Unexpected News: Reading the Bible with Third World Eyes*. Philadelphia, Pennsylvania: The Westminster Press, 1984.

Brueggemann, Walter. *An Introduction to the Old Testament: The Canon and Christian Imagination*. Louisville, Kentucky: Westminster John Knox Press, 2003.

_____. "Biblical Authority", *Struggling with Scripture*. Louisville, KY: Westminster John Knox Press, 2002.

_____. *The Bible Makes Sense*. Winona, Minnesota: Saint Mary's Press, 1977.

_____. *The Creative Word: Canon as a Model for Biblical Education.*
Philadelphia: Fortress Press, 1982.

_____. *The Threat of Life: Sermons on Pain, Power, and Weakness.* Charles L.
Campbell, ed., Minneapolis: Fortress Press, 1996.

Brunner, Emil. *Our Faith.* New York: Charles Scribner's Sons, 1954.

Buchanan, John. "Truth Claims." *Christian Century*, January 28, 2008.

Buechner, Frederick. *A Room Called Remember.* New York, NY: HarperCollins Publisher,
1992.

_____. *Now and Then.* San Francisco: HarperCollins Publishers, 1991.

Cairns, Scott. *Recovered Body.* Wichita, Kansas: Eighth Day Press, 2002. Used by
permission.

Camara, Dom Helder. *The Desert Is Fertile.* Eugene, Oregon: Wipf & Stock Publishers,
1974.

Carter, Sydney. "I Danced in the Morning," www.stainer.co.uk/lotd.html, accessed March
24, 2009. Copyright 1963 Stainer & Bell Ltd. (admin. Carol Stream, IL 60188: Hope
Publishing Company). All rights reserved. Used by permission.

Cash, Roseanne. "The Ear of the Beholder,"
http://measureformeasure.blogs.nytimes.com/2008/05/22the-ear-of-the-beholder/,
accessed June 27, 2008.

Chesterton, G. K. *Orthodoxy.* Peabody, Massachusetts: Hendrickson Publishers, Inc.,
2006.

Chittister, Joan. *Welcome to the Wisdom of the World: and Its Meaning for You.* Grand Rapids,
Michigan: William B. Eerdmans Publishing Company, 2007.

Christian Century, November 13, 2007.

_____, June 3, 2008.

Claypool, John. *God the Ingenious Alchemist: Transforming Tragedy into Blessing.* Harrisburg, PA:
Morehouse Publishing, 2005.

Coffin, William Sloane. *A Passion for the Possible: A Message to U. S. Churches.* Louisville, KY:
Westminster John Knox Press, Second Edition, 2004.

_____. *Credo.* Louisville, Kentucky: Westminster John Knox Press,
2004.

Cox, Harvey. *The Feast of Fools: A Theological Essay on Festivity and Fantasy*. New York: Harper & Row, Publishers, 1969.

_____.*The Seduction of the Spirit: The Use and Misuse of People's Religion*. New York: Simon and Schuster, 1973.

Crim, Keith, ed. *The Interpreter's Dictionary of the Bible, Supplementary Volume*. Nashville, TN: 1976.

Crossan, John Dominic. *A Long Way from Tipperary: A Memoir*. New York, NY: HarperCollins Books, 2000.

Darnton, John. *Mind Catcher*. New York: Onyx, New American Library, Penguin Group (USA), Inc. 2003.

Dellinger, Dave. *Revolutionary Nonviolence*. Indianapolis: The Bobbs-Merrill Company, Inc. 1970.

Donfried, Karl Paul. *The Dynamic Word: New Testament Insights for Contemporary Christians*. San Francisco: Harper & Row, Publishers, 1981.

Duncan, David James. *God Laughs & Plays*. Great Barrington, MA: Triad Books, 2006.

Durham, John I. *The Biblical Rembrandt: Human Painter in a Landscape of Faith*. Macon, Georgia: Mercer University Press, 2004.

Earle, Mary. "A Celtic Christmas," http://www.explorefaith.org/celtic/christmas.html, accessed 9/07/08.

Eck, Diana L. *Encountering God: A Spiritual Journey from Bozeman to Banaras*. Boston, Massachusetts: Beacon Press, 1993, 2003.

Ehrman, Bart. From The Teaching Company, "From Jesus to Constantine," Lecture 6: "Jesus as a Jew."

Fackre, Gabriel. *The Rainbow Sign: Christian Futurity*. Grand Rapids: Wm. B. Eerdmans Publishing Co., 1969.

Fettke, Tom. *The Hymnal for Worship and Celebration*. Waco, Texas: Word Music, 1986.

Forbis, Wesley L. *The Baptist Hymnal*. Nashville, Tennessee: Convention Press, 1991.

Fosdick, Harry Emerson. *The Meaning of Being a Christian*. New York: Association Press, 1964.

_____. *What Is Vital in Religion: Sermons on Contemporary Christian Problems*. London: SCM Press Ltd., 1956.

Fox, Matthew. *Creativity: Where the Divine and the Human Meet.* New York: Jeremy P. Tarcher/Putman, 2002.

Fromm, Erich. *The Revolution of Hope: Toward a Humanized Technology.* New York: Harper & Row, Publishers, 1968.

Gomes, Peter. *Sermons: Biblical Wisdom for Daily Living.* New York: William Morrow and Company, Inc., 1998.

_____. *The Good Book: Reading the Bible with Mind and Heart.* New York, NY: Avon Books, Inc., 1996.

_____. *Strength for the Journey: Biblical Wisdom for Daily Living.* San Francisco: HarperSanFrancisco, 2003.

Harkness, Georgia. *Christian Ethics.* Nashville, TN: Abingdon Press, 1957.

_____. *Toward Understanding the Bible.* Nashville, Tennessee: Abingdon Press, 1952.

Harper, Michael. *A New Way of Living.* Plainfield, New Jersey: Logos International, 1973.

Harrelson, Walter. *Interpreting the Old Testament.* New York: Holt, Rinehart and Winston, Inc., 1964.

Heilbroner, Robert L. *An Inquiry into the Human Prospect.* New York: W. W. Norton & Company, Inc., 1975.

Herzog, Arthur. *The Church Trap.* New York: The Macmillan Company, 1968.

Herzog, William R. II. *Prophet and Teacher: An Introduction to the Historical Jesus.* Louisville, KY: Westminster John Knox Press, 2005.

Heschel, Abraham J. *The Prophets*, Volume I. New York: Harper & Row, Publishers, Inc., 1962.

Horsburgh, H. J. N. *Non-Violence and Aggression: A study of Gandhi's Moral Equivalent of War.* London: Oxford University Press, 1968.

Hromadka, Joseph L. *Theology between Yesterday and Tomorrow.* Philadelphia: The Westminster Press, 1957.

Hunter, Archibald M. *Bible & Gospel.* Philadelphia: The Westminster Press, 1969.

James, William. *The Varieties of Religious Experience.* New York: Collier Books, 1961.

Johnson, James Weldon. *God's Trombones: Seven Negro Sermons in Verse.* New York: The Viking Press, 1927.

Jordan, Clarence and Bill Lane Doulos. *Cotton Patch Parables of Liberation*. Scottsdale, Pennsylvania: Herald Press, 1976.

Kee, Alistair, ed. *The Scope of Political Theology*. London: SCM Press, 1978.

Kee, Howard Clark and Franklin W. Young. *Understanding the New Testament*. Englewood Cliffs, NJ: Prentice-Hall, Inc., 1957.

Keen, Sam. *To a Dancing God*. New York: Harper & Row, Publishers, 1970.

Keyes, Ralph. *The Writer's Book of Hope*. New York: Henry Holt and Company, LLC, 2003.

Kittel, Gerhard, ed. *Theological Dictionary of the New Testament*, Volume IV. Grand Rapids, Michigan: Wm. B. Eerdmans Publishing Company, 1967.

Lamott, Anne. *Plan B: Further Thoughts on Faith*. New York: Riverhead Books, 2005.

Lattin, Don. "Chatting up the man who talks with God." *San Francisco Chronicle*, Sunday, November 17, 2002. Accessed at www.sfgate.com on March 17, 2009.

Laytham, D. Brent. *God Is Not....* Grand Rapids, MI: Brazos Press, 2004.

L'Engle, Madelaine. http://www.storyteller.net/articles/160, accessed 6/20/08.

Levine, Amy-Jill. *The Misunderstood Jew: The Church and the Scandal of the Jewish Jesus*. San Francisco: HarperSanFrancisco, 2006.

Lewis, C. S. *Mere Christianity*. New York: The Macmillan Company, 1960.

Lose, David J. *Confessing Jesus Christ: Preaching in a Postmodern World*. Grand Rapids, Michigan: William B. Eerdmans Publishing Company, 2003.

MacGregor, Geddes. *He Who Lets Us Be: A Theology of Love*. New York: The Seabury Press, 1975.

Macquarrie, John. *Principles of Christian Theology*, Second Edition. New York: Charles Scribner's Sons: 1966.

McLaren, Brian. *A Generous Orthodoxy*. Grand Rapids, MI: Youth Specialties Books, 2004.

Marney, Carlyle. *Priests to Each Other*. Valley Forge, PA: Judson Press, 1974.

Merton, Thomas. *Bread in the Wilderness*. New York: New Direction Books, 1953.

Moltmann, Jurgen. *Religion, Revolution, and the Future*. New York: Charles Scribner's Sons, 1969.

_____. *The Crucified God*. New York: Harper & Row, Publishers, 1974.

_____. *The Passion for Life: A Messianic Lifestyle.* Philadelphia: Fortress Press, 1978.

_____. *Theology of Hope.* London: SCM Press Ltd., 1967.

Morris, Colin. *The Hammer of the Lord.* Nashville, Tennessee: Abingdon Press, 1973.

Mott, Stephen Charles. *Biblical Ethics and Social Change.* New York: Oxford University Press, 1982.

Napier, Davie. *Song of the Vineyard: A Guide to the Old Testament.* Philadelphia: Fortress Press, Revised Edition, 1981.

Newbigin, Leslie. *Open Secret.* Quoted on http://sermonquotes.wordpress.com/category/stories, accessed May 9, 2008.

O'Conner, Elizabeth. *Eighth Day of Creation: Gifts and Creativity.* Waco, Texas: Word Books, 1971.

O'Neill, Eugene. *The Plays of Eugene O'Neill.* New York: Random House, 1910.

Pelikan, Jaroslav. *Whose Bible Is It?: A History of the Scriptures Through the Ages.* New York: Penguin Group (USA), 2005.

Percy, Walker. *The Message in the Bottle.* New York: Picador, 1954.

Peters, Tom. www.tompeters.com, posted 10/15/04.

Peterson, Eugene. *Christ Plays in Ten Thousand Places: A Conversation in Spiritual Theology.* Grand Rapids, Michigan: William B. Eerdmans Publishing Company, 2005.

_____. *Eat This Book: A Conversation in the Art of Spiritual Reading.* Grand Rapids, Michigan: William B. Eerdmans Publishing Company, 2006.

_____. *Tell It Slant: A Conversation on the Language of Jesus in His Stories and Prayers.* Grand Rapids, Michigan: William B. Eerdmans Publishing Company, 2008.

_____. *The Jesus Way: A Conversation on the Ways That Jesus Works.* Grand Rapids, Michigan: William B. Eerdmans Publishing Company, 2007.

Phillips, J. B. *The New Testament in Modern English.* New York: The Macmillan Company, 1962.

Pitzele, Peter. *Our Fathers' Wells: a Personal Encounter with the Myths of Genesis.* San Francisco: HarperSanFrancisco, 1995.

Placher, William. "Struggling with Scripture," *Struggling with Scripture.* Louisville, KY: Westminster John Knox Press, 2002.

Prather, Hugh. *I Touch the Earth, the Earth Touches Me.* Garden City, NY: Doubleday & Company, 1972.

Price, Reynolds. *A Serious Way of Wondering: The Ethics of Jesus Imagined.* New York, NY: Scribner, 2003.

_____. *A Palpable God.* San Francisco: North Point Press, 1985.

Quoist, Michael. *Prayers.* New York: Avon Books, 1975.

Reader's Digest, December 1977.

Sayers, Dorothy. *The Mind of the Maker.* San Francisco: HarperSanFrancisco, 1941.

Schwarz, Hans. *On the Way to the Future.* Minneapolis: Augsburg Publishing House, 1972.

Seeliger, Wes. *Western Theology.* Atlanta: Forum House Publishers, 1973.

Shaull, Richard. "Theology and the Transformation of Society," *Theology Today*, XXV, April, 1968.

Schwartz, Howard. *Reimagining the Bible: The Storytelling of the Rabbis.* New York: Oxford University Press, 1998.

Short, Robert L. *The Gospel According to Peanuts.* Richmond, VA: John Knox Press, 1964.

Smart, Ninian. *Worldviews: Crosscultural Explorations of Human Beliefs.* New York: Charles Scribner's Sons, 1983.

Smith, Wilfred Cantwell. *Religious Diversity.* New York, NY: The Crossroads Publishing Company, 1982.

Spong, John Shelby. *Rescuing the Bible from Fundamentalism: A Bishop Rethinks the Meaning of Scripture.* San Francisco: HarperSanFrancisco, 1991.

Stagg, Frank. *Studies in Luke's Gospel.* Nashville, Tennessee: Convention Press, 1967.

Stassen, Glen. *Living the Sermon on the Mount: A Practical Hope for Grace and Deliverance.* San Francisco: Jossey-Bass, 2006.

Stegemann, Ekkehard W. and Wolfgang Stegemann. *The Jesus Movement: A Social History of Its First Century.* Minneapolis, MN: Fortress Press, 1999.

Suenens, Leon Joseph Cardinal. *A New Pentecost?.* New York: The Seabury Press, 1974.

Sweet, Leonard. *Post-Modern Pilgrims: First Century Passion for the 21st Century World.* Nashville, Tennessee: Broadman & Holman Publishers, 2000.

_____. *Soul Salsa.* Grand Rapids, Michigan: Zondervan Publishing House, 2000.

_____. *Soul Tsunami: Sink or Swim in New Millennium Culture.* Grand Rapids, Michigan: Zondervan Publishing House, 1999.

_____. *The Three Hardest Words in the World to Get Right.* Colorado Springs, CO: WaterBook Press, 2006.

Taylor, Barbara Brown. "Stand and Deliver," *Christian Century.* May 2, 2004.

The Baptist Standard, Volume 90, Number 48.

The Christian Century, January 25, 2005.

Tickle, Phyllis. "Everyday Spirituality," http://www.explorefaith.org/stepstones/everyday.html, accessed 9/7/08.

Tillich, Paul. *Biblical Religion and the Search for Ultimate Reality.* Chicago: University of Chicago Press, 1955.

_____. *Dynamics of Faith.* New York: Harper & Brothers Tourchbook, 1958.

_____. *The New Being.* New York: Charles Scribner's Sons, 1955.

Topol, L. John. *The Way to Peace: Liberation Through the Bible.* Maryknoll, NY: Orbis Books, 1979.

Trueblood, Elton. *The Company of the Committed.* New York: Harper & Row, Publishers, 1961.

_____. *The Humor of Christ.* New York: Harper & Row, Publishers, Inc., 1964.

von Rad, Gerhard. *Genesis: A Commentary.* Philadelphia: The Westminster Press, Revised Edition, 1961.

Westermann, Claus. *A Thousand Years and a Day: Our Time in the Old Testament.* Philadelphia: Fortress Press, 1962.

White, R. E. O. *Biblical Ethics.* Atlanta: John Knox Press, 1979.

Wiesel, Elie. *The Gates of the Forest.* New York: Holt, Rinehart and Winston, Inc., 1966.

Williams, Rowan. "What is the Church? In God's Company", *Christian Century.* June 12, 2007.

Wilson, Sarah Hinlicky. "Plato Was Wrong," *Christian Century.* December 28, 2004.

Woodyard, David O. *Beyond Cynicism: The Practice of Hope.* Philadelphia: The Westminster Press, 1972.

Yoder, John Howard. *The Politics of Jesus.* Grand Rapids, Michigan: William B. Eerdmans Publishing Company, 1972.

Made in the USA
Charleston, SC
30 March 2010